The Politics of Trauma and Peace-Building

In marked contrast to literary, historical and cultural studies, there has been limited engagement with the concepts and politics of trauma by political science and peace-building research.

This book explores the debate on trauma and peace-building and the challenges for democratization that the politics of trauma present in transitional periods. It demonstrates how ideas about reconciliation are filtered through ideological lenses and become new ways of articulating communal and ethno-nationalist sentiments. Drawing on the work of Jacques Rancière and Iris Marion Young and with specific reference to the Northern Irish transition, it argues for a shift in focus from the representation of trauma towards its reception and calls for a more substantive approach to the study of democracy and post-conflict peace-building.

This text will be of interest to scholars and students of peace and conflict studies, ethnic and nationalism studies, transitional justice studies, gender studies, Irish politics, nationalism and ethnicity.

Cillian McGrattan is a lecturer in Politics and a member of the Institute for Research in the Social Sciences at the University of Ulster.

Routledge Advances in European Politics

1 **Russian Messianism**
Third Rome, revolution, Communism and after
Peter J.S. Duncan

2 **European Integration and the Postmodern Condition**
Governance, democracy, identity
Peter van Ham

3 **Nationalism in Italian Politics**
The stories of the Northern League, 1980–2000
Damian Tambini

4 **International Intervention in the Balkans since 1995**
Edited by Peter Siani-Davies

5 **Widening the European Union**
The politics of institutional change and reform
Edited by Bernard Steunenberg

6 **Institutional Challenges in the European Union**
Edited by Madeleine Hosli, Adrian van Deemen and Mika Widgrén

7 **Europe Unbound**
Enlarging and reshaping the boundaries of the European Union
Edited by Jan Zielonka

8 **Ethnic Cleansing in the Balkans**
Nationalism and the destruction of tradition
Cathie Carmichael

9 **Democracy and Enlargement in Post-Communist Europe**
The democratisation of the general public in fifteen Central and Eastern European countries, 1991–1998
Christian W. Haerpfer

10 **Private Sector Involvement in the Euro**
The power of ideas
Stefan Collignon and Daniela Schwarzer

11 **Europe**
A Nietzschean perspective
Stefan Elbe

12 **European Union and E-Voting**
Addressing the European Parliament's internet voting challenge
Edited by Alexander H. Trechsel and Fernando Mendez

13 **European Union Council Presidencies**
A comparative perspective
Edited by Ole Elgström

14 **European Governance and Supranational Institutions**
Making states comply
Jonas Tallberg

15 **European Union, NATO and Russia**
Martin Smith and Graham Timmins

16 **Business, The State and Economic Policy**
The case of Italy
G. Grant Amyot

17 **Europeanization and Transnational States**
Comparing Nordic central governments
Bengt Jacobsson, Per Lægreid and Ove K. Pedersen

18 **European Union Enlargement**
A comparative history
Edited by Wolfram Kaiser and Jürgen Elvert

19 **Gibraltar**
British or Spanish?
Peter Gold

20 **Gendering Spanish Democracy**
Monica Threlfall, Christine Cousins and Celia Valiente

21 **European Union Negotiations**
Processes, networks and negotiations
Edited by Ole Elgström and Christer Jönsson

22 **Evaluating Euro-Mediterranean Relations**
Stephen C. Calleya

23 **The Changing Face of European Identity**
A seven-nation study of (supra)national attachments
Edited by Richard Robyn

24 **Governing Europe**
Discourse, governmentality and European integration
William Walters and Jens Henrik Haahr

25 **Territory and Terror**
Conflicting nationalisms in the Basque country
Jan Mansvelt Beck

26 **Multilateralism, German Foreign Policy and Central Europe**
Claus Hofhansel

27 **Popular Protest in East Germany**
Gareth Dale

28 **Germany's Foreign Policy Towards Poland and the Czech Republic**
Ostpolitik revisited
Karl Cordell and Stefan Wolff

29 **Kosovo**
The politics of identity and space
Denisa Kostovicova

30 **The Politics of European Union Enlargement**
Theoretical approaches
Edited by Frank Schimmelfennig and Ulrich Sedelmeier

31 **Europeanizing Social Democracy?**
The rise of the party of European socialists
Simon Lightfoot

32 **Conflict and Change in EU Budgetary Politics**
Johannes Lindner

33 **Gibraltar, Identity and Empire**
E.G. Archer

34 **Governance Stories**
Mark Bevir and R.A.W Rhodes

35 **Britain and the Balkans**
1991 until the present
Carole Hodge

36 **The Eastern Enlargement of the European Union**
John O'Brennan

37 **Values and Principles in European Union Foreign Policy**
Edited by Sonia Lucarelli and Ian Manners

38 **European Union and the Making of a Wider Northern Europe**
Pami Aalto

39 **Democracy in the European Union**
Towards the emergence of a public sphere
Edited by Liana Giorgi, Ingmar Von Homeyer and Wayne Parsons

40 **European Union Peacebuilding and Policing**
Michael Merlingen with Rasa Ostrauskaite

41 **The Conservative Party and European Integration since 1945**
At the heart of Europe?
N.J. Crowson

42 **E-Government in Europe**
Re-booting the state
Edited by Paul G. Nixon and Vassiliki N. Koutrakou

43 **EU Foreign and Interior Policies**
Cross-pillar politics and the social construction of sovereignty
Stephan Stetter

44 **Policy Transfer in European Union Governance**
Regulating the utilities
Simon Bulmer, David Dolowitz, Peter Humphreys and Stephen Padgett

45 **The Europeanization of National Political Parties**
Power and organizational adaptation
Edited by Thomas Poguntke, Nicholas Aylott, Elisabeth Carter, Robert Ladrech and Kurt Richard Luther

46 **Citizenship in Nordic Welfare States**
Dynamics of choice, duties and participation in a changing Europe
Edited by Bjørn Hvinden and Håkan Johansson

47 **National Parliaments within the Enlarged European Union**
From victims of integration to competitive actors?
Edited by John O'Brennan and Tapio Raunio

48 **Britain, Ireland and Northern Ireland since 1980**
The totality of relationships
Eamonn O'Kane

49 The EU and the European Security Strategy
Forging a global Europe
Edited by Sven Biscop and Jan Joel Andersson

50 European Security and Defence Policy
An implementation perspective
Edited by Michael Merlingen and Rasa Ostrauskaitė

51 Women and British Party Politics
Descriptive, substantive and symbolic representation
Sarah Childs

52 The Selection of Ministers in Europe
Hiring and firing
Edited by Keith Dowding and Patrick Dumont

53 Energy Security
Europe's new foreign policy challenge
Richard Youngs

54 Institutional Challenges in Post-Constitutional Europe
Governing change
Edited by Catherine Moury and Luís de Sousa

55 The Struggle for the European Constitution
A past and future history
Michael O'Neill

56 Transnational Labour Solidarity
Mechanisms of commitment to cooperation within the European Trade Union Movement
Katarzyna Gajewska

57 The Illusion of Accountability in the European Union
Edited by Sverker Gustavsson, Christer Karlsson, and Thomas Persson

58 The European Union and Global Social Change
A critical geopolitical-economic analysis
József Böröcz

59 Citizenship and Collective Identity in Europe
Ireneusz Pawel Karolewski

60 EU Enlargement and Socialization
Turkey and Cyprus
Stefan Engert

61 The Politics of EU Accession
Turkish challenges and Central European experiences
Edited by Lucie Tunkrová and Pavel Šaradín

62 The Political History of European Integration
The hypocrisy of democracy-through-market
Hagen Schulz-Forberg and Bo Stråth

63 The Spatialities of Europeanization
Power, governance and territory in Europe
Alun Jones and Julian Clark

64 European Union Sanctions and Foreign Policy
When and why do they work?
Clara Portela

65 The EU's Role in World Politics
A retreat from Liberal Internationalism
Richard Youngs

66 Social Democracy and European Integration
The politics of preference formation
Edited by Dionyssis Dimitrakopoulos

67 The EU Presence in International Organizations
Edited by Spyros Blavoukos and Dimitris Bourantonis

68 Sustainability in European Environmental Policy
Challenge of governance and knowledge
Edited by Rob Atkinson, Georgios Terizakis and Karsten Zimmermann

69 Fifty Years of EU-Turkey Relations
A Sisyphean story
Edited by Armagan Emre Çakir

70 Europeanization and Foreign Policy
State diversity in Finland and Britain
Juha Jokela

71 EU Foreign Policy and Post-Soviet Conflicts
Stealth intervention
Nicu Popescu

72 Switzerland in Europe
Continuity and change in the Swiss political economy
Edited by Christine Trampusch and André Mach

73 The Political Economy of Noncompliance
Adjusting to the single European market
Scott Nicholas Siegel

74 National and European Foreign Policy
Towards Europeanization
Edited by Reuben Wong and Christopher Hill

75 The European Union Diplomatic Service
Ideas, preferences and identities
Caterina Carta

76 Poland within the European Union
New awkward partner or new heart of Europe?
Aleks Szczerbiak

77 A Political Theory of Identity in European Integration
Memory and policies
Catherine Guisan

78 EU Foreign Policy and the Europeanization of Neutral States
Comparing Irish and Austrian foreign policy
Nicole Alecu de Flers

79 Party System Change in Western Europe
Gemma Loomes

80 The Second Tier of Local Government in Europe
Provinces, counties, départements and Landkreise in comparison
Hubert Heinelt and Xavier Bertrana Horta

81 **Learning from the EU Constitutional Treaty**
Democratic constitutionalism beyond the Nation-state
Ben Crum

82 **Human Rights and Democracy in EU Foreign Policy**
The cases of Ukraine and Egypt
Rosa Balfour

83 **Europeanization, Integration and Identity**
A social constructivist fusion perspective on Norway
Gamze Tanil

84 **The Impact of European Integration on Political Parties**
Beyond the permissive consensus
Dimitri Almeida

85 **Civic Resources and the Future of the European Union**
Victoria Kaina and Ireneusz Pawel Karolewski

86 **The Europeanization of National Foreign Policies towards Latin America**
Lorena Ruano

87 **The EU and Multilateral Security Governance**
Sonia Lucarelli, Luk Van Langenhove and Jan Wouters

88 **Security Challenges in the Euro-Med Area in the 21st Century**
Mare nostrum
Stephen Calleya

89 **Society and Democracy in Europe**
Oscar W. Gabriel and Silke Keil

90 **European Union Public Health Policy**
Regional and global trends
Edited by Scott L. Greer and Paulette Kurzer

91 **The New Member States and the European Union**
Foreign policy and Europeanization
Edited by Michael Baun and Dan Marek

92 **The Politics of Ratification of EU Treaties**
Carlos Closa

93 **Europeanization and New Member States**
A comparative social network analysis
Flavia Jurje

94 **National Perspectives on Russia**
European foreign policy in the making
Maxine David, Jackie Gower and Hiski Haukkala

95 **Institutional Legacies of Communism**
Change and continuities in minority protection
Edited by Karl Cordell, Timofey Agarin and Alexander Osipov

96 **Sustainable Development and Governance in Europe**
The evolution of the discourse on sustainability
Edited by Pamela M. Barnes and Thomas C. Hoerber

97 **Social Networks and Public Support for the European Union**
Elizabeth Radziszewski

98 The EU's Democracy Promotion and the Mediterranean Neighbours
Orientation, ownership and dialogue in Jordan and Turkey
Ann-Kristin Jonasson

99 New Democracies in Crisis?
A comparative constitutional study of the Czech Republic, Hungary, Poland, Romania and Slovakia
Paul Blokker

100 Party Attitudes Towards the EU in the Member States
Parties for Europe, parties against Europe
Nicolò Conti

101 The European Union and Occupied Palestinian Territories
State-building without a state
Dimitris Bouris

102 Portugal in the European Union
Assessing twenty-five years of integration experience
Laura C. Ferreira-Pereira

103 Governance and European Civil Society
Governmentality, discourse and NGOs
Acar Kutay

104 The EU, Migration and the Politics of Administrative Detention
Edited by Michela Ceccorulli and Nicola Labanca

105 Political Representation in the European Union
Democracy in a time of crisis
Edited by Sandra Kröger

106 New Approaches to EU Foreign Policy
Edited by Maciej Wilga and Ireneusz Pawel Karolewski

107 Democracy, Law and Religious Pluralism in Europe
Secularism and post-secularism
Edited by Ferran Requejo and Camil Ungureanu

108 Contemporary Spanish Foreign Policy
Edited by David Garcia and Ramon Pacheco Pardo

109 Reframing Europe's Future
Challenges and failures of the European construction
Edited by Ferenc Miszlivetz and Jody Jensen

110 Italy's Foreign Policy in the 21st Century
A contested nature?
Edited by Ludovica Marchi, Richard Whitman and Geoffrey Edwards

111 The Challenge of Coalition Government
The Italian case
Edited by Nicolò Conti and Francesco Marangoni

112 The Nordic Countries and the European Union
Still the other European community?
Edited by Caroline Howard Grøn, Peter Nedergaard and Anders Wivel

113 Mediating Policy
Greece, Ireland, and Portugal Before the Eurozone Crisis
Kate Nicholls

114 The European Parliament and its International Relations
Edited by Stelios Stavridis and Daniela Irrera

115 Market Expansion and Social Dumping in Europe
Edited by Magdalena Bernaciak

116 The Diplomatic System of the European Union
Evolution, change and challenges
Edited by Michael Smith, Stephan Keukeleire and Sophie Vanhoonacker

117 European Union Enlargement
Material interests, community norms and anomie
Thomas Mehlhausen

118 The Moral Economy of EU Association with Africa
Mark Langan

119 European Space Policy
European integration and the final frontier
Edited by Thomas Hörber and Paul Stephenson

120 Policy Making at the Second Tier of Local Government in Europe
What is happening in Provinces, Counties, Départements and Landkreise in the on-going re-scaling of statehood?
Edited by Xavier Bertrana, Björn Egner and Hubert Heinelt

121 The Politics of Trauma and Peace-Building
Lessons from Northern Ireland
Cillian McGrattan

122 Eurozone Politics
Perception and reality in Italy, the UK, and Germany
Philip Giurlando

123 Politics of Identity in Post-Conflict States
The Bosnian and Irish experience
Edited by Éamonn Ó Ciardha and Gabriela Vojvoda

124 Unequal Europe
Social divisions and social cohesion in an old continent
James Wickham

125 Generations, Political Participation and Social Change in Western Europe
Maria T. Grasso

126 Clientelism and Economic Policy
Greece and the Crisis
Aris Trantidis

127 Challenges to Democracies in East-Central Europe
Edited by Jan Holzer and Miroslav Mareš

The Politics of Trauma and Peace-Building

Lessons from Northern Ireland

Cillian McGrattan

Routledge
Taylor & Francis Group
LONDON AND NEW YORK

First published 2016 by Routledge

2 Park Square, Milton Park, Abingdon, Oxfordshire OX14 4RN
711 Third Avenue, New York, NY 10017

Routledge is an imprint of the Taylor & Francis Group, an informa business

First issued in paperback 2017

British Library Cataloguing-in-Publication Data
A catalogue record for this book is available from the British Library

Library of Congress Cataloging-in-Publication Data
Names: McGrattan, Cillian, author.
Title: The politics of trauma and peace-building : lessons from Northern Ireland / Cillian McGrattan.
Description: Abingdon, Oxon ; New York, NY : Routledge is an imprint of the Taylor & Francis Group, an Informa business, [2016] | Series: Routledge advances in European politics ; 121
Identifiers: LCCN 2015021215| ISBN 9781138775183 (hbk) | ISBN 9781315665344 (ebk)
Subjects: LCSH: Peace-building—Northern Ireland. | Social psychology—Northern Ireland. | Psychic trauma—Northern Ireland. | Northern Ireland—Politics and government—1994–
Classification: LCC JZ5584.N75 M44 2016 | DDC 303.6/609416—dc23LC record available at http://lccn.loc.gov/2015021215

ISBN: 978-1-138-77518-3 (hbk)
ISBN: 978-0-8153-7106-9 (pbk)

Typeset in Times New Roman
by Apex CoVantage, LLC

For Félix and Steffi

Contents

Acknowledgments

This book represents the culmination of a number of years of thought and reading. It dates from Vienna, where I finished my second monograph, to Glasgow, Swansea and Belfast. I have accumulated a great deal of intellectual debts during that journey.

Since moving back to Ulster University I have received encouragement and support from Fidelma Ashe, Arthur Aughey, Máire Braniff, Ruth Fee, Cathy Gormley-Heenan, Carmel Roulston and Kirk Simpson. I have rehearsed the arguments and chapters in this book in innumerable places over the past few years, and I thank Professor Gormley-Heenan and the Institute for Research in the Social Sciences at Ulster University for their support.

The idea from the book arose from discussions with colleagues at Swansea University. I am grateful for the encouragement of that enthusiastic and supportive team, particularly Mark Evans, Jonathan Bradbury and Sophie Williams who encouraged me to develop my ideas towards the form that this book takes.

This book draws on collaborative research funded by the British Academy/Levehulme, and I thank my colleagues in that project.

I thank Routledge's anonymous reviewers whose comments were both helpful and encouraging, and I thank Charlotte Endersby, my editor at Routledge, and her team for their support and help with the process.

My PhD supervisor, Henry Patterson, remains a pivotal influence in my intellectual development. Laura McAtackney, Aaron Edwards, John Coakley, Dr Sara Dybris-McQuaid, Paul Dixon, Catherine Gander, Stephen Hopkins, Eamonn O'Kane, Thomas Hennessey, Professor Elizabeth Meehan, David McCann, Jennifer Todd, Jonathan Tonge and Sophie Williams have all offered invaluable advice that has found its way into this book.

My brother, Brendan, read through and corrected chapters in this book – work that gave me the confidence to proceed towards finishing. I thank my family and extended family for all their support.

Félix arrived in the middle of writing and has influenced this book in innumerable and unimaginable ways. He has changed our lives, filled them with love and joy and made us new people. My appreciation and love, as ever, is dedicated to Steffi who has been, through her love, her support, her critique, her encouragement, her confidence, her engagement and so much more, such an influence on this text.

Introduction

In marked contrast to literary, historical and cultural studies, there has been limited engagement with the concepts and politics of trauma by political science and/or peace-building research. This book suggests that part of that trend is the emphasis within the latter on post-conflict consolidation through institution building. The key insights of, for example, consociational and transitional justice theorizing concern how to establish and regulate bodies to ensure fairness in decision making and accountability in dealing with historical violence. Conversely, the explosion of trauma studies within humanities arguably signals a move away from the specificity of violence towards questions of representation, which in itself may contain a de-democratizing impulse by reducing participation and limiting agency and outcome to somewhat narrow aesthetic concerns. In contrast, I argue that a more substantive approach to democracy and post-conflict peace-building ought to foreground the question of trauma – in its individualized and societal implications. *The Politics of Trauma and Peace-Building*, therefore, seeks to initiate a debate around what going beyond aesthetic or proceduralist concerns might mean; it aims to shift the focus from representation towards reception; and it tries to illustrate these concerns by specific reference to the Northern Irish transition.

In a recent appraisal of that transition, the US diplomat and former senior aide to Bill Clinton, Nancy Soderberg, railed against the seeming lack of policy direction and political progress in Northern Ireland and accused local politicians of an 'abysmal abdication of leadership'. She went on to claim that they were 'far too stuck in the past, making progress vulnerable and even reversible'. A decade and a half after the historic Belfast/Good Friday Agreement of 1998, Soderberg argued that the political leaders were merely reflective of the general public, which had taken peace 'for granted', and stated that the 'the two communities remain far too focused on the injustices of the past'.[1]

Although this book is critical of politicians and attempts at policy implementation and policy design, it is important to remember that, in fact, in the general area of dealing with Northern Ireland's violent past, the region's politicians have made substantial and not inconsiderable progress. A unilateral denunciation of those gains give rise to a twofold danger: first, they may raise expectations to a level that is so high that politicians cannot hope to meet it, into which gap others may step, whether they be self-appointed 'community leaders' or more violent terror groups opposed to peace and the democratic process agreed to by referendum in 1998. The second danger is that the answers provided, in particular by community activists, may be taken so seriously by politicians that they become part of a policy and legislative framework.

This book takes as its point of departure those fears. My focus is on the politics of trauma, which I associate with fundamental democratic and governance problems by viewing them as having to do with a loss of voice; the perpetration of violence, intimidation and terror and the feeling of being betrayed by those in power. My argument essentially is that consideration of the politics of trauma opens space for discussion of the political implications of peace-building, leadership and policy making, reconciliation and truth recovery in deeply divided societies. Such consideration, I suggest, transcends sectional interests of 'community groups' and trains the focus on the possibility of effacing the traces of suffering through the superimposition of institutional management options intended to mitigate inter-bloc, ethno-national struggle and/or ensure juridical accountability for historic offences.

A focus on the political dimensions of trauma troubles structuralist analyses, such as those within critically important literatures on consociationalism and transitional justice, which view peace-building as almost tantamount to institution design. I argue that those tendencies work to constrain the very terms of peace and justice that those literatures are based on. For example, Cathal McLaughlin, a professor of film studies at Queen's University Belfast, has promoted his storytelling video project in which ex-prisoners and gaolers reminisce about the past by suggesting that it represents an alternative to what he sees as politicians' record of failure: 'Telling stories about a politically sensitive past and a contested present is not easy but in the absence of a solution from the top, reconciliation needs to continue at the grass-roots level'.[2] The value in screening these videos, according to McLaughlin, is that '[p]articipants seem to feel validated when their experiences are publicly acknowledged'. However, the limitations of a storytelling project such as this seems to be that the notion of validation is unachievable mainly because it falls short of the so-called 'Hitchens's razor': that 'that which can be asserted without evidence can be dismissed without evidence'.[3] In other words, the subjective nature of such validation renders it prisoner to politically loaded and perhaps even ethnically directed intentions.

The design of institutional mechanisms for dealing with deeply divided countries and divisive, bloodied histories gives way inevitably to strictures in terms of who or what is being excluded and marginalized. As Matthew Flinders points out, this is a general problem of governance: namely, putting shape onto the fractious nature of politics. In this regard, Flinders cites the French philosopher Jacques Rancière that a 'good democratic government is one capable of controlling the evil quite simply called democratic life'.[4] The immediate issue that arises relates to what capable controlling consists of or looks like. (It may be inferred that a bad democratic government exerts control in unethical or suboptimal ways.) I draw on Rancière's notion of the 'part-without-part' – namely, those groups left outwith or at the very margins of political life – to try to elucidate the relationship between peace-building and the politics of trauma. And, in brief, my argument runs as follows: the emphasis within strands of peace-building on management processes and political reconciliation(s) is (unhelpfully) constrictive; for, just as nationalism is inherently exclusionary, any workable conception of peace or justice ought to be about something other than nationalism or, indeed, the reconciliation of nationalist claims. The danger of designing policy around notions of managing division or facilitating some kind of acknowledgement or reconciliation with the past is that it may obscure the demands for justice and truth from those who have suffered the most from terror and political violence. In this way, the very notion of dealing with the past – or working through the past – seems to transcend proceduralist or narrowly institutionalist approaches to democracy to speak to more open-ended, substantive visions of democracy. The danger, as such, may be seen as two-fold – proceduralism can reify and reproduce perpetrators' self-justifications and self-exculpations and the purported historical, ideological and/or societal divisions that those may be based on; and it can reify the experience of victimhood, remarginalizing or rendering agency-less those individuals affected by violence. It can posit unrealistic expectations of politicians and decision makers into which ethnic or community-based entrepreneurs insert themselves, opening space to forward sectional claims and agendas. In positing those expectations, it can also dilute the political and democratic process by creating a culture of cynicism and/or apathy. Rather than attention being focused on the production and publication of identity claims, substantiated by particularistic narratives about the past, the substantivist lens shifts to analyzing reception.

Although Rancière's writings are often more immediately concerned with sensibilities and regimes within post-Marxian philosophy and aesthetics, I suggest that insights from his political philosophy are useful in delineating dynamics within the design of policy in the field of peace-building. These insights proceed from his work on what he refers to as the distribution, or partition, of the sensible (*le partage du sensible*): namely, the processes, shared assumptions and often-unspoken agreements that give rise to a consensus on what is acceptable, visible, sayable and doable in the world of politics. For Rancière, consensus is based on a sharing of sense and is inherently political and social in its implications:

> I do not take the phrase 'community of sense' to mean a collectivity shaped by some common feeling. I understand it as a frame of visibility and intelligibility that puts things or practices together under the same meaning, which shapes thereby a certain sense of community. A community of sense is a certain cutting out of space and time that binds together practices, forms of visibility, and patterns of intelligibility. I call this cutting out and this linkage a partition of the sensible.[5]

This book works obliquely with the latter issue and concerns itself with it by reference to the former. In particular, a central theme refers to what might be termed the ethnicization of peace – by which I mean the harnessing of the rhetoric of peace (and justice, and plurality, and inclusivity . . .) to communal, sectional ends. I wish to go beyond the immediate and somewhat obvious point that that harnessing is part and parcel of ethno-nationalist politics to explore what it means for the design of policy in a situation of a deeply divided society transitioning from violence to peace. This exploration takes as a point of departure the double-edged temptation to reify both violence and peace, both perpetrators and victims and both the past and the present. Writing about the North Atlantic Treaty Organization's (NATO's) intervention in Kosovo, Rancière elucidates this temptation:

> Ethnicism revokes the very space of politics in identifying the people with the race and the territory of exercise of citizenship with the ancestral soil. Ethnic purification does not simply consist in driving an undesirable ethnicity from a territory. It consists in constituting it as an undifferentiated herd, simultaneously denying the collective reality of a people endowed with a public life and the singularity of the individuals comprising it.

Extrapolating from this, a fundamental aim of the book is to explore the tendencies within Northern Irish peace policy and politics to dichotomize and subsume individual experiences and intra-bloc differences within the logic of community cohesion. Importantly, the book aims to avoid the temptation to valorize those distinctions and differences. For, as Rancière goes on to argue, the subject of the 'human' as it features within any such valorization superimposes 'the figure of the victim', working to de-politicize and obscure the very experiences and voices that the project of community cohesion itself, I argue, takes as an end.[6] Rancière's approach stands in contrast to the tendency of claims making and identity politics of focusing on compensation as a means of defining victimhood: where 'victimhood' is something that is constituted or recognized through the admission of culpability. The wrong that created the feeling of victimhood or trauma is, in that regard, offset or displaced relative to the outcome – recognition or compensation. In Rancière's treatment, wrongs are something social, political and societal: the overcoming of wrongs involves the assertion of equality on the part of those affected and the recognition of that fundamental equality by the polity, and in that way, the strictures or policing functions involved in recognition as outcome are transcended. The 'problem' (as such) of trauma and victimhood (and, by extrapolation, peace-building in general) therefore becomes societal in focus rather than procedural or sectional in remit and framing.[7]

The Rancièrean project, if it can be understood as such, involves not only the unveiling of the power structures that give rise to those dichotomies and reifications, but a call or an impetus towards reversal – towards the reassertion of equality.[8] I suggest that it makes three distinctive contributions to the literatures on peace-building and the politics of trauma, which provide undercurrents through this book. First, Rancière's delineation of the notion of distribution goes to the core of political conflicts and is, arguably, exacerbated in places such as Northern Ireland where words (and symbols) are deeply contested – it is the configuration and reconfiguration of the meaning and import attached to words that drives conflict, but also allows for a movement beyond contention. As Rancière points out:

'Politics revolves around what is seen and what can be said about it, around who has the ability to see and the talent to speak, around the properties of spaces and the possibilities of time'.[9] The distribution or sharing out of sensibility, however, works to delimit what it means to participate in a political community – it is both a sharing and a division,[10] and works in variations within communities.[11] As I discuss further in Chapters 3 and 4, the demarcation of community is intrinsic to peace-building in Northern Ireland. The response by some community groups to a recent killing of a former terrorist, for instance, was somewhat revealing: for in the attempt (through a one-page death notice in a Northern Irish paper) to reclaim the 'narrative' surrounding the killing, the groups, in a way, said more about themselves, emphasizing activism, struggle, independence from party affiliation and internationalist focus.[12]

This emphasis on the re/configuration of community gives way to Rancière's second intervention, which concerns his commitment to fundamental equality. As Jean-Philippe Deranty points out, this is founded on Rancière's idea of 'disagreement' and is at odds with both Habermas' emphasis on consensus and communication and Lyotard's stress on incommensurability and the *differend.* Rancière's 'stance', Deranty explains, is 'predicated' on the idea that communication is always possible and is possible outwith pre-established procedures or frameworks. This, Deranty states, is for Rancière the 'very definition of democratic politics, to establish the commonality of experience and thinking between people against the fact of social separation due to hierarchies'. In short, political or democratic 'practice transcends the social destinies and identities imposed by social positions'.[13] That political practice becomes apparent in the unveiling of injustice, hurt or inequality that occurs within disagreement – namely, the denoting of a wrong through a reconfiguration or reinterpretation of the status quo. Rancière's displacement of proceduralism moves the subject of analysis within peace-building from overt conflict towards silence and marginality, where not only traumatic experiences but also much of what constitutes everyday negotiation of peace and transition occur. The focus on the politics of trauma works, I argue, to expand the perspective of peace-building. Typically, the relationship between peace-building and democratization wavers between two poles. On the one hand, there is a suspicion that deeply divided societies are at risk of ethnic 'outbidding', whereby political entrepreneurs radicalize their rhetoric and policy goals, leading to incommensurable differences and widening divergences with other leaders and groups in a polity.[14] Alternatively, ethnic pluralism can be seen as constitutive of a healthy democracy by facilitating social diversity and acting as an impediment against authoritarianism.[15]

The unveiling of inequality and the distribution of sensibility is ultimately a political (and an aesthetic) intervention because it marks a movement from obscurity towards meaning and from mystification and silence towards knowledge and agency. This represents the third area where Rancière's thought complements peace-building and trauma theory. The book, therefore, moves from outlining the linkages between trauma theory and democratization-as-institution-building towards some of the outworkings of those linkages in terms of community politics and ideology in Northern Ireland. The final part of the book explores the implications of restoring agency to dealing with traumatic pasts and divided histories. As such, the principal conclusion of the book is that working by reference to the experience of trauma and victimhood, or speaking *through-but-not-for* that experience, ought to lie at the core of any response to the issue of dealing with divided polities and the legacies of violent histories. In this way, the politics of peace throw light on the often-abstruse critical theorizing of Rancière, but also work to insert a political- and a policy-oriented element to his fundamentally deconstructive impulse.

A key objective of the book is to delineate, through attention to the Northern Irish case, the placement of the politics of trauma within processes of democratic transitions (which can also often have serious de-democratizing elements). I distinguish between democracy as a form of governance and democracy as a set of values and suggest that whereas the former has received enormous attention in political science, sociological and transitional justice literatures, the latter has gone relatively underappreciated. In some respects this is surprising, since ethical values and beliefs always underpin democratic structures; however, it is perhaps to be expected in situations where societies move from violence and division to relative peace. I argue that the pragmatic and expedient ethic of attempting to make societies conform to pre-established visions of peace and reconciliation depends on a post hoc logic; instead, and following the concerns mentioned earlier with regard to the configuring of institutionalized and community-based notions of peace, the book develops the idea that peace and reconciliation should flow from societal cohesion, based on the recognition of fundamental equality and the persistence of inequalities. I suggest that that essentially incremental process may begin with the creation and cultivation of an ethic of social responsibility. Extrapolating from Iris Marion Young's ideas about social connection and the distinction between, on the one hand, the backwards-looking dimensions of blameworthiness and guilt, and the forwards-facing emphasis inherent in responsibility, on the other, the text traces how this ethic might and does look in situations where deeply divided societies seek to move beyond violent pasts.[16]

The Politics of Trauma and Peace-Building, then, represents an engagement with conventional thinking concerning institutionalized peace-building and truth recovery processes. I argue that dominant ideas concerning the management of conflict and transition – particularly those associated with consociational power sharing and certain transitional justice mechanisms (such as truth and reconciliation commissions) – begin with a set of institutional proposals (in effect, a peace-building toolbox) that often results in insulating political elites from ordinary citizens. Deliberative democratic approaches (and storytelling movements), on the other hand, tend to valorize civil society over and above society itself. I suggest that an alternative conceptualization begins by harnessing democracy and justice through an emphasis on ideas of accountability, transparency, scrutiny, oversight and cohesion. This ethic of social responsibility, I argue, moves from society to institutions rather than making society conform to the logic of forms of governance. Although I recognize that the latter may sometimes be necessary in order to regulate violent conflicts, I suggest that the process is interactive and two-way and that unless a concern with social connection is taken into account at one point, conflict and division may continue to be replicated in various forms.

I have alluded to the idea that Northern Ireland is illustrative of these arguments and concerns. My suggestion is that, as a deeply divided society in which the ideological cleavage is fundamentally irreconcilable (Ulster unionists wish to retain the constitutional link with the rest of Britain; Irish nationalists want to break that link and reunify the island of Ireland as one polity), that is transitioning from a history marred with violence, intimidation, exile, exclusion and divisions of various kinds, Northern Ireland represents a difficult case for peace-building. As I point out in subsequent chapters, the South African Truth and Reconciliation Commission has frequently been touted as a model for dealing with Northern Ireland's troubled history. As I also point out in Chapter 5, the tendency of some Northern Irish political actors to mobilize the past through commemoration and memory reflects ethnic dynamics visible in the former Yugoslavia, particularly Bosnia. Although Northern Ireland has not experienced an overarching truth recovery process, the Spanish-type model of agreeing not to make political capital from the past does not seem to be an option favoured by policy makers.[17] Faced with that scenario, I argue that Northern Ireland often reveals the limitations of proceduralist, managerial-type responses to surmounting historic divisions, particularly in the light of the politics of trauma. I do not deny that such a response is at times necessary to consolidate a movement from killing towards democratic politics; rather, my point is that such approaches can neglect the relationship between and among governors and governed that is revealed in the study of the politics of trauma. It suggests that a core element of societal responsibility involves an exploration and an appreciation of how ideas, arguments and beliefs are received and not simply how they are constructed, presented and re/produced.

The Northern Irish 'Troubles'[18] are often read as an ethnic conflict, and the core division certainly centres on ethno-nationalist groupism.[19] The Northern Irish state, which was founded in 1920–1921, was dominated and governed by the Ulster Unionist Party until its prorogation in 1972. As alluded to in parentheses earlier, Ulster unionists, who retain the status of the majority community (constituting just under 50 percent of the population), favour retaining the constitutional link with the rest of the United Kingdom. Mainly Protestant, they espouse an identity that is closely affiliated with British traditions. The Northern Irish nationalist community, who constitute just over 40 percent of the 1.8 million population, on the other hand, strongly identify with the cultural traditions of the Irish Republic; mainly Catholic in religious outlook, they desire the ending of partition and a reunification of the nation-state according to the geographical entity of the island of Ireland.[20] The dynamic between the two groups can be characterized as a problem of double minorities: unionists are in the minority on the island of Ireland, whereas Northern Irish nationalists are in the minority in Northern Ireland itself. The political culture, then, frequently revolves around mutual fears and suspicions founded on zero-sum calculations in which a perceived 'gain' for 'one side' relates to a 'loss' by the 'other'. The precarious balance of minority status, therefore, reinforces an ideological division that is itself a product and a producer of religious and historic antagonisms. The ideological–political–cultural cleavage manifests itself in many ways throughout Northern Irish society, including segregated education and housing – although individuals often find ways to negotiate and even transcend ethno-nationalist taboos in their everyday lives.[21] However, perhaps the most striking indication of that division is in the more than ninety barriers, euphemistically called 'peace walls' or 'peace lines', that divide Catholic from Protestant neighbourhoods in Belfast.[22]

The Northern Irish state began to fragment in the late 1960s under the challenge of the civil rights movement – a mass movement that garnered support for reforms in voting practices, employment, social housing policies and policing from across the two Northern Irish communities. The heavy-handed and cumbersome response by authorities and local Protestant leaders such as the Rev. Ian Paisley inspired a movement towards street politics that was overtaken by militants on both sides of the political divide. With the police stretched to breaking point, London intervened in August 1969 by sending the British army to restore order. However, sensing an opportunity to finish the revolution that was started in 1916, Irish republicans reinstituted armed struggle through the Irish Republican Army (IRA) to, as they saw it, take the 'war to the Brits'.[23] The ensuing conflict, which was largely a history of sectarian assassination and car bombing, resulted in almost 4,000 deaths and upwards of 40,000 people injured until the IRA called a ceasefire in 1997. Republicans were the foremost perpetrators of killings and violence, accounting for just under 60 percent of the deaths; loyalist paramilitaries were culpable of around 30 percent, and state forces just under 10 percent. Although in absolute terms the figures pale in comparison with some other ethnic conflicts, in proportional terms, around one out of every three people was directly affected by the violence in Northern Ireland.

The 1998 Belfast/Good Friday Agreement, which was chaired by Senator George Mitchell, was an exercise in political constraint and represented the culmination of a lengthy process of negotiation between the main political leaders in Northern Ireland and the two governments in London and Dublin.[24] The agreement's aims were set out in the declaration of support, and it is perhaps worth quoting from paragraphs 2 and 3, which epitomized the intentions and aspirations of its designers:

> The tragedies of the past have left a deep and profoundly regrettable legacy of suffering. We must never forget those who have died or been injured, and their families. But we can best honour them through a fresh start, in which we firmly dedicate ourselves to the achievement of reconciliation, tolerance, and mutual trust, and to the protection and vindication of the human rights of all.
>
> We are committed to partnership, equality and mutual respect as the basis of relationships within Northern Ireland, between North and South, and between these islands.[25]

The agreement itself set out an elaborate institutional framework that would provide devolution for Northern Ireland, cross-border cooperation on a consultative basis and fora for discussing issues pertaining to the British Isles as a whole. It also included provisions for the reform of policing, the early release of paramilitary prisoners and the decommissioning of paramilitary weapons and the demilitarization of Northern Ireland. The latter issues were to bedevil the implementation of that framework until 2007 when the two main nationalist and unionist parties, Sinn Féin and the Democratic Unionist Party, agreed to share power and the British government agreed to devolve responsibility for policing and justice to the Northern Irish Assembly. Arguably, since 2007 what have become known as 'legacy issues' pertaining to victims' rights, the possibility of a truth and reconciliation process and public symbolism surrounding the flying of flags and parades have dominated political debate. The first detailed consultation exercise on dealing with the past was carried out by the Consultative Group on the Past in Northern Ireland (CGPNI) in 2008–2009. CGPNI was a body established by the then Labour government and comprised mainly church leaders and civil society spokespersons. Its key proposal of a legacy commission to deal with outstanding issues relating to truth recovery and victims' needs and rights was, however, overshadowed by its call to award a £12,000 compensation payment to the relatives of all the bereaved – a kind of blanket payment that did not discriminate between bystanders, innocent victims and individuals killed while carrying out operations on behalf of paramilitary organizations. Since then there have been two further attempts to provide a roadmap for moving what might be called the politics of the past off the centre stage. First, in the autumn of 2013 Dr. Richard Haass and Professor Meghan O'Sullivan chaired a series of consultations and negotiations with Northern Irish politicians. Their detailed report separated truth recovery or storytelling approaches to the past from the more forensic work of the police and judiciary. News reports suggested that the Northern Ireland parties were largely in agreement about dealing with the past but remained divided on public symbolism. The following year, Northern Irish politicians were again brought into a talks process, this time under pressure from the British and Irish governments. The resulting Stormont House Agreement (SHA) reaffirmed the Haass/O'Sullivan approach, and again the parties seemingly agreed on much of the substance of the proposals surrounding dealing with the past, but strongly disputed the deal's welfare components.

The SHA states that any initiative to deal with the past should promote reconciliation; uphold the rule of law; facilitate justice and information recovery; acknowledge and address the suffering of victims and survivors; be human rights compliant and be based on the principles of balance, proportionality, transparency, fairness and equitableness.[26] Although these are no doubt noble ideals, arguably they set the bar too high for implementation. The SHA, for instance, aims to establish an oral history archive 'to provide a central place for people from all backgrounds (and throughout the UK and Ireland) to share experiences and narratives related to the Troubles'. Submission of testimony, it states, would be voluntary. Yet, it is difficult to predict how that suggestion can be tallied with the principles of proportionality and balance. A definition of inclusive that fits the reality of the Troubles would be proportionate to the killings, so there would be a much higher proportion of IRA victims than deaths linked to the actions of state forces or loyalist terrorists. Again, given the much higher profile sought and given to the republican narrative of the Troubles, it is difficult to be confident that transparency and fairness are being met. Linked with this is the potential for what might be called a Google-ization of suffering whereby the archive is accessed through keyword searches in order to repudiate a particular understanding of history. In addition, republicans (together with other groups) were responsible for almost systematic levels of silencing within their own communities throughout the conflict and into the peace – including covering up a range of child and sexual abuse issues.[27] Furthermore, no doubt many individuals and families may wish to retain their mourning as a private practice and fact rather than divulge their 'stories' to a public archive.

The division of labour in dealing with the past into a forensic- and evidential-based process and a storytelling-type body represents a logical but potentially problematic intervention. For, unlike the South African case, which otherwise seems to provide something of a model, the principle of full disclosure is avoided in the Northern Ireland documents – apart, that is, from a pledge by the UK government only to make full disclosure to the forensic investigatory unit, the Historical Investigations Unit (HIU). This would arguably lead to a mixing of storytelling and evidence that would be detrimental to the objective of adhering to the rule of law. This is because of the possibility of cross-testimony: a statement could be given to the storytelling body, the Independent Commission on Information Retrieval (ICIR), that would not be disclosed to the HIU. The idea behind the ICIR is that the Mafioso-like terror organizations that drove the conflict would conceal evidence to avoid implicating former colleagues and that the only way to find out something of the 'truth' about what happened in the vast majority of killings is through some form of protected immunity. (Precedents have been set when the former IRA leader Martin McGuinness gave limited cooperation to the Bloody Sunday Inquiry citing a code of honour and when the IRA stonewalled inquiries in the Republic of Ireland into police collusion with terrorists in that jurisdiction.)

This book explores the ways in which politicians are facing the difficulties in legislating for dealing with the past in a deeply divided society still transitioning from violence to an uneasy peace. The narrative arc of the book is to set out the challenges for democratization that the politics of trauma present in such transitional situations. I suggest that the division of responsibility to a community level, through rhetorical and analytical devices such as Soderberg's blanket condemnation or McLaughlin's valorization of story, works to insulate policy makers and society in general and, in a way, confers the duty for dealing with the past on those most affected by histories of violence. The book then goes on to explore how ideas about reconciliation are filtered through ideological lenses, becoming new ways of (re)articulating communal and ethno-nationalist sentiments. The final two chapters and the conclusion sketch the possibility of fencing off histories and refocusing the parameters of debate at the societal level.

Notes

1 Gerry Moriarty, "'Absymal' NI politicians too stuck in past, says ex-Clinton aide', *Irish Times*, 28 August 2014. Available at www.irishtimes.com/news/politics/aby

smal-ni-politicians-too-stuck-in-past-says-ex-clinton-aide-1.1910146; accessed on 31 March 2015.

2 Cahal McLaughlin, 'Where politicians fail, storytellers address the Troubles in Northern Ireland', *The Conversation*, 28 October 2014. Available at https://theconversation.com/where-politicians-fail-storytellers-address-the-troubles-in-northern-ireland-33335; accessed on 31 March 2015.

3 Christopher Hitchens, 'Mommie Dearest', *Slate*, 20 October 2003. Available at www.slate.com/articles/news_and_politics/fighting_words/2003/10/mommie_dearest.html; accessed on 20 May 2015.

4 Matthew Flinders, *Defending Politics: Why Democracy Matters in the Twenty-First Century* (Oxford: Oxford University Press, 2012), p. 47.

5 Jacques Rancière, 'Contemporary art and the politics of aesthetics', in *Communities of Sense: Rethinking Aesthetics and Politics*, edited by Beth Hinderliter, William Kaizen, Vered Maimon, Jaleh Mansoor and Seth McCormick (London: Duke University Press, 2009), p. 31.

6 Jacques Rancière, 'The nameless war', in *Chronicles of Consensual Times*, translated by Steven Corcoran (London: Continuum, 2010), pp. 45–46.

7 Todd May, 'Wrong, disagreement, subjectification', in *Jacques Rancière: Key Concepts*, edited by Jean-Philippe Deranty (Durham: Acumen, 2010), p. 75.

8 Samuel A. Chambers, *The Lessons of Rancière* (Oxford: Oxford University Press, 2013).

9 Jacques Rancière, *The Politics of Aesthetics: The Distribution of the Sensible*; translated by Gabriel Rockhill (London: Bloomsbury, 2004), p. 8.

10 Davide Panagia, '*Partage du sensible": the distribution of the sensible' in *Jacques Rancière: Key Concepts*, edited by Jean-Philippe Deranty (Durham: Acumen, 2010), p. 96.

11 Samuel A. Chambers, 'Police and oligarchy', in *Jacques Rancière: Key Concepts*, edited by Jean-Philippe Deranty (Durham: Acumen, 2010), p. 62.

12 See *Irish News*, 9 May 2015, p. 24.

13 Jean-Philippe Deranty, 'Introduction: a journey in equality', in *Jacques Rancière: Key Concepts*, edited by Jean-Philippe Deranty (Durham: Acumen, 2010), p. 10.

14 See, for example, Donald L. Horowitz, *Ethnic Groups in Conflict* (London: University of California Press, 1985); or Alvin Rabushka and Kenneth A. Shepsle, *Politics in Plural Societies: A Theory of Democratic Stability* (Columbus, OH: Charles E. Merrill Publishing Co., 1972).

15 See, for instance, Mark R. Beissinger (2008) 'A New Look at Ethnicity and Democratization', *Journal of Democracy*, 19(3): 85–97; or David D. Laitin, *Nations, States and Violence* (Oxford: Oxford University Press, 2007).

16 Iris Marion Young, *Responsibility for Justice* (Oxford: Oxford University Press, 2013).

17 For an exception, see Owen Paterson, 'Leonard Steinberg memorial lecture: Building the future, dealing with the past, Owen Paterson MP, Secretary of State for Northern Ireland', November 2010; author copy.

18 The application of the term 'conflict' to the recent history of killing is disputed by some victims' groups who hold that it affords retrospective legitimacy on terror organizations. Within the academic literature, the term 'conflict' has, arguably, become a more common way of referring to that history. I avoid this debate over nomenclature and use the terms 'Troubles' and 'conflict' interchangeably throughout the book; my intention is to avoid repetition and not to give offense.

19 Cillian McGrattan, *Northern Ireland, 1968–2008: The Politics of Entrenchment* (Basingstoke: Palgrave Macmillan, 2010), pp. 7–33.

20 At the 2012 census Protestants accounted for 48.56 percent and Catholics for 45.14 percent. Catholics outnumber Protestants in the under-40-year-old cohorts. Although recent surveys suggest that people identifying with a 'British only' category constitute 40 percent of the population and 'Irish only' 25 percent, Protestants tend overwhelmingly to give their votes to parties favouring maintenance of the Union as a primary

policy objective, whereas Catholics overwhelmingly give their votes to parties favouring reunification as a primary policy goal. See Tom McGurk, 'No certainties any more in the new North', *Sunday Business Post*, 17 May 2015, p. 20.

21 See Cillian McGrattan and Elizabeth Meehan, *Everyday Life after the Irish Conflict: Devolution and North-South Cooperation* (Manchester: Manchester University Press, 2013).

22 Cathy Gormley-Heenan and Jonny Byrne (2012) 'The Problem with Northern Ireland's Peace Walls', *Political Insight*, 3(3): 4–7.

23 Thomas Hennessey, *Northern Ireland: The Origins of the Troubles* (Dublin: Gill & Macmillan, 2005); see also Paul Bew, Peter Gibbon and Henry Patterson, *Northern Ireland, 1921–2001: Political Forces and Social Classes* (London: Serif, 2002). For introductory guides to the Northern Ireland conflict and Northern Irish politics, see Aaron Edwards and Cillian McGrattan, *The Northern Ireland Conflict: A Beginner's Guide* (Oxford: Oneworld, 2012); Paul Dixon and Eamonn O'Kane, *Northern Ireland Since 1969* (Abingdon: Routledge, 2011); Jonathan Tonge, *The New Northern Irish Politics?* (Basingstoke: Palgrave Macmillan, 2004).

24 Joseph Ruane and Jennifer Todd, *After the Good Friday Agreement: Analysing Change in Northern Ireland* (Dublin: UCD Press, 1999).

25 The Agreement (April 1998). Available at www.gov.uk/government/publications/the-belfast-agreement, accessed on 23 May 2015.

26 The Stormont House Agreement (December 2014). Available at www.gov.uk/government/uploads/system/uploads/attachment_data/file/390672/Stormont_House_Agreement.pdf; accessed on 3 April 2015.

27 See Liam Kennedy, 'They shoot children don't they? An analysis of the age and gender of victims of paramilitary "punishments"', Report to the Northern Ireland Committee Against Terror and the Northern Ireland Affairs Committee of the House of Commons, 2001. Available at http://cain.ulst.ac.uk/issues/violence/docs/kennedy01.htm; accessed on 3 April 2015. Paramilitaries are currently carrying out an average of two punishment-beatings per week; see Chris Kirkpatrick, 'Two "punishment-style" attacks carried out every week in Northern Ireland', *Belfast Telegraph*, 3 November 2014. Available at www.belfasttelegraph.co.uk/news/northern-ireland/two-punishmentstyle-attacks-carried-out-every-week-in-northern-ireland-30712724.html; accessed on 3 April 2015.

1 The politics of trauma

The politics of trauma are central to ideas about democracy and – by extrapolation – to processes of peace-building and democratization in post-conflict societies.[1] Trauma recurs in such societies in various ways, but always involves concerns over loss, grievance, culpability and complicity in the hurts and injustices caused by terror and political violence in the past. I wish to suggest that to speak of the politics of trauma does not mean to devalue the unfathomability and sense of powerlessness that constitutes the legacy of terror upon individuals; instead, I argue that a framing that emphasizes inarticulacy at the expense of working through and beyond violence works to leave victims as marginal, peripheral and without voice. The legacy of hurt and inarticulacy that is produced by the sudden imposition of violence cannot easily be done away with, but I argue that unless responses to that imposition form part of the politics of peace-building, then societies transitioning away from conflict risk basing their new dispensation on the exclusion of the most vulnerable.

What, then, do the politics of trauma look like? More specifically, what do they look like in the context of a peace-building situation or a society transitioning from violence to a democratic settlement process? The aim of this chapter is to begin to sketch an outline of an answer to those questions based on the notion that, in the first instance, the political dimensions of trauma involve a response. In other words, how do we begin to respond to trauma at a political level? I suggest that that framing involves something more than the exuberant aestheticized representations that constitute one form of analysis of engagement with trauma. More specifically, as I go on to point out, it also involves looking beyond platitudinous efforts to try to invest peace-building and, in particular, transitional justice, with rounder, more empathetic edges; to that end, I point out that although the effort may result in a broadening of the discipline, in practical and social terms, it indulges the conceit of pity.

I suggest that the political response may be distinguished from, for example, those approaches and the psychoanalytic treatment of individual trauma cases in that it addresses and positions itself directly in front of questions of power, agency, society and perspective. By this, I mean to shift focus, or, more precisely, to broaden the viewpoint, to incorporate issues to do with knowing about trauma (something that is, by nature, a pain that is private, recurring and silencing). In other words, the focus of this chapter (and the rest of the book) is not simply the question regarding how we know what we are talking about when the subject is intrinsically linked to inarticulacy. It also speaks to what follows from that question – for in asking it, we already imply an answer and a response. Thus, the second question relates to how can we incorporate that ambiguity of knowledge into our response? To what extent does that haziness forestall attempts to respond? The chapter describes how the politics of trauma initially involve recognition of those fissures and the consideration of ways of dealing and coping with them. In so doing, the politics of trauma essentially circle around questions of meaning and reception.

This exploration provides the basis for later discussions concerning how post-conflict societies understand themselves as societies or as political communities, and it aims to clear the ground on which to address understandings and representations of social and societal responsibility for the victims of historic violence. The discussion of the politics of trauma, then, involves the tackling of inarticulacy through the restoration of voice and agency, while working within the confines of what Gilles Deleuze described as 'the indignity of speaking for others', that is, the appreciation of 'the theoretical fact that only those directly concerned can speak in a practical way on their own behalf'.[2]

The politics of trauma in transitional societies

The focus of what might be termed 'mainstream' approaches to post-conflict democratization – namely, those relating to peace-building in general and its constituent and cognate disciplines of political science and transitional justice in particular – tend to obscure or ignore the relationship between trauma and democracy. For example, the United Nation's definition of transitional justice supports a procedural approach, defining transitional justice as 'the full range of processes and mechanisms associated with a society's attempt to come to terms with a legacy of large-scale past abuses, in order to ensure accountability, serve justice and achieve reconciliation'.[3] In this view, democracy is chiefly associated with the protocols, rules and institutions that provide for checks and balances against abuses of power and for accountability and oversight of policy makers. Arguably, because of this focus, the relational aspects of democracy become downplayed – that is, the notion that exclusion and even injustice can occur not only in the absence of a system of protocols and scrutiny mechanisms, but through their very operation. Likewise, it can lead to ignoring the idea that behavioural norms and expectations exist not simply within the territory of ideas, beliefs and prejudices but are created through the very guidelines established to constrain injustice and facilitate reconciliation. Of course, the institutional and rule-based aspects of democracy are of vital importance and play a determining role in shaping the outcomes of, for example, elections or other forms of political contestation. But a framing that focuses on those aspects, I suggest, tends to overshadow other important elements, in particular, the ethical or social ties that constitute the fabric of political transition. One effect of this tilt in post-conflict situations is that the political and ethical ramifications of post-conflict trauma remain under-researched and underappreciated.

I suggest that political and policy-oriented responses within post-conflict societies to dealing with contentious, violent pasts require careful (re)calibration to more fully take into account the *political* dimensions of trauma. This may be achieved in several practical ways, such as the enshrining of victims' experiences at the heart of society through positive discrimination, the valorization of victims' experiences within truth and reconciliation processes over those of perpetrators and the fencing in of historical narratives to delimit the number of permissible 'lies' that circulate in post-conflict societies.[4] The chapter is concerned primarily with the *ethos* of responding to trauma: as such, it argues that trauma demands a response and a recognition of the imperative involved in extending societal responsibility for those individuals affected by political violence and terror.

In constructing this argument, I make two distinctions regarding the political and societal implications of trauma in post-conflict situations and divided societies. First, I deliberately sidestep questions concerning the actual practice of psychiatric work on post-traumatic stress disorder (PTSD) or intergenerational transfer of traumatic memories. Although I understand that these questions cannot be divorced from a political or the social context,[5] the essentially epistemological and methodological issues involved in establishing what that context or set of relations involves seems to me to be analytically separate from the exploration of the trauma/peace-building relationship, which is concerned with how peace is built at a political and societal level. Second, the chapter is not immediately concerned over the debates within psychoanalysis over the changing clinical definition of trauma and PTSD.[6] Instead, I wish to explore the politics of trauma within societies that are transitioning from conflict to peace. Standard approaches to settlement processes, or building peace and deepening democracy in such societies, focus on institutional engineering; that is, on the designing of bodies and rules to encourage, for example, power sharing among elites and/or participation in the decision-making process among various sectors of society. To return to the United Nations example: for the UN, the demilitarization, demobilization and reintegration (frequently abbreviated to DDR) of former combatants are also seen as intrinsic to building inclusive, peaceful societies.[7] The two approaches can be exclusive and suboptimal: the focus on perpetrators of violence, for instance, may inhibit notions of inclusivity and power sharing among their victims. Put crudely, the essential choice between peace and stability now (with the focus on elite compromise and perpetrator-centred processes) and justice later, or justice and peace now (with the danger being that holding perpetrators accountable for their actions risks destabilizing the peace, or is unrealistic and remains unfulfilled). Both despite and because of these problems, I suggest that any attempt to conceive democratization processes within such societies needs to be aligned with an awareness of trauma in a political sense. I argue that this incorporates and yet goes beyond procedural definitions of democracy to include a sense of social responsibility for those who have suffered from terror and political violence.

The politics of trauma involves the imposition of powerlessness through the irruption of overwhelming violence that is both unexpected and involves a breach of trust and security.[8] Veena Das points out that pain 'makes a claim asking for acknowledgement'; in other words, despite its ostensible subjective and private nature, the very inarticulateness involved with trauma works as a call, an expression that demands an answer.[9] Trauma, in a political sense, incorporates this societal imperative, but also questions the power relations involved in the perpetuation and recurrence of injury. The politics of trauma, then, involve asking what underpins the return of collective grievances in transitional societies. They examine the power asymmetries and persistent injustices (and perceived wrongs) that lie behind unresolved fissures. Since trauma involves the loss of articulateness in a political sense, it incorporates questions of democracy-as-voice and democracy-as-access. By working with and through the hurts and the forcible removals of the words that could be used to explain the injuries, the politics of trauma always also revolve around questions concerning the restoration of voice, the facilitation of access to power and decision makers and the demand for transparency in the political process. It asks fundamental questions about the relationship between political leaders and elected representatives and the citizens they serve; as such, the politics of trauma emphasizes the ability of politicians to try to rebuild broken relationships and repair fractured trust.

An immediate problem that arises in talking about the politics of trauma is that of what constitutes 'talk'; in other words, how can we apply the empirical approach of 'mainstream', positivistic methodologies of social science to investigate something that, by its nature, evades assimilation and representation?[10] This is because trauma is not only a recurring pain that is subjective, individual and privatized, but it also involves the loss of means to assimilate that recurrence (thereby repeating the search for meaning). In other words, it is characterized by repetition: an intermittent but ever-present living out and acting out of an injury in the past and a recurring attempt to come to terms with the legacy of pain, which can itself be hindered and frustrated by the overwhelming nature of the initial hurt. Trauma, then, involves interior haunting(s) and is seemingly defined by the removal of the means to exorcize. In other words, the damage cannot be simply worked through and healed – the damage itself recurs and frustrates the process of articulating hurt and locating pain.

Elizabeth Bennett has argued that trauma is never truly subjective – it is never completely interior or exterior – but involves relational dynamics in which the silenced strain for vocalization. Bennett's key concern is with artistic representational engagements with trauma, which she sees as inherently political in that it works against privilege and power by drawing its audience into an awareness of pain and pain's incommunicable nature.[11] In a similar way, the critical re/presentation of trauma necessitates awareness of political and ethical factors. One of the immediate and most fundamental of these factors relates to questions of manipulation, appropriation and usurpation of the pain of others. Neutrality can, in this regard, be seen perhaps as 'patronizing' with the resort to aestheticized renderings of trauma being tantamount to some kind of post-modern spectacle.[12] However, although trauma frustrates healing, it does not negate progress. This point is clarified by Dominick LaCapra, who argues that

> . . . [t]rauma brings about a dissociation of affect and representation . . . Working through trauma involves the effort to articulate or rearticulate affect and representation in a manner that may never transcend, but may to some viable extent counteract, a re-enactment, or acting out, of that disabling dissociation.[13]

Exploring the politics of trauma, then, implies an interrogation of what the disempowerment consists of and how it is maintained; however, it also involves looking at the imperative of the idea of taking responsibility for restoring voice.

The idea that trauma is political – that it revolves around issues to do with power and betrayal and centres, therefore, on fundamental democratic issues – brings it firmly into the sphere of the study of societal transition and democratization. The consequent idea that trauma compels a response suggests that it should be a key concern of academics interested in and working within societies that are moving from violence to some form of peace and stability. However, trauma's ambiguous, politically and morally charged nature requires alternative methods to the tendency within the study of peace-building and democratization in general towards problematizing issues in terms of quantitative, objective or 'scientific' responses. Although, as LaCapra points out, empirical evidence is absolutely necessary in trying to work through and redress traumatic injustices, it can also do violence to the liminal perspective and position in which victims, in part, reside – the 'absolute fundamental', alluded to by Deleuze, of recognizing the potential for research and commentary on vulnerable subjects to (pretend to) speak on their behalf. Yet, the deferral of the implications of that absolute with regard to the politics of trauma within the peace-building literatures of political science and transitional justice reflects a disciplinary bias towards positivism; but it may also contribute to a neglect of fundamental issues concerning democratization in post-conflict societies to which those disciplines broadly aim to further and deepen.

The political responses to trauma are, of course, different from those relating to conflict more generally – indeed the idea of a 'tool-box' or 'best practice' that are prevalent within the peace-building literature[14] may do damage to the traumatized individual. If those approaches are reproducing limited visions of democracy by virtue of their lack of a serious engagement with the politics of trauma, then a more rounded picture may be achieved by the incorporation of that politics into their discussions, analyses and practices. The study of the politics of trauma is not inherently or intrinsically opposed to sub-disciplines within peace-building; rather, the deferral of consideration of the political dimensions of trauma within peace-building risks the recycling of constrained, unbalanced and perhaps unjust and untenable notions of peace.

Troubling trauma

As mentioned earlier, trauma is often represented as unintelligible – as a limiting event or an excess that stands outside of the bounds of normal human explanation. The logic that seems to follow from this is that trauma is an imprisoning event; it not only escapes the bounds of intelligibility, but it is an inescapable event that, once experienced, returns to haunt individuals and that is capable of being transmitted across societies and across time. Cathy Caruth's work is emblematic of this way of framing trauma. As she explains:

> For history to be a history of trauma means that it is referential precisely to the extent that it is not fully perceived as it occurs; or to put it somewhat differently, that a history can be grasped only in the very inaccessibility of its occurrence.[15]

Caruth's work, which (together with that of Dori Laub and Shoshana Felman)[16] has been influential in the field of literary studies, arguably takes as its point of departure Freud's early (1917) essay on trauma, 'Mourning and melancholia'.[17] In this work, Freud contrasts mourning, which he views as the process of working through and moving beyond grief, with melancholia, which he sees as being recurrent and, to an extent, overwhelming of personality. Freud subsequently revised this binary and saw the relationship as less rigid. In the 1923 essay, 'Ego and the id',[18] for example, he argued that bereavement endures in the psyche and that rather than a setting aside of the past, the mourning process always retains an element of identification with the lost object/person. Although a locking in may occur for psychological and emotional reasons,[19] as Freud points out, people are able to move forward with their lives as survivors of loss and trauma – in other words, the hurt is endured but the individual is not eternally overwhelmed by it. Although Freud's work remains focused on the individual, it may be seen to give way to ethical obligations to care for and protect vulnerable members of society – that is, to provide a means of restoring voice and of overcoming and working through loss.

Caruth's approach has been severely criticized for working effectively to forestall such progress. Wulf Kansteiner and Harald Weinböck have, for instance, criticized the focus on abstraction and downplaying of empirical assessment of actual and perceived hurt as positively deleterious to healing and survival. The 'formidable moral conundrum' that they see as lying at the heart of Caruth's deconstructivist project lies in the limits of the project's own presentation of representation: in other words, the focus on the depiction (or lack thereof) of trauma occurs at the cost of consideration of lived experience. As they explain:

> . . . [f]rom the perspective of the trauma victim whose very survival might depend on his/her ability to repair his/her trust in human systems of signification as quickly as possible, Caruth's exuberant aestheticization and valorization of trauma appears ruthless, perhaps even cynical.[20]

Jeffrey Alexander retains Caruth's concern with the mediated aspects of trauma but seemingly invests it with a greater degree of agency than Caruth seemingly allows for in her own framing. Trauma occurs, he argues, when 'members of a collectivity feel they have been subjected to a horrendous event that leaves indelible marks upon their consciousness . . . and will change their future in fundamental and irrevocable ways'.[21] In this understanding, trauma as a concept moves from being simply about perception or inarticulacy towards being construal and constitutive of identity – it resides in emotions but is also capable of being mobilized.[22] In other words, trauma, when placed in a socio-political setting, is not only something ambiguous and haunting but also something that is pliable. Yet in both Alexander's and Caruth's understandings – that is, trauma as nebulous but real and trauma as chosen and structured – arguably, an emphasis on powerlessness is retained. Trauma is framed as a form of silence and a practice of silencing. The indelibility and irrevocability of trauma in Alexander's formulation goes some way, however, to explaining how it often manifests itself and plays a critical role in transitional societies insofar as legacies from the past go unresolved or come back to haunt the present.

Alexander's sociological approach can be distinguished from the rarefied readings of Caruth by situating trauma in a concrete setting that involves actual individuals. As such, it provides the basis for thinking about trauma politically in terms of voice, power and democracy. And this is essentially the point of departure for Jenny Edkins for whom traumatic recurrence involves implications for how society and democracy function. In exploring these implications, Edkins argues that the majority of politics occurs in routinized, regulated practices – most political activity, in other words, fits into patterns and, in turn, a central impulse within this is to make events fit similar patterns: the smoothing out of difference and distinction under legislation and regulative policies or the annexation and explanation of change and alteration within ideological or narratival frames represent central tools in the repertoire of both politicians and ordinary citizens for ensuring a semblance of continuity. Edkins places questions of memory at the centre of the study of politics – the maintenance of legitimacy and authority across time requires continuity in community and collective narratives;[23] in addition, memory acts as a kind of metaphor for core political dynamics of opening up (remembering) or shutting down (forgetting). As such, she contrasts 'politics' – the everyday routines of legislating and conducting ordered debate – with 'the political', 'where established ways of carrying on . . . are challenged and ruptured'.[24] 'Politics' is underpinned and maintained by such ruptures and, as she points out, it may be more accurate to think in terms of politicization and de-politicization rather than in a narrow frame.

Instead of linearity and continuity, trauma introduces a fractured temporality – the past recurs and invades the present in an unpredictable and profoundly unsettling fashion and, in so doing, calls attention to the power plays that reside within 'normal' politics. Edkins contrasts what she calls trauma-time with the linear temporality of normal politics. Trauma, for her, is a breach of that linearity and an imposition of powerlessness; but the politics of trauma, she argues, 'has to entail something else. It has to involve a betrayal of trust as well'. This betrayal, she points out, is the eruption of violence – unexpected and non-assimilable – into everyday life.[25] Trauma involves questions of power – abuse occurs at the hands of those with authority and control, and the failure to protect or abide by protocols and rules of best practice is ultimately the responsibility of those tasked with overseeing and policing. Thus, betrayal involves not only a 'giving away' or abandonment, but also a revelation of power: it calls into question our confidence in authorities, it taints the certainty that we have delegated and entrusted to leaders and officials and it exposes the flimsiness on which we base our convictions and beliefs in established orders. Thus, trauma is not just an isolating, atomizing and radically destructive event – it also involves the shattering of identity at a social level and the fragmentation of societal cohesion.[26] As Hutchison explains, traumatic events may be reproduced and engendered at a public level. Due to the representation of 'shock, vulnerability and confusion', she argues, individuals 'strive to make sense of what they are seeing, being affected by emotional responses and drawing upon prevailing discourses and symbols to [make] sense of what they see and feel'. Because of that desire to find meaning in extreme events, shared tropes are utilized, and the events themselves 'become perceived as a collective experience'.[27]

Hutchison's insight that an important part of the politics of trauma has to do with its mediation and representation tells only half the story; arguably, it reproduces the same logic that helps to defer considerations of the relationship between democracy and trauma. For a focus on the representational side of trauma can lead to a downplaying of the role that political elites can play in dealing with and working through traumatic events. The objectification of pain and suffering through mediation and representation works to focus attention on the Otherness of victims – on the monstrosities of human beings to other human beings and on the atrocities inflicted and suffered. As LaCapra points out, this emphasis on what might be called the exoticism of trauma works to displace the human and the individual. For instance, it harnesses feelings of pity (and condescension) at the expense of critical empathy, which involves the unsettling and exposing of the self. LaCapra argues that the evocation of pity through representation in effect re-victimizes victims by eulogizing suffering as a kind of vicarious end in and of itself – that is, as something redemptive and uplifting.[28] This sentiment is a common refrain within what might be called the Northern Irish victims' lobby or sector[29] or within statements by Northern Irish victims' spokespersons and groups. For example, the umbrella organization Justice for Innocent Victims of Terror continually repudiates platitudinous sympathy: 'Innocent victims and survivors of terrorism do not want your pity; they seek your understanding, your support and your commitment to do right by them in ensuring that Justice and Accountability prevails'.[30]

The key point is that the politics of trauma imply an awareness of the potential of power dynamics (whether implicit or overt) to reproduce the sense of betrayal, silencing, marginalization and hurt that the original interruption of violence brought about. Second, it means paying attention to the effects of those dynamics in shaping, colouring and determining identity – analyzing and exploring how traumatized identities and victimhood can be reinforced through representational frames and tropes, which are perhaps even the unintended consequence of a policy design and direction that is dedicated towards achieving justice and information retrieval. Finally, the politics of trauma involves a movement beyond representation and inarticulacy towards inclusion in society of those groups and individuals who have suffered the impact of terror and political violence. As LaCapra points out, the politics of trauma involve critical empathy and the avoidance of empty condolences and the exploration of how traumatized identities based around ideas of victimhood need not remain marginal and muted. As such, the politics of trauma involve exposing and revealing power disparities that result from political violence and peace settlements; it incorporates discussion not only of procedural but also substantive methods of including victims within peace-building; and it establishes the idea that some kind of imperative exists to encourage and facilitate that work.

Responding to trauma: representation, resilience, restoration, justice

The only way to challenge the objectification of trauma through the kinds of representations that LaCapra argues against is to try to recover or restore the individual victim at the centre of our attention.[31] This does not preclude critical analysis, argues LaCapra, but instead invests it with a degree of empathy that can be missing from or that can be manipulated by performance or – in the related concern of Sontag – that can be viewed as nothing other than representation by performance studies.[32] Michael Humphrey argues that the generalization and objective analysis of grievance is often the effect of truth commissions, where the intention is to restore societal stability. At the centre of this movement is the resort to performance as a form of truth creation: '[t]estimonies to suffering before tribunals are not aimed at securing justice but at constructing the victim as the foundation for moral and social reconstruction'.[33] Victims are thus constituted as such through performative displays that are often highly structured, ritualized and institutionalized. In such a way, the politics of trauma are inverted: societal responsibility for individual victims is replaced by victims' responsibility for healing society. As Fiona C. Ross (2003) points out in relation to the case of the South African Truth and Reconciliation Commission, for example, the disregard of women's experience of violence and rape within the remit of the commission represented a form of marginalization that helped to undermine efforts to integrate gendered issues into South African society.[34] The South African example speaks to the point that it is not simply representation but the authorization and legitimization of representation that seemingly lead to a deepening of democracy. However, these are the very terms that a politics of trauma challenges because trauma reminds us that violent experiences remain disempowering and retain the fractures created by betrayal. Although ideas about authorization and the canonization of legitimate representation work to silence those fractures, they are ultimately (to a degree) counterproductive and ineffective, for, to repeat the arguments of Das, individual hurt nonetheless remains and resides and continues to call out for recognition and voice.

The procedural approach to democratization deals with the possibility of and potential for trauma with a number of answers. These range from the mechanistic legalism of transitional justice initiatives with a focus on truth recovery and healing towards the practical importance of not reawakening old hurts by carefully managing institutional change, along with a legislative recognition of trauma through the provision of psychiatric care. 'Transitional justice' itself remains a disputed term – the idea of 'transition', for example, can be seen to denote a politically directed movement, and its linking to 'justice' might be seen to give way to an 'altered – and lesser – form of justice', a form linked to a particular historical moment.[35] However, as the forward-moving dynamic regarding the logic of transition itself – the movement from violence to peace – can be seen to offset the avowed victim-centred goals and approach. This is because it depends on a fashioning of versions of the past that appear to best fit contemporary settlement processes.[36] Regardless of this nuance, the International Center for Transitional Justice (ICTJ) offers a catch-all definition that stresses the importance of rules, roles and procedures: Transitional justice 'measures', it avers, 'include criminal prosecutions, truth commissions, reparations programs and various kinds of institutional reforms'. Transitional justice, the Center states, 'is not a "special" kind of justice'; it is, rather, 'an approach to achieving justice in times of transition from conflict and/or state repression'. The objective, it goes on to claim, is that by 'trying to achieve accountability and redressing victims, transitional justice provides recognition of the rights of victims, promotes civic trust and strengthens the democratic rule of law'.[37]

Although the transitional justice approach to peace-building begins with a concern for victims' rights, it is essentially structuralist and statist in focus. That is to say, it broadly looks to patterns of causation as distinct from a methodology that traces acts and omissions by individual actors – or even elite groups – and its focus has tended towards crimes perpetrated by authoritarian regimes. Of course, these tendencies can be traced to the fact that transitional justice takes its *raison d'être* from the Nuremburg trials after World War II and is seen to encompass a range of judicial mechanisms, such as the International Criminal Tribunal for the Former Yugoslavia (ICTY), and quasi-judicial institutions based on storytelling and emphasizing restorative justice, such as the South African Truth and Reconciliation Commission. The focus, therefore, has been on instances of regime change rather than post-conflict scenarios. However, even with that proviso, the narrative is patchy: the example of the Tokyo tribunal is largely forgotten, whereas

> [t]he long and exhaustive process of confrontation of the Nazi past in Germany is better traced as beginning from the activation of domestic judicial institutions in the 1960s than to a military tribunal founded by occupying powers in the 1940s.[38]

The structuralist and state-directed bias is made clear in the ICTJ's description of the activities of transitional justice. 'Because systemic human rights violations affect not just the direct victims, but society as a whole,' the organization argues, 'states have duties to guarantee that the violations will not recur, and therefore, a special duty to reform institutions that were either involved in or incapable of preventing the abuses'. The organization's description of its objectives goes on to contend that a 'history of unaddressed massive abuses is likely to be socially divisive, to generate mistrust between groups and in the institutions of the State [*sic*], and to hamper or slow down the achievement of security and development goals'.[39]

Although transitional justice theorists try to answer these questions through pleas to justice, the links between democracy and justice are often assumed rather than theorized or subjected to robust testing.[40] Following the ICTJ's approach the basic idea seems to be that securing justice through the recovery of truth(s) about past crimes and bringing perpetrators to justice will facilitate democratization by encouraging openness, accountability and transparency ('commitment to the rule of law') in post-conflict and post-authoritarian societies. Where political considerations are taken into account in this type of analysis they relate to the contestation between different versions of history or 'the truth'. The harnessing of justice to truth displaces questions of social responsibility for traumatized victims and confines societal transition within the framework of institutions and procedures. For example, in what has become one of the seminal works in contemporary transitional justice, Ruti Teitel asks what happens when the shared understandings on which every polity (she argues) is based break down. Situating transitional justice with a constructivist understanding,[41] her objective is 'to resituate the rule-of-law dilemma by exploring societal experiences that arise in the context of political transformation . . . [and] to attempt to understand the meaning of the rule of law for societies undergoing massive political change'.[42]

The inarticulacy of trauma and the politics of betrayal are seemingly not included in this understanding – breakdown instead is equated with the need to cultivate consensus, and the juridical process is held to be the key mechanism of transition: '[i]t is through the framework of law, the language, procedures and vocabulary of justice, that . . . reconstruction is advanced'.[43] Following from this, democratization must be seen to consist of the restoration of stability. The proscription is curiously homeopathic: the rationale or logic seems to be that 'like cures like' – in other words, because violence is the result of the absence of 'The Law', then peace must be fostered with the creation of justice. For example, Teitel argues that '[transitions] are periods when shared notions of political truth and history are largely absent'; she claims '[i]n transition, the very foci of shared judgement that form the basis for a new social consensus are expected to emerge through the historical accountings'.[44] In what historians (in a post–Hayden White era) would arguably find as rather passé, 'history' in Teitel's account is something that is contested but nevertheless remains objectively discernible. History, in her view, seems to be something beyond mere facts on which a consensual interpretation can be placed. Political development, then, is linked to uncovering truths about the past, for, as Teitel argues, '[t]he notion is that had this knowledge been known, then matters would have been different and, conversely, that now that the 'truth' is publicly known, the course of events will be different'.[45] Teitel's vision is compelling until issues concerning the publication and assimilation of truth are taken into account – and instances where both the authority of 'History' and 'The Law' remains subject to continued revision, contestation and competition. However, the political nuances involved in such issues are easily set aside in what is an essentially legalistic understanding of political transition in which 'History' exists to underpin 'The Law'. Thus, for Teitel,

> [w]hat makes for transitional accountability is generated by forms and practices within a legal system. Transitional histories reveal how certain legal forms and practices enable historical productions and transformed truths, shedding new light on our intuitions about the role of history in liberalising political change. Collective memory is created in frameworks and through symbols and rituals. In transition, the oft-shared frameworks – political, religious, and social – are threatened; so it is the law, its framework, and processes that in great part shape collective memory. In transitions, the pivotal role in shaping social memory is played by the law.[46]

The idea here is seemingly that legal frameworks are central to transitions because they are constitutive of political reality – they say what is acceptable and what is out of bounds; they establish preferred norms of belief and behaviour. However, the causality could easily be reversed and law might be seen as following historical interpretations and whoever can mobilize enough opinion behind her understanding of history may get the chance to make the law. In Teitel's understanding, justice is best served in periods of transition through selecting appropriate stories from the past. What she calls 'transitional histories' work to 'reveal how certain legal forms and practices enable historical productions and transformed truths, shedding new light on our intuitions about the role of history in liberalizing political change'. The notion does not seem too far removed from the Spanish novelist Javier Cercas' definition of myth: '[a] popular story that is true in part and false in part and that tells a truth that cannot be told only with the truth'.[47] Historical experiences that do not fit this prearranged order must be silenced in pursuit of truth, and the idea of trauma, replete as it is with ideas about inarticulacy, does not seem to have a place in Teitel's transitional justice schema.

Transitional justice as homeopathic peace-building, therefore, emphasizes storytelling as a way of recovering voice and establishing accountability.[48] PTSD and transgenerational transmission of traumatic narratives are, likewise, viewed as battles over control of the past[49] or sociological concerns to do with cyclical patterns of marginalization and alienation.[50] However, the underlying traumatic events may be rarely touched upon in such practices: they may be neatly bracketed in narratives of healing or acknowledgement under storytelling projects, or they may be placed at the service of nation building within truth and reconciliation processes – often to the exclusion of contexts and questions surrounding gender, class, age or locale.[51]

This is not to discount the genuinely therapeutic effects that truth recovery or storytelling or related initiatives and interventions may cultivate – storytelling and other practices that relate or devolve from Rogerian, person-centred therapies may well assist individuals come to terms with the traumas that they suffered. They can also give way to models of poor practice, such as the suggestion that a conflict transformation centre on the site of the former prison where the majority of paramilitary prisoners were confined would be a place that their victims could go to share their memories and reach some kind of closure. Other examples of bad practice include the restorative justice projects that have placed rape victims in the same room as their perpetrators, which extends to the notion that space be created for victims and those who inflicted terror and political violence.[52] What I wish to suggest, however, is that the politics of trauma, while encompassing aspects of truth recovery and, obviously, the articulation of historic hurts, also involves issues to do with processes of democratization. The standard proceduralist responses then work to assimilate trauma into something comprehensible and something that can be dealt with and legislated for.

The provision of psychiatric care response, or the 'medicalization' of victimhood, involves the positing that trauma is 'an "illness" that can be "cured" within existing or slightly modified structures of institutionalized medicine and psychiatry'.[53] Medicalization typically occurs through the exertion and expansion of state power into the lives of individuals by dislocating them from their local communal or familial support networks and requiring them to attend courses of cognitive-behavioural therapy (CBT) – funding is withdrawn from the former and the process is effectively privatized by awarding it to professionals trained in the latter. Northern Ireland, for example, represents a key example of what Humphrey has described as the 'therapeutic state':[54] community-based and cross-community organizations face funding cuts, and in order for victims to retain social security benefits, they must agree to be 'treated' by approved agencies. The idea is that government can provide a series of 'packages of care' that correspond to individual needs. Thus, resources are 'directed' or 'targeted' at specific needs, which provides not only 'value-for-money', but also access to services for individuals.[55] However, the expansion of state power occurs at the same time as the withdrawal of state responsibility:[56] 'access' is granted or afforded following consultation with a range of approved assessors (including general physicians and psychiatrists). Several implications follow, including the removal of resources and state recognition of alternative ways in which individuals have been seeking support, such as painting classes or local volunteering or charitable work. More problematic is the implication that if an individual is not 'cured' following his or her six sessions of CBT, then, in effect, the 'problem' lies with the individual and the state can claim it has done all it can.

The legislative construction of victimhood and trauma represents a means of applying order and predictability to an area that is, by its nature, highly ambiguous, inherently conflictual and incredibly complex. The rationalization (in both the sense of cost cutting and clarifying) of responsibility into service simplifies the role of the state and serves to harness and constrain risk by bringing vulnerable groups and individuals within a legislative framework, transforming them from damaged persons to being 'clients' or 'stakeholders'. Humphrey's 'therapeutic state' is, then, an extension of the general movement from top-down, accountable and scrutinizable (in theory at least) government towards structures of governance where policy making and implementation are dispersed (although power, as in this case, often remains solidly within the grasp of those who set legislation).[57] These governance trends have led to a reframing of the politics of trauma in terms of everyday resilience. This involves emphasizing what might be termed the 'reverse side' of trauma – for example, rather than concentrating on its inexplicability and creation of inarticulacy, the traumatic event, from the point of view of resilience, is seen as banal and rendered governable through a language of 'shock, devastation, anger, and blame'. As Brassett and Vaughan-Williams explain, the logic dictates that '[p]olitical energy is drawn to a specific and limited narrative of disaster and response where human experience is portrayed in universal terms'. The implications are that an 'ethics of pity is quickly marshalled, a politics of empathy constructed: something of the human persists and such events remind us of that'. The controlling and constraining of trauma, then, becomes part of the governance response.[58] In turn, reconstruction involves mobilizing the citizen, the subject or coherent pre-existing groups of citizens as agents in a process of dealing with and overcoming trauma.[59] The question of 'justice' for hurts suffered becomes filtered through or, more accurately, elided with transitional justice procedures and placed within a broader vision of (post)liberal peace-building.[60] Although much of this literature focuses on procedural or institutional aspects of post-conflict reconstruction, it does not specifically address the question of responsibility for trauma or the issue of the ethics that attach to trauma in the political arena. The focus often remains on the institutional – Pupavac and Pupavac, for instance, rely on James Nolan's ideas about the 'therapeutic state'[61] to argue in a rather predictable and pedestrian fashion that Croatian politics can be characterized as inert due to the privileged position afforded to war veterans within Croatian society.[62] As alluded to earlier, the idea of the therapeutic state fundamentally gives rise to questions of societal and political responsibility. One alternative way of thinking about this is to focus on how resilience actually functions. For Neocleous, for instance, governance in the aftermath of traumatic events harnesses a language and an expectation of individual's and communities' resilience in the interests of constructing and propagating a 'deeply conservative mode of thinking' that ultimately works as 'a means of cutting off political alternatives'.[63] Thus, resilience operates to usher in the political understandings gleaned from behavioural psychology regarding our capacity to cope with untoward events and, in the process, turns attention away from the past towards the future – preparedness and prevention for uncertainty and potential traumas yet to come, he argues, become pivots of political discourse and function as ways of structuring new conceptions of citizenship: '"Resilience" . . . designates an aptitude for little other than keeping things exactly as they are. We can expect to be traumatized collectively but not mobilized politically'.[64]

Given the limitations of a procedural approach to the experience of trauma, which, by definition, is resistant to attempts to give meaning or legislate for, some scholars writing within the field of transitional justice have sought to expand the paradigm. Catherine Cole, for example, has asserted that

> . . . [i]f, as Caruth says, the 'task of learning to listen anew calls for different ways of thinking about what it means to understand and what kinds of truth we are looking for', [then] transitional justice has much to gain from a deeper engagement with art.[65]

Cole argues that the aesthetic can achieve 'the goals of transitional justice',[66] despite alluding to criticism made against Antjie Krog for manipulating testimony in her book *Country of My Skull*. 'Art', she argues, possesses, 'a powerful ability to reveal depth, complexity and the affective and embodied dimensions, helping us to know these things as historical fact and lived experience'. Artistic practice, therefore, 'can signal presence, highlight absence and tolerate silence without necessarily trying to fill it'. The idea seems straightforward – artistic practices (and engagement with art) can reveal new ways of voicing and perceiving an experience. But, of course, artistic practice and engagement also involve judgment, assessment, preference and even bias. Cole shrewdly gives no criteria for negotiating the problems that artistic evaluation may present were truth commissions to use artistic 'tactics'. Neither does she offer assistance to the problem of misrepresentation – instead, Cole seems relaxed about the prospect for artists to manipulate victims' testimony and/or historical events. The problem seems not to be temptation, but the valorization of such artistic interventions emptied of their political implication. Although Cole remarks on the distinction between art and transitional justice, the parallels seem clear and are revealed again in Cercas' notion that some 'truths' can best be expressed through myth, which is something less than the truth. In fairness, Cole seems to acknowledge this issue and reverts to the notion of 'read[ing] critically' because of 'the western and northern hemispheric bias of trauma studies as well as its tendency to focus on individual experiences of violence, when often the causes and consequences of violence are systemic and structural in nature'. This may well be the case – though Cole does not go into any detail to substantiate her claims; however, when politics become detached from economic bases and nationalism is preponderant, then notions of post-coloniality can work to replicate rather than deconstruct established power relations.[67] This can occur through the framing of reform or intervention within pre-established notions of colonizers, subject groups and neo-imperialism or neo-liberalism when, in fact, the dynamics that these terms can imply do not always play out as the theory would suggest (for example, it does not make sense for nationalistic elites to jettison their working classes in case more radical groups mobilize those left behind and work to 'outbid' their intra-bloc rivals).[68]

Stories and responsibility

The direction that this taking of sides means as a response to trauma is inherent in the political writings of Jacques Rancière. The limitations of a procedural, institutional and legalistic approach to democratization are the central concern of Rancière's writings on politics – and, in part, his alternative emphasizes the political and ethical importance of art as a way of transcending grievance and imparity. To some extent this idea speaks to the notion that the political effect of methodological mainstreaming is not simply to place an emphasis on one type of system of problem setting and problem solving and the marginalization of alternatives – it actively works to displace and silence alternative ways of thinking about the world. Rancière describes this process as the 'the distribution of the sensible" (*le partage du sensible*). As he puts it,

> I call the distribution of the sensible the system of self-evident facts of sense perception that simultaneously discloses the existence of something in common and the delimitations that define the respective parts and positions within it. A distribution of the sensible therefore establishes at one and the same time something common that is shared and exclusive parts. This apportionment of parts and positions is based on a distribution of spaces, times, and forms of activity that determines the very manner in which something in common lends itself to participation and in what way various individuals have a part in this distribution.[69]

The distribution of the sensible, he goes on to argue, relates not only to the individuals who form a self-governing community, but also the preceding act that 'determines those who have a part in the community of citizens'.[70] The sharing out, therefore, refers to practices of exclusion and inclusion and is associated with what is 'capable of being apprehended by the senses'[71]. For Rancière, the process involves a shutting down of the political, which he associates with dissensus – debate beyond or resistant to juridical foreclosure[72] – by the establishment and maintenance of an order that aims for consensus in terms of acceptable beliefs, values and behaviours. Rancière equates this state of shutting down with the metaphor of the police, which constitutes the first of the two ways that 'community' can be ascertained. He distinguishes the police order from that of actual policing work: Rancière describes the order of the police as the way of counting; that is, of ascertaining only the 'empirical parts – actual groups defined by differences in birth, by different functions, locations, and interests that constitute the social body'.[73] He argues that this approach actually demarcates not only what is acceptable, but also what is knowable about politics: 'the police is a partition of the sensible whose principle is the absence of a void and of a supplement'.[74] As Samuel Chambers explains: '[t]he police order distributes bodies without remainder and without exclusion . . . there is nothing it does not account for, nothing left over or external to its process of counting'.[75] In other words, 'the supplement', the extra or the disagreement and difference that seemingly constitute the core of politics, is subsumed within a form of politics that seeks to maintain order or contain debate within institutions and procedures. Rancière is explicit about the implications for democratization: 'Democracy', he argues, 'is not a political regime . . . [it] is the very regime of politics itself'.[76] Democracy, then, is to be 'outside of the count'[77] – in other words, it is found beyond the movement towards proceduralization.

Rancière's play of politics/police proceeds from what he sees as the ambiguity inherent in the concept of equality, which depends on legislating or inscribing a certain order – that is, a certain balance between specific groups and individuals. It is for this reason that he distinguishes between politics and the political, with the political or the beginnings of politics involving perceptions of inequality or grievance. The contention that follows from that is worked out through politics; that is, it is given meaning and resolution, but gives way to further claims making. Politics, then, he argues, is 'heterogenous' with the police:

> Politics acts on the police. It acts in the places and with the words that are common to both, even if it means reshaping those places and changing the status of those words. What is usually posited as the space of politics, meaning the set of state institutions is precisely not a homogenous place. Its configuration is determined by the state of relations between political logic and police logic.[78]

The drifting that is inherent in the political from openness to closure marks the effort towards ending debate and the beginnings of the realm of the police. That realm, for Rancière, ends the political insofar as it involves the subsuming of support *and* opposition, the incorporation of inclusion *and* exclusion, and the annexation of agreement *and* dissent. Democracy as a practice and an ethos, he argues, can be made subject to these processes but fundamentally is concerned with a broadening of 'the political stage' and the making visible of the almost imperialistic enclosure of the realm of the police.[79]

For Rancière, democratization, or 'politics', represents the second way of counting 'the community'. Having placed most of the everyday within the realm of 'the police', he equates 'politics' with the disruption of the police order: '[p]olitics is specifically opposed to the police'.[80] For Rancière, the struggle for democracy is integral to the overcoming of inequality, which, in turn, can collapse into an anti-democratic or oligarchic project that installs ideological visions onto society and on to the state. 'Democracy', in this understanding, is to be sought after but is forever unachievable; as such, it is linked to competitions over ascribing meaning to events and inequities or imparities, but also to a struggle against the confusion over the drift between dissensus and consensus, debate at the ever-present possibility of foreclosure: 'What democracy means is precisely this: the juridico-political forms of State constitutions and laws never rest upon one and the same logic'.[81]

The inverse, the return of the political, involves dissensus – the questioning of presumed equality, interruption and the challenging of systems of domination.[82] Despite the subsuming nature of the order of the police, Rancière argues that it can be confounded by the aesthetic, which becomes political when it calls into question our assumptions of what seems self-evident, recasting them to focus on what lies beyond, what underpins and what is excluded.[83] He distinguishes his idea of disagreement and the supplement (the extra, the beyond) from Lyotard's much-cited *le différend*: disagreement is, for Rancière,

> . . . neither a misunderstanding nor a general lack of comprehension. It is a conflict over what is meant "to speak" and over the very distribution of the sensible that delimits the horizons of the sayable and determines the relationship between seeing, hearing, doing, making, and thinking. In other words, disagreement is less a clash between heterogeneous phrase regimes or genres of discourse than a conflict between a given distribution of the sensible and what remains outside it.[84]

Extrapolating from Rancière, we might suggest that trauma works in a political sense towards the same end as aesthetics – it reveals the sensation at the heart of Rancière's *sensible* as hurt and betrayal and in so doing exposes the erstwhile hidden effects of power and the fragility of the relationship between elites and those they represent. Rancière explains the inversion by juxtaposing the noun 'politics' with the adjective 'the political' in the sense that '[p]olitics is the art of suppressing the political'.[85] However, it is precisely this juxtaposition that, when extrapolated to the sphere of the politics of trauma, victimhood and peace-building, seemingly leads quickly to dead ends. In short, when placed in that realm, Rancière's thought would seem to have little to contribute beyond a critical analysis of power and representation. For example, the application of the 'police logic' may be seen to disenfranchise victims and traumatized individuals by filtering their concerns and needs along juridico-institutional pathways or within discourses that are underpinned by pre-determined outcomes in the forms of ethical demands for reconciliation or compromise – demands that may require victims to engage with the perpetrators of political violence on terms favourable to the latter (in other words, implicitly requiring victims to reconcile themselves to perpetrators' explanations).

On the other hand, the logic of dissensus may create an equivocation between terms such as victim and perpetrator that may similarly replicate pre-existing power relations. Thus, perpetrators may claim victimhood or subaltern status of one kind or another, and those individuals who directly suffered their violent acts may find themselves forced to admit the demands of recognition by their perpetrators in ways that water down their own calls for justice and reparation. This debate has, for example, surfaced in Northern Ireland in several ways over the issue of compensation and reparation, with some victims arguing against inclusion of paramilitaries in state payouts to the families of the deceased (for instance, when the deceased may have been blown up by his or her own bomb) and others questioning what they perceive to be unequal treatment between security force victims and survivors and individuals in the general public. In some ways, the debate over recognition echoes similar concerns in the former Yugoslavia regarding the payment of pensions to 'veterans' who may have been culpable of egregious acts of violence and terror.[86] Often, the concern goes beyond monetary issues and speaks instead to a demand for recognition and a fear of equivalence between victims and perpetrators (or perpetrators and state security forces in Northern Ireland) and the creation of a discourse of relativism – based around the idea that 'if you had been there, you would have done the same'.[87]

I wish to suggest, however, that one avenue within Rancière's thought allows a circumnavigation of these concerns and addresses the problem highlighted by Deleuze. This avenue also avoids the aesthetic politicizations inherent in transitional justice, which are encapsulated in Cercas' notion of a myth – in the case of transitional justice as articulated by Cole and Teitel, of a transitional truth made up of something less than the truth. The point of departure is Rancière's conception of democracy, which he fundamentally locates in the disruption of the police order. He rejects the idea that democracy is present when the individual is rendered subject or subordinate to the universal, and instead argues that democracy occurs at the point of contention between what he calls the *demos* and the *ochlos* – that is, between 'the people' as a sharing community and the 'throng of people' of the community 'obsessed with its own unification'.[88] For Rancière, democracy is found in the interruption of the police order – the logic that establishes communities that enjoy particular rights and that excludes others. As he describes it, this interruption is achieved through 'a singular mechanism of subjectification' – the revelation (or making visible) of those people who have no share in the community-based distribution of the sensible.[89] This making visible occurs through the manifestation or perception of a grievance, an imparity/inequality or a wrong. The dissensus that occurs within society (that divides 'the people') is supplementary to legislation in that it acts as a discord against the obsession with unity among those who wish to sublimate disagreement within or into a cohesive community. For Rancière, 'community', then, operates in two senses – an anti-democratic, populist tendency towards unity that is based on processes of inclusion and exclusion; and a division, where those outside of that process question its basis. 'The invention of community', he writes, 'the ever-to-be-recommenced invention of the community of equals – is kindled in the disjointed and random relationship between what is there and what forces change; in the facticity of the process of sharing'.[90]

It is for this reason that Rancière writes about the 'hatred of democracy' among political classes. For example, he writes of how '[d]emocrats themselves have always remained suspicious of democracy' [91] and how the ' "government of anybody and everybody" is bound to attract the hatred of all those who are entitled to govern men by their birth, wealth, or science'.[92] In contrast to sociological work on post-democracy as an age in which ideology and division have been filtered from the public arena, [93] in which parties become obsolete or media for maintaining policy while changing personnel,[94] or where notions of freedom and choice are meaningless,[95] Rancière places the notion in relation to his distinction between forms of community:

> Postdemocracy is the government practice and conceptual legitimization of a democracy *after* the demos, a democracy that has eliminated the appearance, miscount, and dispute of the people and is thereby reducible to the

> sole interplay of state mechanisms and combinations of social energies and interests.

He goes on to argue that it is not found simply in institutions; rather, it is

> . . . an identifying mode, among institutional mechanisms and the allocation of the society's appropriate parts and shares, for making the subject and democracy's own specific action disappear. It is the practice and theory of what is appropriate with nothing left over for forms of the state and the state of social relations.[96]

Rancière's thought resists the relativism of myth making and transitional norms and opens the possibility of defending marginalized individuals and groups through its defence of democracy. He places democracy in contrast to power and wealth. 'It is not based on any nature of things nor guaranteed in any institutional form', he writes. It is relational and is in constant need of defence:

> It is not borned along by any historical necessity and does not bear any. It is only entrusted to the constancy of its specific acts . . . among those who know how to share with anybody and everybody the equal power of intelligence, it can conversely inspire courage, and hence joy.[97]

The implications of Rancière's thought, then, for the politics of trauma seem to lie in the notion that a response to trauma does not simply consist of reconfiguring the meaning of the experience and the event that caused trauma – it is not simply performative nor deconstructive; it is both but more. It is also not simply reconstitutive of relations through social or political mechanisms or institutions – it is that and more. It is critical of modes of inclusion and exclusion, but it is also more than this. Instead, it provides for a response based on the facticity of experience and the interrogation of where the distribution of the sensible occurs. It also provides for a response that questions the power of community to curtail, forestall and contain experiences and points of view that may strike discordant notes.

Conclusion

The procedural and legalistic approach is, at its core, based on the premise that truth recovery facilitates democratization by holding political elites accountable for previous human rights abuses and by opening up discursive space for citizenry to debate ideas and reach some kind of consensus.[98] As I point out in more detail in the next chapter, whereas deliberative democracy is more relaxed about the opening up of dialogue – provided, of course, that mechanisms are in place and proper rules of debate are followed – than alternative approaches to managing ethnically divided and transitioning societies, the resort to regulations and institutions does not really tackle the core problems to do with betrayal and responsibility that are posed in the politics of trauma. Although these problems may be fundamental to a vision of democratization, they are not easily quantifiable; nor are they subject to simple cultivation through institutions. Arguably, betrayal, complicity and responsibility lie at the nexus of the relationship between democracy and justice. For if democracy and justice are taken to be in the first instance values before they are practices,[99] then questions concerning betrayal at the hands of political authorities and responsibility towards our fellow citizens seem to encapsulate the impulse towards democratization. The *ressentiment*/trauma binary explored and exposed by Jeffrey Olick may well be a valid and radical response to the imposition of violence, but seems to reside at the level of the individual and may not be carried through to a societal or democratic level:[100] the obverse of trauma-as-betrayal and trauma-as-silencing is not an ethos of a demand for justice; rather, the demand for justice forms part of a broader societal imperative to remedy grievances, arbitrary or prejudicial exclusions and injustices.[101] *Ressentiment* as a prerogative towards seeking redress and reparation forms part of that imperative, but the politics of trauma do not need to end in a kind of identity politics as Olick sees it.[102] Indeed, a politics of reparation may seem to serve as a metaphor for trauma-as-group claims making may continue to recur in a slow process of upward mobility or as an unending process of zero-sum ethnic politicking.[103] Olick's idea of historical responsibility, then, in that case may become expanded and linked to a politics of responsibility in the present – a politics of redress and rebalance and a politics of critical empathy.

Olick points out that the social sciences have failed to take trauma as a concept as seriously as psychiatry, history or literary studies.[104] As a result, these links between democratization processes within societies moving away from violence tend to be seen in terms of institutions. Where trauma does feature, it does so at a practical level with regard to the ever-present possibility that institutionalization of truth recovery may re-traumatize their respondents or may open up wounds that could lead to a return to conflict.[105] Although this may well be the case, at the level of democracy – or, rather, democratization – what this re-traumatizing involves is a silencing, an exclusion and a removal of agency. In other words, the practical concern with avoiding the mistakes of the past or the procedural concerns with establishing workable democratic or truth recovery institutions do little to answer the basic questions posed by traumatic events: namely, those involving the betrayal of trust and the exposing of political power. I have suggested that these questions can be displaced by standard, 'mainstream' positivistic approaches to analyzing transitional politics.

As Rancière suggests, although positivism is subsuming, it is not totalizing, and although alternative political experiences (such as those of individuals who have been alienated from political elites) exist in the margins, their very existence calls into question the assumptions upon which routinized, 'normal' politics operates. Neither is the recognition of that liminality an admission of recurring and inescapable inarticulacy. The political dimension of trauma, rather, calls out for recognition and, as such, a kind of admission into society: as an injustice, it demands reparation; as an exclusion, it demands acknowledgment; as a muting, it demands voice. The politics of trauma, then, are intimately bound up with an ethics of responsibility. I have suggested that, fundamentally, politics revolves around the construction of an ethos that takes seriously trauma and victimhood as societal issues. Victimhood is, of course, a notoriously slippery term (one person's victim may be another's oppressor). However, the response to trauma that this chapter proposes involves recognition of responsibility. That response echoes Judith Butler's analyses of grief, mourning, vulnerability and the 'precarious life'. Butler argues that the recognition or the 'mindfulness' of vulnerability 'can become the basis of claims for non-military political solutions . . . We cannot . . . will away this vulnerability. We must attend to it'.[106] And from that attentiveness, she argues, can arise a radical political ethos centered on inter-dependence – a new conceptualization of community based on mutual need rather than competition.

The core lesson of such a politics, this chapter has suggested, is that democratization processes need to incorporate not only procedural dimensions, but also a consideration of the core values that transitional societies wish to hold about themselves. The Rancièrean 'supplement' that trauma constitutes – namely, the inarticulacy of experience and the perception of betrayal by political power – stands outside of this process. Instead, it calls for a different form of democratization – one based, not on individual victims' responsibilities towards societies, but on societies' responsibilities to those who suffered most from the effects of political violence. Trauma, in a political sense, stands outside the subsuming efforts of dominant approaches to peace-building in that it retains the memory of fissured relationships and fractured trust. It resists attempts to establish prefabricated 'solutions' which can result in a speaking for or on behalf of marginalized individuals, thereby compounding their loss of voice and agency. And it evades the similar notion to apply a lens and politicize it by emphasizing it as mediated or performative. Instead, I have suggested that the political dimension of trauma, then, works to restore societies' responsibilities for individuals to the heart of democratization processes. What this looks like in terms of peace-building and the practical issues involved in establishing post-conflict societies are the themes of the next chapters.

Notes

1 Duncan Bell, 'Introduction: Memory, trauma and world politics', in *Memory, Trauma and World Politics: Reflections on the Relationship between Past and Present*, edited by Duncan Bell (Basingstoke: Palgrave Macmillan, 2010), pp. 1–29; Jenny Edkins *Trauma and the Memory of Politics* (Cambridge: Cambridge University Press, 2003); Jenny Edkins 'Remembering relationality: Trauma time and politics', in *Memory, Trauma and World Politics: Reflections on the Relationship between Past and Present*, edited by Duncan Bell (Basingstoke: Palgrave Macmillan, 2010), pp. 99–115; Michael Humphrey, *The Politics of Atrocity and Reconciliation: From Terror to Trauma* (London: Routledge, 2002); Michael Humphrey, 'Reconciliation and the Therapeutic State' (2005) *Journal of Intercultural Studies*, 26(3): 203–220; Dominick Lacapra, *Writing History, Writing Trauma* (Baltimore: The Johns Hopkins University Press, 2001).

2 Deleuze cited in Michel Foucault and Gilles Deleuze, 'Intellectuals and power', in *Language, Counter-Memory, Practice: Selected Essays and Interviews*, edited by D. F. Bouchard (Ithaca: Cornell University Press, 1977), p. 209.

3 United Nations, 'Guidance note of the Secretary-General: United Nations Approach to transitional justice' (N.P., 2010). Available at www.unrol.org/files/TJ_Guidance_Note_March_2010FINAL.pdf; accessed on 27 August 2013.
4 Michael Ignatieff, *Warrior's Honor: Ethnic War and the Modern Conscience* (London: Vintage, 1999), p. 173; see also Aleida Assmann (2007) 'Europe: A community of memory?' *GHI Bulletin*, No. 40: pp. 11–25.
5 For a critical overview of the political assumptions underpinning mental health care work, see, for example, Chris Gilligan (2006) 'Traumatised by Peace? A Critique of Five Assumptions in the Theory and Practice of Conflict-Related Trauma Policy in Northern Ireland', *Policy & Politics*, 34(2): 325–345.
6 Ian Hacking (8 August 2013) 'Lost in the Forest', *The London Review of Books*, 35(15): pp. 7–8.
7 See the United Nations, Disarmament, Demoblization and Reintegration Resource Centre, www.unddr.org; accessed on 25 February 2015.
8 See Edkins, *Trauma*.
9 Veena Das (1997) 'Language and Body: Transactions in the Construction of Pain', *Daedalus*, 125(1): 70.
10 This seems to be the impulse behind the seminal works of Cathy Caruth: *Trauma: Explorations in Memory* (Baltimore: Johns Hopkins University Press, 1995); *Unclaimed Experience: Trauma, Narrative, and History* (Baltimore: Johns Hopkins University Press, 1996); see also her recent short monograph/collection of essays, *Literature in the Ashes of History* (Baltimore: Johns Hopkins University Press, 2013).
11 Elizabeth Bennett, *Empathic Vision: Affect, Trauma, and Contemporary Art* (Stanford: Stanford University Press, 2005), p. 12.
12 Susan Sontag, *Regarding the Pain of Others* (London: Penguin), p. 99; Sontag excoriates the theorizing of Guy Debord and Jean Beaudrillard that, for 'the West', war and suffering are mediated: 'To speak of reality becoming a spectacle is a breathtaking provincialism. It universalizes the viewing habits of a small, educated population living in the rich part of the world, where news has been converted into entertainment – that mature style of viewing which is a prime acquisition of "the modern", and a prerequisite for dismantling traditional forms of party-based politics that offer real disagreement and debate'; ibid, pp. 98–99.
13 LaCapra, *Writing History*, p.42.
14 For an overview, see David P. Barash and Charles P. Webel, *Peace and Conflict Studies* (London: Sage, 2014).
15 Caruth, *Unclaimed Experience*, p. 18.
16 Shoshanna Felman and Dori Laub, *Testimony: Crises of Witnessing in Literature, Psychoanalysis, and History* (London: Routledge, 1992).
17 Sigmund Freud, 'Mourning and melancholia', in *On Murder, Mourning and Melancholia*, translated by Shaun Whiteside (London: Penguin, 2005), pp. 201–218.
18 Sigmund Freud, 'Ego and the id', in *Beyond the Pleasure Principle: And Other Writings*, translated by John Reddick (London: Penguin, 2003), pp. 103–150.
19 LaCapra argues that individuals may 'resist working through' because they retain a 'fidelity to trauma, a feeling that one must somehow keep faith with it' (*Writing History*, p. 22). Similarly Andrew Rigby argues that it seems 'commonsense' for people to 'want to forget the pains of the past and get on with their lives', but that those people 'whose core identity is as a victim' find it impossible to break with what occurred to them or their loved ones; see Andrew Rigby, *Justice and Reconciliation: After the Violence* (London: Lynne Rienner, 2001), p. 1.
20 Wulf Kansteiner and Harald Weilnböck, 'Against the concept of cultural trauma (or how I learned to love the suffering of others without the help of psychotherapy)', in *A Companion to Cultural Memory Studies*, edited by Astrid Erll and Angsar Nünning (Berlin: De Gruyter 2010), pp. 230.

21 , Jeffrey C. Alexander, 'Towards a theory of cultural trauma', in *Cultural Trauma and Collective Identity*, edited by Jeffrey C. Alexander, Ron Eyerman, Bernhard Giesen and Neil J. Smelser (London: University of California Press), p. 1.
22 Ibid, p. 22.
23 Edkins, 'Remembering', p. 101.
24 Ibid, p. 108.
25 Edkins, *Trauma*, p. 4.
26 Piotr Sztompka (2000) 'Cultural Trauma: The Other Face of Social Change', *European Journal of Social Theory*, 3(4): 449–466.
27 Emma Hutchison (2010) 'Trauma and the Politics of Emotions: Constituting Identity, Security and Community after the Bali Bombing', *International Relations* 24(1): pp. 65–86.
28 LaCapra, *Writing History*, pp. 41–42.
29 The terms are used with the admission that many people who consider themselves victims resist seeing themselves as part of a 'lobby' or 'sector', holding that their needs and rights are distinct from other societal stakeholders; furthermore, some utilize the language of governance and policy instrumentally in order to engage with civil servants and elected representatives.
30 *The Impartial Reporter*, 'Fermanagh witnesses say Blair should give OTR evidence', 12 June 2014. Available at www.impartialreporter.com/news/roundup/articles/2014/06/12/405474-fermanagh-witnesses-say-blair-should-give-otr-evidence/; accessed on 13 June 2014. Capitalization in original.
31 Humphrey, *The Politics of Atrocity*, p. 103.
32 LaCapra, *Writing History*, pp. 86–113.
33 Humphrey, *The Politics of Trauma*, p. 107.
34 Fiona C. Ross, *Bearing Witness: Women and the Truth and Reconciliation Commission in South Africa* (London: Pluto Press, 2003).
35 Tricia D. Olsen, Leigh A. Payne, and Andrew G. Reiter, *Transitional Justice in Balance: Comparing Processes, Weight Efficacy* (Washington, DC: United States Institute for Peace, 2010), p. 10.
36 See, for example, Eric Gordy, *Guilt, Responsibility, and Denial: The Past at Stake in Post-Milošević Serbia* (Philadelphia, PA: University of Philadelphia Press, 2013); Cillian McGrattan (2009) '"Order Out of Chaos": The Politics of Transitional Justice', *Politics*, 29(3): 164–172; Jelena Obradović-Wochnik (2013)'The "Silent Dilemma" of Transitional Justice: Silencing and Coming to Terms with the Past in Serbia', *International Journal of Transitional Justice*, 7(2): 328–347; Jelena Obradović-Wochnik, *Ethnic Conflict and War Crimes in the Balkans: The Narratives of Denial in Post-Conflict Serbia* (London: IB Tauris, 2013).
37 International Center for Transitional Justice [ICTJ], 'What is transitional justice?' Available at http://ictj.org/about/transitional-justice; accessed on 17 June 2014.
38 Gordy, *Guilt*, p. 169; see also John Dower's conclusion that in regard to the Tokyo Tribunal, '[s]o substantial . . . [were the] omissions that it does not seem too harsh to speak of criminal neglect, or even collusion, on the part of the prosecution itself'; John Dower, *Ways of Forgetting, Ways of Remembering: Japan in the Modern World* (New York: The New Press, 2012), p. 124.
39 ICTJ, 'What is transitional justice'.
40 David Mendeloff (2004) 'Truth-Seeking, Truth-Telling and Postconflict Peacebuilding: Curb the Enthusiasm?' *International Studies Review* 6(3): 355–380.
41 Ruti G. Teitel, *Transitional Justice* (Oxford: Oxford University Press, 2000), p. 6.
42 Ibid, p. 12.
43 Ibid, p. 72.
44 Ibid, p. 71.
45 Ibid, p. 111.
46 Ibid, p. 71.

47 Javier Cercas, *Outlaws*, translated by Anne McLean (London: Random House, 2014), p. 177.
48 Jennifer Curtis, *Human Rights as War by Other Means: Peace Politics in Northern Ireland* (Philadelphia, PA: University of Pennsylvania Press, 2014).
49 See, for instance, Vamik Volkan's ideas about 'chosen trauma' and the valorization of victim-cults in order to justify and claim legitimacy for contemporary claims making; Vamik Volkan 'Chosen trauma, the political ideology of entitlement and violence'. Available at www.vamikvolkan.com/Chosen-Trauma,-the-Political-Ideology-of-Entitlement-and-Violence.php; accessed on 29 July 2013.
50 See, for example, Ereshee Naidu and Cyril Adonis, 'History on their own terms: The relevance of the past for a new generation' (N.P., 2004). Available at www.gsdrc.org/go/display&type=Document&id=3138; accessed on 29 July 2013.
51 See, for instance, Paul Gready, *The Era of Transitional Justice: The Aftermath of the Truth and Reconciliation Commission in South Africa and Beyond* (Abingdon: Routledge, 2011); Greg Grandin (2005) 'The Instruction of Great Catastrophe: Truth Commissions, National History, and State Formation in Argentina, Chile, and Guatemala', *American Historical Review*, 110: 46–67; Cillian McGrattan, *Memory, Politics, Identity: Haunted by History* (Basingstoke: Palgrave Macmillan, 2013); Jelena Obradović-Wochnik, 'The "Silent Dilemma" '; Ross, *Bearing Witness*.
52 For example, the non-governmental organization Healing Through Remembering has run several storytelling and archiving projects whose underlying goal seems to be to 'open up a platform in which diverse voices and experiences of the conflict can be heard by all members of the public'; see www.healingthroughremembering.org/projects/Everyday_Objects; accessed on 15 June 2014. For a critique of restorative justice practices, see Cillian McGrattan (2010) 'Community-Based Restorative Justice in Northern Ireland: A Neo-Traditionalist Paradigm?' *British Journal of Politics and International Relations*, 12(3):408–424.
53 Kali Tal, *Worlds of Hurt: Reading the Literatures of Trauma* (Cambridge: Cambridge University Press, 1996), p. 6.
54 Humphrey, 'Reconciliation'.
55 Barry McCaffrey, 'What is the future for victims' groups here?' *The Detail*, 30 July 2013. Available at www.thedetail.tv/issues/245/victims/what-is-the-future-for-victims%E2%80%99-groups-here; accessed on 15 June 2014. The quotations are taken from a video clip on the webpage of an interview with Mrs. Ann Dorbie, the director of the Northern Ireland Victims and Survivors Service.
56 Humphrey, 'Reconciliation', p. 217.
57 Nikolas Rose, *Powers of Freedom* (Cambridge: Cambridge University Press, 1999).
58 James Brassett and Nick Vaughan-Williams (2012) 'Governing Traumatic Events', *Alternatives: Global, Local, Political* 37(3): pp. 183–184.
59 Vanessa Pupavac (2012) 'Global Disaster Management and Therapeutic Governance of Communities', *Development Dialogue*, 58: 81–97; Mladen Pupavac and Vanessa Pupavac (2012) 'Trauma Advocacy, Veteran Politics, and the Croatian Therapeutic State', *Alternatives: Global, Local, Political* 37(3): 199–213.
60 Chandra Lekha Sriram (2007) 'Justice as Peace? Liberal Peacebuilding and Strategies of Transitional Justice', *Global Society*, 21(4): 570–591.
61 James L. Nolan, *The Therapeutic State: Justifying Government at Century's End* (New York: New York University Press, 1998). Pupavac and Pupavac ignore the fact that Nolan's text does not concern itself in any way with the dynamics of deeply divided or post-conflict societies.
62 Pupavac and Pupavac, 'Trauma Advocacy', p. 200.
63 Mark Neocleous (2012) ' "Don't Be Scared, Be Prepared": Trauma-Anxiety-Resilience', *Alternatives: Global, Local, Political* 37(3): 198.
64 Ibid, p. 196.
65 Catherine M. Cole (2014) 'At the Convergence of Transitional Justice and Art', *The International Journal of Transitional Justice*, 8(2): 322.

66 Ibid, p. 316.
67 The application of post-colonial theory to Ireland was spearheaded by Edward Said and Seamus Deane during the 1980s, but has been the subject of both damning and constructive critique; see, for example, Stephen Howe, *Ireland and Empire: Colonial Legacies in Irish History and Culture* (Oxford: Oxford University Press, 2000). Stefanie Lehner, for example, brings together the Marxist roots of some of post-colonialism, with a focus on 'the network of power structures' – particularly with regard to gender inequalities – with a Levinasian focus on the individual as an 'Other'. What she terms a 'subaltern ethics' is based on a 'sensibility and responsiveness to the *ethos* of the other, namely the specific position and place that a subaltern other occupies in a given society'; Stefanie Lehner, *Subaltern Ethics in Contemporary Scottish and Irish Literature: Tracing Counter-Histories* (Basingstoke: Palgrave Macmillan, 2011), p. 22; emphases in original. The starting point of this project is the philosophy of Emmanuel Levinas, whose own foundation lies in the Dostoyevsky quote from *The Brothers Karamzov*: 'We are all responsible for all [and] for all men before all, and I [am] more responsible than all the others'. As Lehner explains, although this responsibility is detached from reciprocity, it remains a political and a social act because, for Levinas, 'it is the encounter with the face of the Other that also confronts one with all the innumerable others that make up society' (cited in ibid, p. 22). The subaltern ethics inherent in this approach avoids a political programme beyond the imperative placed on 'the critic' of 'careful scrutiny and negotiation of power relations [and] a deliberate taking of sides' in favour of the marginalized; see also Colin Graham, *Deconstructing Ireland: Identity, Theory, Culture* (Edinburgh: Edinburgh University Press, 2001).
68 Donald L. Horowitz, *Ethnic Groups in Conflict* (London: University of California Press, 1985).
69 Rancière, *The Politics of Aesthetics*, p. 7.
70 Ibid.
71 Gabriel Rockhill, 'Appendix 1', in Rancière, *The Politics*, p. 89.
72 Rancière offers the following explanation of what constitutes 'the political': 'The same thing – an election, a strike, a demonstration – can give rise to politics or not give rise to politics. A strike is not political when it calls for reforms rather than a better deal or when it attacks the relationships of authority rather than the inadequacy of wages. It is political when it reconfigures the relationships that determine the workplace in its relation to the community. The domestic household has been turned into a political space not through the simple fact that power relationships are at work in it but because it was the subject of argument in a dispute over the capacity of women in the community'. Jacques Rancière, *Disagreement: Politics and Philosophy*, translated by Julie Rose (London: University of Minneapolis Press, 1999), pp. 32–33.
73 Jacques Rancière, 'Ten theses on politics' in *Dissensus: On Politics and Aesthetics,* translated by Steven Corcoran (London: Continuum, 2010), p. 36.
74 Ibid.
75 Chambers, *Lessons*, p. 43.
76 Rancière, 'Ten theses', p. 31.
77 Ibid, p. 32.
78 Rancière, *Disagreement*, p. 33.
79 Jacques Rancière, 'Does democracy mean something?' in *Dissensus: On Politics and Aesthetics,* translated by Steven Corcoran (London: Continuum, 2010), p. 54.
80 Rancière, 'Ten theses', p. 36.
81 Jacques Rancière, *Hatred of Democracy*, translated by Steve Corcoran (London: Verso, 2006), p. 54.
82 Chambers, *Lessons*, p. 43.
83 Jacques Rancière (2002) 'The Aesthetic Revolution and Its Outcomes: Emplotments of Autonomy and Heteronomy', *New Left Review* 14 (March-April): 133–151.

84 Gabriel Rockhill, 'Editor's introduction: Jacques Rancière's politics of perception', in Rancière, *The Politics*, p. xiv.
85 Jacques Rancière, *On the Shores of Politics*, translated by Liz Heron, (London: Verso, 1995), p. 11.
86 Pupavac and Pupavac, 'Trauma advocacy'.
87 McGrattan, 'Politics'.
88 Rockhill, 'Appendix 1', p. 92.
89 Rancière, *Disagreement*, p. 99.
90 Rancière, *Shores of Politics*, p. 90.
91 Rancière, *Disagreement*, p. 96.
92 Rancière, *Hatred*, p. 94.
93 Colin Crouch, *Postdemocracy* (London: Polity, 2004).
94 Peter Mair, *Ruling the Void: The Hollowing of Western Democracy* (London: Verso, 2014).
95 David Chandler, *Freedom and Necessity in International Relations: Human-Centred Approaches to Security and Development* (London: Zed Books, 2013).
96 Rancière, *Disagreement*, p. 102.
97 Rancière, *Hatred*, p. 97.
98 Lauren K. Taylor and Alexander Dukalskis (2012) 'Old Truths and New Politics: Does Truth Commission "Publicness" Impact Democratization?' *Journal of Peace Research* 49(5): 671–684; Charles Tilly, *Credit and Blame* (Oxford: Princeton University Press, 2008).
99 See Ian Shapiro, *Democratic Justice* (London: Yale University Press, 1999).
100 Jeffrey K. Olick, *The Politics of Regret: On Collective Memory and Historical Responsibility* (Abingdon: Routledge, 2008).
101 Young, *Responsibility*.
102 Olick, *Politics*, p. 173.
103 See, for instance, Timothy Kubal, *Cultural Movements and Collective Memory: Christopher Columbus and the Rewriting of the National Origin Myth* (Basingstoke: Palgrave Macmillan, 2008).
104 Olick, *Politics*, p. 154.
105 See, for example, Helena Cobban, *Amnesty after Atrocity? Healing Nations after Genocide and War Crimes* (Boulder, CO: Paradigm Publishers, 2007).
106 Judith Butler, *Precarious Life: The Powers of Mourning and Violence* (London: Verso, 2004), p. 29.

2 Peace-building and the politics of responsibility

This chapter looks at the implications of the politics of trauma for building and sustaining peace. Drawing in particular on the Northern Irish example, it argues that articulating a commitment to societal responsibility is essential to building a peaceful democracy. The previous chapter emphasized the idea that trauma is characterized by inarticulacy, grievance and betrayal but that aestheticization of that silencing equates to a form of depoliticization that works to reify or abstract individual hurt from historical, societal and political contexts. The politics of trauma, then, involve restoring an awareness and perhaps even an engagement and articulation with the broader landscape within which the hurt and injustice have occurred. This chapter aims to develop that argument by bringing together recent work on political responsibility by Iris Marion Young and Eric Gordy to explore how models for building democratic peace (consociationalism, deliberative democracy and agonistic democracy) may be reinforced and complemented with a consideration of ideas concerning social ties and connections. Although these ideas are implicit within the 1998 Northern Irish peace accord, I suggest that the practice of governing Northern Ireland frequently clashes with what can be seen as the 'stickiness' of the past. The chapter suggests that a policy of placing responsibility at the forefront of any policy or political initiative to build and foster peace may work to constrain these clashes.

Trauma and democracy

The relationship between the retrieval of information about historic crimes and human rights abuses and peace-building is complex. As pointed out in the previous chapter, the growth of research in the field of transitional justice (arguably a sub-discipline of peace studies) in the past two decades is in part a response to the idea that accountability and justice should be key elements of any transitional society.[1] As pointed out in Chapter 1, a dilemma remains regarding the possibility that too much truth can be destabilizing.[2] The dilemma resides unresolved at the heart of the United Nations' peace-building protocols. For example, the UN advocates 'the right to truth', including the 'right of families to know the fate of their relatives'.[3] On the other hand, the Oslo protocols of 2010 require states to '[r]ecognise the rights of victims of armed violence in a non-discriminatory manner, including provision for their adequate care and rehabilitation, as well as their social and economic inclusion'.[4] A potential conflict of interests may, it could be argued, result in the 'truth' that some victims hold regarding their innocence of any violence and against the need for a 'non-discriminatory' approach that could include perpetrators who may also consider themselves to be victims.

A number of responses have been suggested to these troubling issues with one prominent example being the South African model of a truth recovery process that offers amnesties in return for truth. Mark Osiel, for instance, has argued that when accompanied by a range of obligations that tie new regimes and leaders to human rights protocols, amnesty processes can provide some level of the truth about crimes being achieved.[5] The point seems to be that amnesty serves power interests and fosters a *carte blanche* attitude to violent pasts that inevitably bolsters the interests of perpetrators over their victims. This was roughly the approach of the South African Truth and Reconciliation Commission (TRC). As Mahmood Mamdani has recently pointed out, the South African transition was planned before the TRC was set up and that amnesty was promised to perpetrators

> . . . not in exchange for truth-telling but, crucially, for joining the process of political reform. The negotiations were conducted with the aim of ending political and juridical apartheid. They involved inevitable compromises on both sides, without which the transition could not have been achieved.[6]

As such, amnesty as a set of policy tools for moving societies beyond violence goes beyond proceduralism to incorporate substantive issues concerning ethical principles and long-term, transgenerational judgments. These issues lie at the heart of Paul Ricoeur's alternative and critical views on amnesty, which he defined as 'organized forgetting'. Ricoeur claimed that they 'do wrong at once to truth, thereby repressed and as if forbidden, and to justice, as it is due to the victims' [7]; instead, he advocated a historically and empirically informed approach in which critical history becomes married with a sense of justice.[8]

Another response is to aim for something less than a truth recovery process. Whereas some socio-psychological scholars speak of the need to cultivate empathy, acknowledgement and understanding among antagonistic groups,[9] some political theorists aim for a middle ground based on what might be termed the development of a political culture of consensus and dialogue. Amy Gutmann and Dennis Thompson, for example, have argued that '[c]omprehensibility of conflicting claims is far less final than reconciliation, and far more accepting of the kind of continuing moral controversy that is not only inevitable but desirable in a democracy'.[10] They contend that

> . . . the goal of creating a society with commonly shared values still lacks moral content and therefore cannot justify the sacrifice of criminal justice. At minimum, the content of the new society's shared values must be incompatible with continuing the morally abhorrent practices of the past.[11]

In other words, a new constitution or agreed-upon framework of democratic principles ignores the ideological reality that differing views on the past will prevail even after violence has ended. Gutmann and Thompson are critical of attempts to solve this conundrum that stresses the importance of reconciliation, which they argue should not be defined or framed in terms of 'seeking some comprehensive social harmony, whether psychological or spiritual . . . Reconciliation is an illiberal aim if it means expecting an entire society to subscribe to a single comprehensive moral perspective'.[12] They suggest that although democratic societies ought to strive for reconciliation on some matters (freedom of speech, non-discrimination and equality measures), the notion of consensus on any matter or a closing down of debate is antipathetic to a healthy democracy where conflict is essential but filtered through appropriate channels.[13]

Some transitional justice theorists have also advocated a mixed approach. For example, in a recent survey of transitional justice mechanisms, Olsen et al have argued that '[t]rials and amnesties proved inconclusive for improving democracy. Truth commissions, when used alone, have a significant, negative effect'.[14] The underlying idea seems to be that there is a nebulous but very real link between democratization, peace and justice (all broadly conceived). This chapter addresses the link from an alternative angle – and one that remains somewhat under-researched and underappreciated in the peace-building and transitional justice literatures: namely, the implications for democratization that are involved in the politics of trauma. Following the discussion of Rancierè's thought in Chapter 1, I wish to argue that the key dilemma in building peace between a notion of 'positive peace' (justice, societal reconciliation, social inclusion and so on) and 'negative peace' (slowly building institutions, delayed truth recovery or simply the absence of war) sidesteps the notion that regimes of appropriateness are inherent in each pathway. This is not to suggest that the dichotomy, undoubtedly expressed with a certain lack of finesse, between positive and negative peace is false; rather, the argument suggests that peace-building and democratization work to create distributions of the 'sensible' that reproduce self-referencing logics. The effect of these distributions is to risk not only reifying the discourses and forms and modes of identity that precipitated and drove forward conflict, but the continued marginalization of individuals, social groups and identities that resist or stand outside of mainstream political configurations. I argue that an alternative begins not simply from a critical deconstruction of the power disparities that inhabit dominant modes of belonging or those that ensue from peace-building strategies. That approach in turn risks reifying through inversion: namely, the valorization of other identities or communities. The alternative approach, instead, I suggest, begins with a reversion; it begins with what is *outwith* the domain of the sensible – what Rancierè calls the '*demos,* the poor or *une part des sans-part,* a part without part, a part with no part'. As Chambers explains:

> [T]he *part des sans-part* cannot be contained by or included within the police order; it is the part that has no part *within* the police order. It is the part that

only comes to be through politics. Thus, the unintelligible part is not *hidden* and for that reason unseeable; rather, the unintelligible is not there at all.

The point of critical engagement, therefore, is not to unmask or make visible, since the police order renders it invisible. Rather, it is to emphasize and expose the points at which the marginal makes its presence felt – in other words, the points at which those outwith legislative frameworks or what is considered appropriate begin to make claims on the status quo.

It is at this point that the politics of trauma become important for peace-building and democratization. This is because, and as Jenny Edkins's work points out, the politics of trauma represent an unveiling of the relationship between those with power and those without, between those in the centre of the decision-making process and those on the margins of society and between political elites and victims of political violence.[15] I suggest that what this unveiling gives way to is a consideration of a societal responsibility to include its most disenfranchised members.

Proceduralist peace-building

For purposes of clarity, I focus on how that consideration applies to peace-building efforts, particularly how democratization processes are framed in societies transitioning from violence to peace. The intention is not to re-run debates over the merits of one type of democratic vision over another, but rather to suggest that unless the politics of trauma is taken seriously within peace-making (whether that is institutional design, international involvement or grassroots initiatives) then it is somewhat premature to speak of justice or reconciliation. The chapter does not question the arguably tendentious division between peace and justice[16]; instead, the argument, simply put, is that the links between peace-building and democratization can be strengthened if the politics of trauma are taken more seriously. The chapter represents a sketch at such an integration. The focus is on the Northern Irish case where in many ways the implications of not taking such an integration seriously are becoming increasingly clear: namely, the change process becomes jeopardized by the traumatic return of ghosts from the past in numerous and varied ways, ranging from enduring sectarianism and social segregation to debates over victims' rights; from controversies over public symbolism and political culture to the recurring revelations of spies, informants and deals made between governments and paramilitaries.[17] I recognize that the institutional form of the Northern Ireland Assembly – a consociational structure (see below) – may lend itself to a divided (elite) political culture and policy process. However, I suggest that an underappreciated element in the tendency for elements of the past to dominate contemporary politics lies in the failure to incorporate an awareness of the political implications of trauma – in particular, the demand for some kind of acknowledgment of societal responsibility that accrues from these politics.

The relationship between the politics of trauma and democratization is founded on the idea that political legitimacy, stability and authority are closely aligned with memory. Thus, Edkins argues that 'memory is not an add-on to the study of politics': it does not simply concern identity issues; instead, it is integral to 'the form of political authority that the nation represents is intimately tied up with, and made possible by the way in which it invokes its memories, and with what it remembers and why'.[18] Edkins' arguments echo those of J.G.A. Pocock, who sees memory, or what he calls historical consciousness, as the juncture at which high politics and everyday life meet together with the historical and the sociological.[19] For Pocock, historical awareness and memories of the past flow from and into 'tradition' – the narratives that shape society and govern its expectations are also shaped and formed by society in turn. And it is a similar concern with the politics of the past that allows Edkins to infuse memory studies with a political edge. Thus, she argues that trauma is not just psychological: although it is individual and involves oppressive tendencies of incommensurability and voicelessness, it is also in large part related to others – to society and to political power. As pointed out in Chapter 1, Edkins argues that although traumatic events are characterized by (recurring) powerlessness, they also involve betrayals.[20]

Traumatic experiences and traumatic memories involve existential threats – they change the meaning of identity at a fundamental level since self-perception is closely linked to social context. Edkins argues that traumatic events 'strip away the diverse commonly accepted meanings by which we lead our lives in our various communities. They reveal the contingency of the social order and in some cases how it conceals its own impossibility'. In other words, the politics of trauma reveal the ways 'in which the social order is radically incomplete and fragile. It demonstrates in the most shocking way that what we call social reality is nothing more than a fantasy'. As Edkins continues, the politics of trauma 'question our settled assumptions about who we might be as humans and what we might be capable of. Those who survive often feel compelled to bear witness. On the whole, the rest of us would rather not listen'.[21]

The themes of silence and silencing recur in testimonies of victims and survivors of Northern Ireland's conflict. In a book compiled by the Wave Trauma Centre, the two themes coincide in the story of one survivor of a bombing:

> Before the bomb, I was bubbly, outgoing, and confident. It has been an uphill struggle for me to remain that way. I have become withdrawn, with no confidence, I am shy, depressed and suffer from insomnia among other things. Deafness is lonely and isolating. It's only since meeting with others who are affected by the 'Troubles' that I am getting any help or recognition. My husband and children are victims too because of my deafness . . . The two older girls were in drama groups putting on musicals and my son was lead vocalist in the school choir, I went to see them but couldn't hear them singing, that is the saddest thing of all.[22]

Although it manifests itself at the individual and familial level in the first instance, trauma is inherently disruptive of individuals and society. The disruption proceeds from the radical (re)conceptualization of history that traumatic events engender. Following the work of Vladimir Jankelivitch, Berber Bevernage alludes to this break in his analytical dissection of how we experience the past. Bevernage argues that a dominant mode of articulating the experience of 'pastness' utilizes the language of historiography and law: it views the past as irreversible, 'having-been' (*avoir-eu-lieu*), transient or fleeting. Crimes and hurts are revisited in order to consign them more firmly to the past: judgments are made and historical events are deemed finished with, 'done-and-dusted'. An alternative mode views the past as irrevocable, a 'having-been-done' (*avoir-fait*) and as something stubborn and tough. Bevernage explains that people

> . . . experience the past as irreversible if they experience it as fragile and as immediately dissolving or fleeting from the present. They experience the past as irrevocable if they experience it as a persistent and massive depository that sticks to the present.[23]

This 'stickiness' is, evidently, a dominant element of the traumatic experience. As a response to history, it informs how we interpret, re-present and reconstruct violence and injustice.

Whereas transitional justice is a direct attempt within peace-building to tackle the 'stickiness' of the past, there is no reason to suppose that either securing peace and/or deepening democracy requires some kind of reckoning with the past. In response to this and to the perhaps overly procedural basis of early formulations such as Teitel's, the scholarly and practitioner-based sides of the transitional justice movement have broadened to incorporate bottom-up or localized initiatives. However, as Jelena Obradović-Wochnik has pointed out, despite this increasing reach, the impetus remains the same and 'still carries a strong focus on silence-breaking activities'.[24] In an important critique, Obradović-Wochnik demonstrates how despite this aim, transitional justice works to reinforce the silence(s) that it wishes to expose. 'Selective academic engagement', occurs she argues, by the prioritization of 'activists' voices', thereby privileging certain types of stories and reproducing power dynamics that are founded on self-serving political narratives about the past: transitional justice practitioners, concerned with public participation, often fail to consider the context that make such participation and speaking (im)possible'.[25]

Obradović-Wochnik's work discusses several ways in which such silencing practices occur, including the allocation of collective blame; the construction of an imaginary, simplified 'public' audience or the ethnicization of social groups or entire populations. She concludes, however, that transitional justice practices can nevertheless be reformed to ameliorate the tendency towards silencing by focusing on the exposure of the 'mechanisms that exclude' and the revelation of the 'complexities inherent within silences'.[26] The danger, of course, is that attempts to rebalance the deficit may create further regimes of exclusion. However, Obradović-Wochnik's prescription that 'silence' ought to be decoupled from 'denial' seems pertinent to the Rancierean approach: the latter, as she points out, is typically tackled with recourse to a discourse of truth recovery that is in actuality closer to truth imposition in the form of coerced or cajoled reconciliation. Silence, on the other hand, may stand closer to the Rancierean part-without-part, in that it may be not simply an appropriate but the only response available to acts of political violence, terror, corruption and intimidation.

The extent to which transitional justice is struggling to come to terms with its built-in bias towards exclusion and deferral of silencing and trauma is, arguably, reflected in alternative strategies of peace-building. This is apparent in the practice and literature of consociationalism. Although the institutional engineering of this theory is premised on the idea that it is better to build a democratic peace than risk a return to violence through a process of coming to terms with the past, I wish to suggest that the links between it and transitional justice are substantial and problematic, but they are largely ignored in the literature. For example, the discipline's key journal, *The International Journal of Transitional Justice* (published by Oxford University Press), regularly features articles appraising the purportedly expanding nature of the field and offering reconceptualizations of what transitional justice is or suggestions about what it should be doing. Yet even when the focus of those articles is on division, the methodological impulse remains naively and simplistically segregationist and proceduralist. A case in point is Khanyisela Moyo's passing allusion to substantive democracy in her exploration of the limitations of transitional justice in dealing with reparations in racially divided societies (South Africa and Zimbabwe); her rather insipid suggestion is that the policy goals of transitional justice ought to be reframed to prioritize land redistribution in truth recovery processes. What this redistribution might mean in normative terms or what it would look like practically or how it would be implemented is seemingly deemed outwith consideration.[27] Yet the underlying logic is decidedly structuralist – 'redistribution' in this case echoes consociationalists' emphasis on 'autonomy' and the unquestioning faith in group cohesion. This is unsurprising given that Moyo's point of departure is another re-imagining of transitional justice – Nevin Aiken's recent monograph *Identity, Reconciliation and Transitional Justice* in which 'constructivist' theorizing is mentioned but the structuralist critique of constructivism is missed. The 'gap' in reasoning leads to what may be viewed as a significant misinterpretation and misrepresentation of reality: Nevin, for instance, complains about the 'failure to gain any significant cross-community support for otherwise well-regarded initiatives for addressing the past such as those suggested by Healing Through Remembering [a non-governmental lobby group] and the Consultative Group on the Past [a governmental consultation exercise]'.[28] Not only was the latter's report deeply controversial,[29] but Aiken appears to be setting these bodies' work apart from the 'highly polarized lines of group identity' that he argues characterizes the Northern Irish political culture. The reasoning is devoid of irony and recalls Brecht's 'solution': 'To dissolve the people / And elect another'.[30] My point is that transitional justice tends to operate according to the same logic as consociationalism – but, critically, without consociationalists' realism that division needs to be recognized rather than wished out of existence or ignored. In other words, it operates according to a relatively strict and underarticulated distribution of appropriateness: ethno-nationalism is reified, if not valorized, and alternative experiences of the past or of marginalization or trauma in the present are displaced. This is key to understanding the links between consociationalism and transitional justice. The exclusionary regime drawing that typifies both theories is often overlooked in the counterfactual reasoning that is typically used to both justify and attack consociationalism. I suggest that this reasoning depends on a false dichotomy between consociationalism and 'integrationism'.

Consociationalism refers to a set of ideas about conflict regulation. Essentially, it states that if two or more contending groups exist in a region, then violent conflict can be reduced or ended by channeling disputes through political institutions. Drawing on the work of the Dutch political scientist Arend Lijphart,[31] consociationalists assert that in such cases, institutions should be designed according to an established set of principles: for example, majoritarianism should be avoided and instead power should be shared out between the contending groups, a series of checks and balances should be set up to allow groups the opportunity to veto legislation that may discriminate against their interests, elections should be held within proportional systems and bloc autonomy should be emphasized – particularly over issues affecting specific regions or regarding institutions such as the courts and the police. Consociationalists argue that in situations of ethnic conflict, identity tends to be difficult to change, deep rooted within culture and history and multifaceted, being reinforced within a number of overlapping socio-cultural networks (for example, language, sport, religion, political association). They contend that this durability has to be worked with rather than ignored or imagined out of existence. In a robust defence of the theory, Jonathan Tonge goes further and charges critics with 'elitism': '[i]nstead of accepting and cherishing diversity, identity is seen [by such critics] as an affliction held by people, requiring remedial treatment'.[32] On the other hand, as two transitional justice-oriented scholars have argued in a complementary fashion, 'strong and secure identities . . . can also serve as the basis for political generosity' and may assist attempts at challenging 'sectarian attitudes and practices'.[33]

Lijphart first applied consociational theory to Northern Ireland in 1975[34]; since the mid-1980s it has informed the joint and separate work of John McGarry and Brendan O'Leary. O'Leary and McGarry distinguish themselves from Lijphart on the basis that whereas 'Lijphart makes no important distinction between polities that are linguistically, ethno-nationally, or religiously divided', they view division in Northern Ireland as originating primarily from a 'self-determination dispute spanning two states'.[35] McGarry and O'Leary have used the provisions of the Good Friday Agreement and procedures of the Northern Ireland Assembly to revise consociational theory and, in particular, Lijphart's idea concerning 'conducive conditions'. In contrast, Paul Dixon has pointed to several features of the agreement that suggest it is not consociational in intention or application. Thus, the Northern Irish executive never operated as an integrated body, proportional allocation of resources and services was not provided, the British government possesses an external veto and the agreement promoted integrative measures.[36]

A number of criticisms have been levelled at consociational theorizing. A fundamental objection is that it is not a theory at all, but is in fact an example of post hoc or even circular reasoning. In other words, consociationalism is a cure for a problem that it defines – it is a description turned into a prescription.[37] Because of this, consociationalism is seen as tending to reinforce and reproduce conflict-based and socially divided identities – both at an everyday level and within the culture of political leadership.[38] In addition, the principles upon which consociationalism are built are nothing more than principles – that is, notions about 'strong and secure identities' being useful for building peace are untested and unverifiable, and the theory does not specify how, why or when that usefulness can be triggered.[39] Other critics have argued that the empirical evidence shows that rather than regulating or ending conflict, consociationalism provides the opportunities for bloc identities to become useful once more for waging violence, in that it valorizes segregationist leaderships and provides such leaders time to regroup.[40] Critics of consociationalism tend to favour alternative approaches and strategies such as deliberative democracy, electoral plurality and proportional representation, the integration of contending groups and policies aimed at the watering down of the importance of boundaries and symbols, along with an emphasis on civic society rather than ethnic leadership elites.

The counterfactual that both consociationalism and integrationism depend on is that unless their policies are implemented as the core part of peace-building, then the risk is that conflict may recur or that policy will be ignored (in the face of the historical reality of division or changeable identity). The underlying point is that each framing works to harness a set of ideas about appropriateness; or, put another way, each school of thought constitutes its own distribution of the sensible. The counterfactual works because of this harnessing. In other words, both consociationalist and integrationist proposals are possible because they depend on establishing some kind of centre: for consociationalists, this centre is divided into autonomous ethno-national blocs, whereas for integrationists, it is created out of a new identity. Tonge's critique of integrationism hints at this idea but does not follow its logic towards consociationalism: '[T]he collectivization of identities into a single core begs the question, which core? Integrationists may deny that their project is assimilationist, arguing that a core single national, or post-national identity does not entirely eradicate previously-held identities'.[41] Tonge goes on to criticize integrationists for their 'lack of clarity' over these terms and over their projects. He may well have a point, but even though consociationalists are more up-front about taking ethno-nationalist identities at face value and working with those deeply held beliefs, that does not really mitigate the tendency towards centrism or core building. The critique that integrationism is elitist or paternalistic – given the tendency of academics or liberals to urge others to give up what are perceived as nationalistic prejudices – may well be levelled at consociationalism, where the tendency is to valorize particular aspects of identity that academics and practitioners see as important. The flat-packed version of peace-building that both depend on – that is, the notion that some kind of pre-established entity can be constructed from a range of objects – is ultimately exclusivist; the question, then, of whether consociationalism or integrationism is more or less elitist is a matter of degrees or perception. Moving beyond what might be called the Ikea logic of peace-building requires investing the design phase with a concern for the parts of society left out – in particular, those groups on the margins of political deliberations, victims and the traumatized. The following sections locate some of where these exclusions occur within peace-building in Northern Ireland.

Governing Northern Ireland

The Northern Ireland Assembly was established under the peace accord of 1998. It is a 108-seat body with a wide range of primary and secondary legislative powers that have been devolved from London. The Assembly is elected by proportional representation and the executive constituted through the d'Hondt mechanism – excepting, that is, the ministry with responsibility for policing and justice, which was awarded outwith d'Hondt to the cross-community Alliance Party. This section explores how assumptions about justice underpin the workings of the Assembly and governance in Northern Ireland in general and how those mechanisms work to constitute a realm of appropriateness. The 1998 agreement has almost facilitated a definitive break with the violence of the past (which has continued at a much reduced level in the form of republican anti-agreement shootings and bombings, and which obviously retain the potential to cause massive loss of life), and it would most likely have been impossible to agree on a mechanism for dealing with the past at the time of the signing; however, the recurrence of historic issues can be linked to the outworkings of the peace settlement. Although the agreement pledged parties to 'firmly dedicate ourselves to the achievement of reconciliation, tolerance, and mutual trust, and to the protection and vindication of the human rights of all',[42] I wish to argue that these sentiments need to be buttressed with a commitment to societal responsibility as a first step to creating stability around the politics of the past. This can be seen in alternative visions of democracy at work in Northern Ireland – in particular, consociational and deliberative democratic schemes. The final section sketches alternative visions.

As alluded to earlier, consociationalism is among the most prominent visions of democratization and peace-building, particularly in the case of ethnic conflict. Consociationalists argue that ethnic division needs to managed and filtered into political processes through institutional frameworks that guarantee shares of power and protected autonomy. The Northern Ireland peace settlement has been seen as emblematic of these ideas and is suggestive of the need to create a robust structure to contain and manage ethnic division.[43] Consociationalism is traditionally critiqued along the lines that it reifies and perpetuates division; it tends to take ethnic identification as a given and does not allow for fluidity or a breaking down of strongly held views.[44] Indeed, this is seen as a strength: Clancy and Nagle, for example, argue that 'it is a quixotic undertaking to try to redirect ethno-national identities; it is possible, though to try to make them more benign and less threatening . . . Conflict remains, but it is channelled [*sic*] through democratic institutions'.[45]

In evidence to the Northern Ireland Assembly's Assembly and Executive Review Committee, Professors Brendan O'Leary and Christopher McCrudden argued for the maintenance of the consociational governance structures.[46]

Referring to the on-going debate over whether one of the executive parties should leave to become an unofficial opposition, O'Leary claimed that 'the existing arrangements are better than they might appear, even to those schooled in the orthodoxies of the Westminster model. We think that it is politically inappropriate to prefer the Government and opposition model for Northern Ireland'. He recommended 'enhancing MLAs' policy and administrative scrutiny capabilities through increasing resources available for expert assistance, which is also good for building party capacity'. O'Leary and McCrudden's evidence reflects the fundamental consociationalist idea that stability is key to peace-building and that even if it means delimiting political opposition or potentially delaying truth recovery mechanisms, those concessions are the price that must be paid in order to ensure the end of violence. It is ostensibly unfair, then, to criticize consociationalism for not paying attention to victims' issues. The point is subtler: despite the emphasis on post-war or post-conflict institutional engineering, nevertheless an idea of justice underpins consociationalism – namely that the best that can be hoped for is to end violence and filter contention through a network of political institutions. Justice occurs through constraining democracy. The focus on managing division by bolstering intra-bloc politics neglects the question of the responsibility that those blocs have to each other to govern and work within the same polity. Regardless of whether it is the ultimate desire of groups to reform or end that polity (the Irish nationalist parties in Northern Ireland, for example, wish to end the current constitutional settlement and reunify the island of Ireland under one jurisdiction), that issue of working, governing and living within a current polity remains. The politics of trauma work to reveal that issue, and questions of responsibility pervade post-conflict societies. Arguably, those politics logically precede institution building (whether those institutions are consociational or truth recovery commissions) precisely because they speak to cultural attitudes and informal practices, which institution building seeks to constrain, circumscribe, harness or police. As Vivian Lowndes and Mark Roberts have recently pointed out, in situations of institutional constraint, it is not sufficient simply to focus on rules or protocols. Although these are important, the 'narrative' that attaches to an institution must also be taken into account because any change process must involve the developments of new understandings.[47] The point being that the narrative underpinning consociationalism remains the understanding that unless a 'core' is established out of ethno-nationalist political leaders who can 'carry' their constituencies, then the risk of falling back into violence remains. That narrative works to frame key actors within the public sphere as critical to peace-building and allocates them roles within a set of rules.

The issue that characterizes much of the debate over consociationalism is what follows from that narrative – as McCrudden and O'Leary's intervention in Northern Ireland demonstrates: the key questions seem to be how fair and transparent are the rules and procedures? Ian O'Flynn sidesteps the type of institutional problems that preoccupy consociationalism: '[C]itizens will not be able to think of themselves as sharing a common national identity unless there is some common basis upon which they can engage with one another on non-ethnic terms'.[48] In contrast to consociationalists' emphasis on rules and elites, engaging civil society lies at the heart of O'Flynn's vision:

> [D]eliberative democracy requires us to shift away from an elite-driven process towards a process in which the decisions that result can, in a meaningful sense, be understood as expressions of the will of the people – where "the people" is construed, not narrowly in terms of ethnic leaders and those they purport to represent, but in terms of the full diversity of views and positions in society'.[49]

What happens, however, where 'the people' can be extended to include their 'ethnic leaders', where, for example, electoral returns broadly mirror other societal divisions (including education, housing and culture)? In other words, what happens when 'elites' do not 'purport to represent' *their* 'people' but largely coincide with them? Luskin et al have recently tackled this problem in relation to Northern Ireland, arguing that '[o]rdinary citizens may actually have less intractably opposing views than the elites who speak for them, and the experience of grappling together with policy issues may both help them to see this and bring their views still closer'.[50] Sustained engagement in deliberation may, they argue, make it harder for elites to ' "play the ethnic card" '. These arguments seemingly have merit, and other evidence from Northern Ireland reveals the multiple ways in which people negotiate, transcend and transgress ethnic boundaries in their everyday lives.[51] Deliberative democrats have also recently explored ways in which identities can be articulated in a non-confrontational fashion that does not need to be buttressed by consociational architecture. John Boswell, for example, has suggested that narrative provides an alternative to deliberative democracy theorists' usual emphasis on argumentation. For Boswell, the concept of 'narrative' lies between anecdote and discourse: like the former, they display discernible structural features and have plots that link events; they frame particular concerns or protagonists as important and become reified and 'canonical'. As with the latter, they are fluid and are built up in a performative fashion over numerous interactions and iterations.[52] Following John Dryzek's critique of Jurgen Habermas,[53] Boswell argues that deliberation does not in reality only take place in single spaces and in a monologic fashion; instead, it occurs in 'complex systems' and involves 'take as well as give'.[54] He argues that narrative plays a crucial role in facilitating these conditions and that, furthermore, it provides for communication and sense making. Although Boswell views narrative as a 'rationalis[ing]' device that provides space for discussion and deliberation,[55] he also admits that its 'structuring role may also work to exclude certain individuals or marginalise their claims'. More problematically for divided societies in particular, Boswell admits that the 'danger is that mutual adherence to a vague narrative may result in apparent consensus, while still allowing conflict to fester unresolved'.[56]

The idea that a deliberative democratic approach can be brought to bear in such societies and that it may contribute positively to moving beyond the impasse of entrenched narratives lies at the heart of many approaches to truth recovery and transitional justice. Leigh Payne, for example, argues for a 'contentious co-existence' in post-conflict societies, which she describes as an approach that

> . . . does not require elaborate institutional mechanisms, but rather is stimulated by dramatic stories, acts, or images that provoke widespread participation, contestation over prevailing political viewpoints, and competition over ideas . . . in other words . . . democracy in practice.[57]

Payne works in a somewhat sceptical fashion, breaking down conceits and deconstructing self-serving apologies, and her idea of competing narratives works to open debate: '[u]nsettling accounts do not replace one prevailing political view with another. Instead, they generate political competition over how to interpret dramatic political events, how to use them, and what they mean for contemporary political life'.[58] This seems rather unsatisfying, particularly for societies where openness and democracy might be seen to be the problem rather than the solution. The politics of trauma in such societies can be harnessed to democratic and institutional politics in ways that actually close down and exclude victims' voices. In Northern Ireland, as was mentioned earlier, the 1998 institutional arrangements were established with a view to moving forward as opposed to revisiting the past. Again, this point is indirectly but critically linked to Payne's theorizing because in polities such as Northern Ireland, the idea of open political competition may be a misnomer: political competition may occur within progressivist discourses that sideline or defer consideration of ideas about historical truth recovery or justice. Payne, understandably perhaps, avoids prescriptions: '[u]nsettling accounts and contentious coexistence do not heal democracies. Indeed they cannot even guarantee particular policy changes. What they do is change the political context and put into practice the democratic art of participation, contestation, and competition'.[59]

In Payne's account it is assumed that competition is good and that openness is conducive to democratic deepening. These assumptions are intuitively attractive, but what happens in asymmetric relationships such as those that occur between perpetrators and their victims? Once intrinsic and established unfairness in voice and experience is taken into account, the risk then arises that the deliberative democratic presumption of politics may actually work to undercut the possibility of politics. In short, appeal to narrative is never enough in divided societies. Kirk Simpson's work on victims in the Northern Ireland context represents one attempt to circumvent the inherent problems within deliberative democratic theory.[60] Simpson argues that law and governance 'only accrue validity and potency by acquiring the consent of the governed', which, in the context of divided societies, necessarily entails issues of accountability and scrutiny of past violence and historic conflict.[61] Simpson borrows from Habermas's writings on 'ideal speech situations' and argues that 'competing truth claims can only be resolved through rational discussion aimed at the creation of a consensus'.[62] For this to take place, a series of steps needs to be adhered to: first, he writes 'an objective speech act can be considered "true" when it is accepted as referring to a [state] of affairs in the world'. Second, 'a normative speech act is considered to be correct whenever it fits within a complex array of competing social values and norms'. Finally, 'evaluative speech acts are considered to be truthful when they are made by sincere communicative actors'.[63] Simpson points out that such a model requires a number of other conditions to function, including equal participation, freedom from constraint and authentic engagement by participants. I suggest that, at a minimum, these terms need to be underpinned by a narrative sense and a political commitment to societal responsibility; otherwise, they remain open to interpretation and politically informed revision. That is to say, the invisible or the part without part will remain outwith the speech act simply because of the possibility that perpetrators may feel that they are being sincere, whereas their victims may feel humiliated. Despite this possibility, Simpson's model seems to be one of the most nuanced and far-reaching schemas devised in relation to the Northern Ireland transition. His model proceeds from an emphasis on victims' rights and an appreciation of victims' choices and thus provides a basis for securing recognition of the stories and experiences that remain otherwise invisible within frameworks derived from transitional justice, consociationalism and deliberative democracy.

One vision of democracy that seems able to incorporate these divided, contentious politics of Northern Ireland is that suggested by Chantal Mouffe. In part, Mouffe's point of departure is a critique of the Habermasian and liberal democratic faith in reason that she sees as underpinning deliberative democratic approaches. She argues, via Wittgenstein, that agreement on the procedures of dialogue presumes agreement on the language to be used; rules and institutions, then, cannot be divorced from the practices and modes of behaviour that constitute everyday life: 'distinctions between "procedural" and "substantial" or between "moral" and "ethical" that are central to the Habermasian approach cannot be maintained and one must acknowledge that procedures always involve substantial ethical commitments'.[64] For Mouffe, everyday life is centred around and saturated with questions of power – and, in particular, asymmetric power relations: 'if we accept that relations of power are constitutive of the social, then the main question of democratic politics is not how to eliminate power but how to constitute forms of power that are compatible with democratic values'.[65] Her alternative is to implicate each individual within the political – since power is all-embracing and all-invasive, we cannot escape it through systems of rules; instead, we must learn to ameliorate its oppressive tendencies by cultivating agonistic, pluralist democratic values. She locates agonism in

> . . . a different mode of antagonism because it involves a relation not between enemies but between "adversaries", adversaries being defined in a paradoxical way as "friendly enemies", that is, persons who are friends because they share a common symbolic space but also enemies because they want to organize this common space in a different way'.[66]

Mouffe's schema allows for the persistence of conflict alongside democratic openness in ways that neither consociationalists nor deliberative democrats could feasibly or plausibly tolerate (given their fundamental insistence on filtering contention through particular channels). However, when viewed through the lens of post-conflict and deeply divided societies, agonistic democracy's very openness may result in the reproduction of inequities and injustices. A key element of victimhood, for example, will always be political powerlessness, marginality and being in a position of unequal voice and agency vis-à-vis perpetrators. For victims to move beyond and through trauma necessitates complex processes of working through their pasts; inevitably the negotiation of the stultifying nature of trauma involves political dynamics as new ways of articulating identity are found. Mouffe's notions of contestation and fluidity of power either speak past this process or may actually work to reinforce disparities. In other words, victims become re-victimized through the ostensible focus on contest and plurality.

Andrew Schaap has attempted to develop Mouffe's formulations towards the area of reconciliation after conflict.[67] He contends that she overstates her argument in a number of ways. First, her reading of deliberative democratic theorists (particularly the key text by Amy Gutmann and Dennis Thompson)[68] is misleading. Even if such theorists downplay the contested nature of reasonableness and rationality, neither they nor Mouffe's alternative of respect can be worked out in advance. Second, he argues that 'the kind of vibrant clash of identities that Mouffe advocates may be more likely to harden or reify existing identities than to transform them'.[69] Finally, he argues that Mouffe's schema does not really provide for decision making. In this, he builds on Dryzek's idea of distinguishing between sites of deliberation and decision; however, helpful and clarifying as his intervention undoubtedly is, it seems that Schaap does not really get around the 'stickiness' that the past exerts in divided societies. In part, the problem lies with Dryzek's idea – it does not apply to places such as Northern Ireland where the very nature of the state is the object of contestation, where ethnic competition is about inscribing ideas about the past and the future onto the decision-making apparatus. In other words, the delineation between decision making and deliberation only confuses analysis of and does not really apply to places where decision making reflects partisan (ethnicized) interests and where legislation, in turn, contributes to the reproduction of those voices. Again, the deferral of consideration of these issues works to usher in a regime of appropriateness – contention is viewed as a positive force without regard to those remaining outside of the realms in which democratic debate is cultivated.

Guilt and responsibility

An alternative vision is, however, implicit within Mouffe's ideas and is perceptible in her allusion to sharing. If Mouffe is correct and some kind of basis is needed outside of cognitive or legalistic strategies and frameworks for contestation and debate, then what might that foundational agreement or that shared space look like? Again, is it possible to ameliorate the exclusionary effects of the kind of predominating approaches to peace-building and democratization that I have described in this chapter? I want to suggest that Iris Marion Young's work on political responsibility provides one answer to these questions. Although Young does not specifically locate her work in deeply divided societies, her ideas on responsibility and guilt seem to have some implications for post-conflict arenas. Young situates her reflections, for example, in a structuralist understanding of politics – responsibility for the well-being of society is, in part, shared by all its members. Responsibility is, however, limited – as members of society, we share in an imperative to try to end injustice, but the fact of injustice occurring does not make us personally liable – unless, of course, we can be 'specifically identified as causing the harm' and know what we are doing.[70] What she calls the 'social connection model of responsibility' sees responsibility as deriving 'from belonging together with others in a system of interdependent processes of cooperation and competition through which we seek benefits and aim to realize projects'. Responsibility for injustice, then, is not simply the result of living together within a legally or constitutionally defined polity; rather, it results from 'belonging together' – in other words, from 'participating in the diverse institutional processes that produce structural injustice'. Thus, she concludes that responsibility 'is essentially shared. It can therefore be discharged only through collective action'.[71]

Young's model of social responsibility depends on five elements: First, whereas responsibility is general, guilt is particular – individuals are culpable and blameworthy for their actions and omissions. Second, in ascribing guilt and blame, it is important to be precise about the context in which harm or injustice occurs. Third, the emphasis on responsibility rather than guilt necessitates the adoption of a forward-looking lens that focuses on resolving injustice. Fourth, responsibility is therefore shared by individuals and finally it is discharged collectively. The individualizing of responsibility and guilt enables Young to avoid the trap of watering down blame – that is, if everyone is responsible for injustice, then, by definition, no one is culpable and nothing has to be done to remedy it. She asserts that the emphasis on society defers the possibility of absolving some people by blaming others. Thus, although individuals may be culpable and liable for injury and injustice, everyone is implicated in resolving as far as possible the wrongs that have been caused: 'Responsibility spreads', she writes, 'it isn't confined'.[72]

Young's emphasis on the future-orientation of responsibility serves to distinguish it from and delimits the more backwards-looking tendencies of blame and guilt. However, in post-conflict and deeply divided societies, the emphasis may work to undercut Young's key concern with developing shared obligations; for in those situations, the future tends to be justified through historical narratives that often act as taboos on belief and behaviour – the teleological urge of nationalism, in other words, fills ideas of responsibility and the future with received truths regarding historical obligations relating to the past. The answer to this problem may be located in Young's early work on difference politics, which fundamentally serves to justify practices of positive discrimination. In that work, Young conceives justice in terms of oppression and domination and argues that these are socially prior to individuals.[73] Compensation, in her view, is not simply a matter of repairing past injustice, but of correcting its legacies in the present.

Young's views have been criticized as being inherently essentializing and implicitly unhelpful to the Northern Irish situation. For instance, Carmel Roulston has argued that at the core of Young's early writings lies the notion that 'exclusion and subordination' can be countered by 'facilitating and encouraging the oppressed to organise and articulate their needs, interests and values, but also of recognising identities'. For Roulston, this is similar – 'a variant' – on the consociational impulse to 'attempt to find ways of making liberal democracy work in states divided by ethnicity, language or religion'. She concludes that whereas consociationalism stresses elite accommodation, Young suggests 'that governments and states should create mechanisms which would allow all oppressed or minority groups to meet, discuss and formulate policy'.[74] As Roulston points out, Young does not intend that groups be closed or become reified, but that risk remains in deeply divided societies; it also requires groups and individuals on the fringes of power and the margins of society to assert their own identities and make claims for rights and resources. Yet, in the case of the politics of victimhood and individuals who may have been traumatized by violent events, such a course seems somewhat idealistic.

A similar or related argument has been proposed by Adrian Little in relation to Mouffe's theorizing. He, for example, suggested that the radical reconceptualization of the political located in Mouffe provides the beginnings of an answer to the question 'how do we proceed to debate on institutional design if we do not have a sufficiently mature conception of democracy?'[75] This vision ultimately leads towards civil society as an alternative to elite and popular division; but even in societies such as Northern Ireland, where vibrant civil society/societies exist, government continues to act as the main repository of resources and, as the victims' debates show, easily legislates groups into and out of existence. Little also points to a further vision of democracy that may at first glance circumvent that limitation and, although he points out the difficulties involved in application of the principle, he approvingly refers to Dryzek's idea of 'workable arrangements' that are agreed to by participants 'for different reasons'.[76] This seems to place working prior to agreement and as such can be seen as analogous to (or at least a thin version of) the consociational-type approaches Little and Dryzek challenge insofar as it begins with an idea of what works and shapes society to fit. This actually overturns Mouffe's introduction of sharing, which starts (in an almost Rawlsian 'original position' fashion) with an idea of shared values that are built from rather than towards. The same impulse lies at the heart of Young's other work on communication[77] in which she broadens the idea of justice to include not simply issues of distribution, regulation and redistribution, but also is concerned with voice, marginalization and recognition. Democracy, then, becomes not about maturation or depth, but just, fair, open and balanced relationships between and among elites and ordinary citizens. If trauma is taken as a form of disarticulation, a rupturing of communication and a forcible removal of understanding,[78] then the political science/legalistic debates between consociationalism, deliberative democracy and agonism will never really speak to questions of historic grievances.

Proponents of these theories could easily suggest that they were never designed to tackle historic grievances and that, even in the case of consociationalism, which is the field of thought most particularly dedicated to peace-building, the preference is clearly for peace and stability over justice. The point of exploring the issue from the point of view of the politics of trauma is to highlight the fact that that type of argument does not really hold in societies transitioning from violence to peace; or, rather, it sits alongside the argument from the politics of trauma, which focuses on issues of betrayal, trust and accountability. The point, then, is not to suggest an overhauling of these theories, but rather to reinvest them with an emphasis upon societal responsibility; where those theories work to exclude marginalized groups and individuals through the institution of regimes of the sensible, the impetus then must be to reverse their logics. In other words, if democracy is to mean anything beyond formalistic principles, then it must be invested with a sense of justice as reparation, communication and positive and affirmative discrimination. In the Rancierean sense, this implies going beyond procedural definitions of democracy to look at the general political culture.

This point is underscored in a recent book on the attempts to come to terms with the past in Serbia, in which Eric Gordy refers to the idea of the German sociologist Max Weber that 'bureaucracies once founded tend to take on a life and logic of their own'.[79] The sentiment is, arguably, reflective of the main lessons of the book in which Gordy maps the 'genuine achievements' of transitional justice in the region together with its demonstrable inability to really tackle received wisdoms about the past and the resilience of sectarian and segregated ideologies in the present. For Gordy, the institution of a trial process at the International Criminal Tribunal for the former Yugoslavia and, specifically, the prosecution of Milošević – despite his evading justice through his suicide – worked to 'set a precedent for the reach of legal responsibility'[80] Yet, as he points out, despite – or perhaps because of – pressure from the international community and influential organizations such as the United States Institute for Peace, the impact at an everyday level is negligible: 'Memories of the past remain disputed, and transitional justice initiatives have not bridged those cognitive divisions. In this regard it could be said that legal "truth" has not contributed to social "reconciliation"'.[81]

As the institutional roll-out of transitional justice mechanisms gathered pace in the first decade of the 21st century, Gordy argues, so, too, did stories about the conflict(s) of the 1990s become more and more entrenched. The problem, as he sees it, lies in the sectional focus of transitional justice initiatives in Serbia or, more precisely, the confinement of activity to targeted groups. The paradoxical effect of institution building has become a filling out of a legal space with little or no impact on the political or social realms. Gordy explains the limitations of the law as follows: 'While it is not wholly implausible that a legal cause could lead to a social or cultural effect, a deeper understanding of the environment is required'.[82] For Gordy, the implication is clear: it is in the cultural processes of understanding that the past becomes salient and divisive.[83] As he explains, 'responsibility has to do with our sense of who we are, our sense of one another, and people's sense of us. Collective perceptions and feelings are involved at all these levels'.[84]

Gordy's vision of responsibility is based on a reframing of Karl Jasper's ideas about guilt – particularly his notion of metaphysical guilt, which he views as stemming from the 'co-responsibility' that individuals bear for tackling 'injustice and unfairness'. The notion of responsibility, for Gordy, works to emphasize the importance of 'states of feeling or judgment operating on the level of relationships, perceptions, and individual self-assessment'.[85] As such, it corresponds to Young's vision and is suggestive of an incrementalist approach to building peace based on an acknowledgement of the shared nature of politics and democratization. Although her final book circles around a handful of hypothetical examples of 'real world' situations, the one compelling empirical example she offers of this type of model in action relates to an ordinance passed by the city of Chicago requiring firms to state whether they benefitted from the slave trade. She argues that although this ordinance might be construed as blaming corporations, what it also does is 'encourage public discussion of the historic injustice of slavery among Americans, not only in schools and universities, but also in commercial and industrial enterprises'.[86] To this we might add that it also sets down a benchmark: that is to say, responsibility is not simply about the re/production of ideas, but an awareness of their reception, and reception itself is, therefore, not simply to do with perception of validity but an inter-subjective relationship. The notion of a benchmark enters into that relationship to demarcate something (benefiting from slavery) as wrong, as beyond the pale, and it firmly establishes a clear chain of responsibility – in this case between citizens (through their public representatives and public bodies) and capital.

Conclusion

Young's example echoes the attempts to legislate for lustration-type mechanisms in Northern Ireland. It allows us to see how once a first step is taken to admit and proffer responsibility, that, in itself, acts as a catalyst and triggers a dynamic of social connection. The point echoes a recent conclusion by Landon Hancock where he argued that there are few lessons to be learned from the Northern Irish experience of building peace. One exception to this is that in order to 'maintain support for peace and to provide the space for further shifts in identity salience', a key policy aim should be 'to reduce the focus on political concerns'. He goes on to explain that it 'is not as though highly contentious political issues are going to disappear, nor are they going to become easier to solve'. However, a failure to shift emphasis to 'bread and butter' issues may result in further alienation of sections of the Northern Irish community from (peaceful and democratic) politics and 'may contribute to the sense that the peace process is stalling instead of moving forward'.[87] The sentiment seems reasonable, but politicians may, in practice, find it difficult to distinguish between 'political' (symbolic and emotive) issues and 'bread and butter' (routine) ones. This may be due, perhaps, to voter pressure and/or the possibility that in places such as Northern Ireland where the nature and shape of the state itself (such as it is) is the subject of competition, questions of resource allocation or (re)distribution are in essence zero-sum calculations (what one 'side' gets or is conceded, the 'other side' loses).

In cases such as Northern Ireland's, where the 'stickiness' of the past continues to inspire divided identities and hold individuals trapped in traumatic prisons, the potential for factionalism seems inherent. I have argued that Iris Marion Young's late description of social responsibility may serve in some way to fill that gap by precipitating an outward movement of connection, attention and awareness of injustice, along with the imperative of attempting to remedy it. The emphasis on a connected model of responsibility may work to forestall some of Hancock's fears through a kind of path-dependent fashion, such as that envisaged in the work of Jennifer Todd on political change in Northern Ireland. Todd, for instance, has argued that ideas can work as 'wedges' or 'footholds' within political discourses, making their effects felt gradually over time.[88] This notion coincides with Hancock's proposal and the central premise of this chapter – that building peace requires some kind of articulate and articulated commitment to connection and responsibility. Of course, that idea may be rebuked on the grounds that not everyone in ethnically divided societies professes social responsibility. After all, the idea of clan, tribe, family or blood underpins the logic of us/them that characterizes contention in such arenas. I have argued that rather than presenting a limitation or a stumbling block, such a reservation actually enhances the necessity for articulating a commitment to the principle of social responsibility. The idea is implied but not articulated in the Belfast/Good Friday Agreement of 1998 in committing politicians to peace, tolerance and human rights; whether that vision is worked out according to consociational, deliberative democratic or agonistic principles, I have argued that it is imperative that that outworking give serious attention to the question of societal responsibility.

Notes

1 See, for example, Jon Elster, *Closing the Books: Transitional Justice in Historical Perspective* (Cambridge: Cambridge University Press, 2004); Ruti Teitel (2003) "Transitional Justice Genealogy", *Harvard Human Rights Journal* 16: pp. 69–94.
2 Andrew Rigby, *Justice and Reconciliation: After the Violence* (London: Lienne Rienner, 2001).
3 UN Human Rights Resolution 2005/66 'Right to Truth'. Available at http://ap.ohchr.org/documents/E/HRC/resolutions/A_HRC_RES_9_11.pdf; accessed on 8 May 2014.
4 See www.osloconferencearmedviolence.no/pop.cfm?FuseAction=Doc&pAction=View&pDocumentId=24790; accessed on 8 May 2014.
5 Mark Osiel, *Making Sense of Mass Atrocity* (Cambridge: Cambridge University Press, 2009), p. 224.
6 Mahmood Mamdani (November 2013) 'The Logic of Nuremburg', *The London Review of Books*, 35(21): 34.
7 Paul Ricoeur and Sorin Antohi, 'Memory, History, Forgiveness: A Dialogue between Paul Ricoeur and Sorin Antohi'. Available at www.janushead.org/8–1/ricoeur.pdf; accessed on 8 May 2014.
8 See Paul Ricoeur, *Memory, History, Forgetting* (Chicago: University of Chicago Press, 2004).
9 See, for example, Daniel Bar-Tal, 'Collective Memory of Physical Violence: Its Contribution to the Culture of Violence', in *The Role of Memory in Ethnic Conflict*, edited by E. Cairns and M. D. Roe (Basingstoke: Palgrave Macmillan, 2003), pp. 77–93.
10 Amy Gutmann and Dennis Thompson 'The Moral Foundations of Truth Commissions', in *Truth V. Justice: The Morality of Truth Commissions*, edited by R. I. Rotberg and D. Thompson (Princeton, NJ: Princeton University Press, 2000), p. 35

11 Ibid p. 28.
12 Ibid, p. 35.
13 Daniel Philpott argues that this kind of thinking is too prescriptive of change. 'Liberal skeptics' of reconciliation practices, such as Gutmann and Thompson, he believes, 'implicitly propose a wall that seems to divide transformations of moral outlooks into a politically legitimate sort that involves respect, reciprocity, and trust and a sort that does not belong in politics, like forgiveness, repentance, and harmony'. For Philpott, this conceptualization of reconciliation is too 'thin': 'It does not deal with the past. Each of the wounds of political injustice uniquely diminishes the human flourishing of the several parties involved in the injustice'. Here the emphasis seems (in my reading) to be not so much on liberalism versus illiberalism (despite the framings by Gutmann and Thompson and Philpott), but more on distinctions or gradations within a liberal approach to dealing with the past: societal reconciliation at one end of a continuum and justice for individual victims at the other. See Daniel Philpott, *Just and Unjust Peace: An Ethic of Political Reconciliation* (Oxford: Oxford University Press, 2012), p. 85.
14 Olson, Payne, and Reiter, *Transitional Justice,* p. 153.
15 See Edkins, *Trauma;* Edkins 'Remembering Rationality'.
16 See David Mendeloff (2004) 'Truth-Seeking, Truth-Telling, and Postconflict Peace-building: Curb the Enthusiasm?' *International Studies Review*, 6: 355–380.
17 A voluminous literature now exists on these ongoing events. For introductions to the Northern Ireland conflict and peace process, see Arthur Aughey, *The Politics of Northern Ireland: Beyond the Belfast Agreement* (Abingdon: Routledge, 2005); Joseph Ruane and Jennifer Todd, *The Dynamics of Conflict in Northern Ireland: Power, Conflict and Emancipation* (Cambridge: Cambridge University Press, 1996) or Tonge, *The New Northern Irish Politics?*. For a detailed insight into the 3,603 deaths that resulted from the conflict between 1966 and 1999, see David McKittrick, Seamus Kelters, Brian Feeney and Chris Thornton, *Lost Lives: The Stories of the Men, Women and Children Who Died as a Result of the Northern Ireland Troubles* (Edinburgh: Mainstream, 1999). For two overviews of the 'legacy debates', see John Nagle and Mary-Alice C. Clancy, *Shared Society or Benign Apartheid? Understanding Peace-Building in Divided Societies* (Basingstoke: Palgrave Macmillan, 2010) and McGrattan, *Memory.*
18 Edkins, 'Remembering Rationality', p. 101.
19 J.G.A. Pocock, 'Time, Institutions and Action: An Essay on Traditions and Their Understanding', in *Political Thought and History: Essays on Theory and Method* (Cambridge: Cambridge University Press, 2009), p. 187.
20 Edkins, *Trauma*, p. 4.
21 Edkins, *Trauma*, p. 5.
22 Wave Trauma Centre, 'Angela's Story', in *Injured . . . On That Day*. (Belfast: Community Relations Council, 2011), p. 53.
23 Berber Bevernage, *History, Memory, and State-Sponsored Violence: Time and Justice* (London: Routledge, 2011), p. 4.
24 Obradović-Wochnik, 'The "Silent Dilemma" ', p. 334.
25 Ibid, p. 330.
26 Ibid, p. 347.
27 Khanyisela Moyo (2015) 'Mimicry, Transitional Justice and the Land Question in Racially Divided Former Settler Colonies', *International Journal of Transitional Justice,* 9(1): 70–89.
28 Nevin T. Aiken, *Identity, Reconciliation and Transitional Justice: Overcoming Intractability in Divided Societies* (Abingdon: Routledge, 2013), p. 197.
29 McGrattan, *Memory*, p. 133.
30 Bertolt Brecht, 'The Solution' [*Die Lösung*] in *Poems: 1913–1956*, edited by John Willet and Ralph Manheim (London: Methuen, 1976), p. 430.
31 See, for instance, Arend Lijphart, *Democracy in Plural Societies – A Comparative Exploration* (Yale University Press, New Haven, 1977).

32 Jonathan Tonge, *Comparative Peace Processes* (London: Polity, 2014), p. 50.
33 Peter Shirlow and Kieran McEvoy, *Beyond the Wire: Former Prisoners and Conflict Transformation in Northern Ireland* (London: Pluto Press, 2008), p. 4.
34 Arend Lijphart (1975) 'The Northern Ireland Problem: Cases, Theories, and Solutions', *British Journal of Political Science*, 5(1): 83–106.
35 John McGarry and Brendan O'Leary, *The Northern Ireland Conflict: Consociational Engagements* (Oxford: Oxford University Press, 2004) p. 2; see also. John McGarry and Brendan O'Leary, *Explaining Northern Ireland: Broken Images* (Oxford: Blackwell, 2000); Brendan O'Leary and John McGarry, *The Politics of Accommodation: Understanding Northern Ireland* (London: Athlone Press, 1993).
36 See Paul Dixon (2005) 'Why the Good Friday Agreement Is Not Consociational', *Political Quarterly*, 76(3): 357–367.
37 Matthijs Bogaards (2000) 'The Uneasy Relationship between Empirical and Normative Types in Consociational Theory', *Journal of Theoretical Politics*, 12(4): 395–423.
38 Duncan Morrow, 'Breaking antagonism? Political leadership in divided societies', in *Power Sharing: New Challenges for Divided Societies*, edited by Ian O'Flynn and David Russell (London: Pluto, 2005), p. 56.
39 Sue M. Halpern (1986) 'The Disorderly Universe of Consociational Democracy', *West European Politics*, 9(2): 181–197.
40 Denis M. Tull and Andreas Mehler (2005) 'The Hidden Costs of Power-Sharing: Reproducing Insurgent Violence in Africa', *African Affairs*, 104: 375–398.
41 Tonge, *Comparative Peace Processes*, p. 49.
42 'The Agreement' [1998]. Available at http://cain.ulst.ac.uk/events/peace/docs/agreement.htm; accessed on 9 May 2014.
43 Brendan O'Leary and John McGarry (2006) 'Consociational Theory, Northern Ireland's Conflict, and Its Agreement. Part 1: What Consociationalists Can Learn from Northern Ireland', *Government and Opposition*, 41(1): 43–63.
44 See, for example, Paul Dixon (2011) 'Is Consociational Theory the Answer to Global Conflict? From the Netherlands to Northern Ireland and Iraq', *Political Studies Review*, 9(3): 309–322.
45 Nagle and Clancy, *Shared Society*, p. 219.
46 Northern Ireland Assembly Official Report: Hansard. 'Assembly and Executive Review Committee: Review of d'Hondt, Community Designation and Provision for Opposition: Briefing from Professor Christopher McCrudden and Professor Brendan O'Leary, 5 March, 2012'. Available at www.niassembly.gov.uk/Assembly-Business/Official-Report/Committee-Minutes-of-Evidence/Session-2012–2013/March-2013/Review-of-dHondt-Community-Designation-and-Provision-for-Opposition—Briefing-from-Professor-Christopher-McCrudden-and-Professor-Brendan-OLeary/; accessed on 9 May 2014.
47 Vivien Lowndes and Mark Roberts, *Why Institutions Matter: The New Institutionalism in Political Science* (Basingstoke: Palgrave Macmillan, 2013).
48 Ian O'Flynn, *Deliberative Democracy and Divided Societies* (Edinburgh: Edinburgh University Press, 2006), p. 141.
49 Ian O'Flynn (2007) 'Divided Societies and Deliberative Democracy', *British Journal of Political Science*. 37(4): 733.
50 R. C. Luskin, I. O'Flynn, J. S. Fishkin, and D. Russell (2014) 'Deliberating across Deep Divides', *Political Studies*, 62(1): 116–17.
51 See McGrattan and Meehan, *Everyday Life*.
52 John Boswell (2013) 'Why and How Narrative Matters in Deliberative Systems', *Political Studies*', 61: 623.
53 John Dryzek (2010) 'Rhetoric in Democracy: A Systematic Appreciation', *Political Theory*, 38(3): 319–339; Jurgen Habermas, *The Theory of Communicative Action – Vol. 1: Reason and the Rationalization of Society* (London: Heinemann, 1984).
54 Boswell, 'Narrative', p. 12.

55 Ibid, p. 632.
56 Ibid, p. 13.
57 Leigh A. Payne, *Unsettling Accounts: Neither Truth nor Reconciliation in Confessions of State Violence* (London: Duke University Press, 2008), p. 281.
58 Ibid, p. 285.
59 Ibid, pp. 288–289.
60 Kirk Simpson (2007) 'Victims of Political Violence: A Habermasian Model of Truth Recovery', *Journal of Human Rights* 6: 325–343; Kirk Simpson, *Unionist Voices and the Politics of Remembering the Past in Northern Ireland* (Basingstoke: Palgrave Macmillan, 2009).
61 Simpson, 'Victims', p. 327.
62 Ibid, p. 331–332.
63 Ibid, p. 332.
64 Chantal Mouffe (1999) 'Deliberative Democracy or Agonistic Pluralism?' *Social Research*, 66(3): 749.
65 Ibid, p. 753.
66 Chantal Mouffe, *The Democratic Paradox* (London: Verso, 2005), p. 13.
67 Andrew Schaap (2006) 'Agonism in Divided Societies', *Philosophy & Social Criticism*, 32(2): 255–277.
68 Amy Gutmann and Dennis Thompson, *Democracy and Disagreement* (Cambridge, MA: Belknap Press of Harvard University Press, 1996).
69 Schaap, 'Agonism', p. 270.
70 Young, *Responsibility*, p. 104.
71 Ibid, p. 105.
72 Ibid, p. 180.
73 Iris Marion Young, *Justice and the Politics of Difference*. (Princeton, NJ: Princeton University Press, 1990), p. 8
74 Carmel Roulston, 'Democracy and the challenge of gender: New visions, new processes', in *Gender, Democracy and Inclusion in Northern Ireland*, edited by C. Roulston and C. Davies (London: Palgrave 2000), p. 34.
75 Adrian Little, *Democracy and Northern Ireland: Beyond the Liberal Paradigm?* (Basingstoke: Palgrave Macmillan, 2004), p. 189.
76 Cited in ibid, p. 107.
77 Iris Marion Young, *Inclusion and Democracy* (Oxford: Oxford University Press, 2000).
78 Caruth, *Unclaimed Experience*.
79 Eric Gordy, *Guilt, Responsibility, and Denial: The Past at Stake in Post Milošević Serbia* (University of Pennsylvania Press, 2013), p. 59.
80 Ibid, p. 60.
81 Ibid, p. 68.
82 Ibid, p. xiv.
83 Ibid, p. 68.
84 Ibid, p. 19.
85 Ibid, p. 18.
86 Young, *Responsibility*, p. 183.
87 Landon E. Hancock, 'Peace from the people: Identity salience and the Northern Irish peace process', in *Lessons from the Northern Ireland Peace Process*, edited by Timothy White (Madison, WI: University of Wisconsin Press, 2013), p. 85–86.
88 See, for example, Jennifer Todd, 'Elite intention, public reaction and institutional change', in *The Anglo-Irish Agreement: Re-thinking Its Legacy*, edited by Arthur Aughey and Cathy Gormley-Heenan (Manchester: Manchester University Press, 2011), pp. 50–63.

3 Peace-building as community politics in Northern Ireland

This chapter explores the emergence of community-based democracy in Northern Ireland. As pointed out in the introduction, Rancière's political philosophy foregrounds the notion of community as critical to democracy and governance and that governance depends on distributions of sensibility. As Matthew Flinders points out, the implication of that intervention is to highlight the 'controlling' paradox of governance: namely, the capacity to promote participation and voice by offsetting the demands of collectives and the withdrawal of individuals.[1] The analytic movement, then, involves a shift in focus from groupist or identity-based politics towards questions of knowledge, understanding, representation and reception of ideas and arguments.[2] The act or process of depoliticization, then, is associated with the retrenchment of community or groupist logics.[3] This chapter explores these tensions and suggests that a new emphasis is being placed on community in the design and implementation of policy and charts how ideas from community policing are echoed in public arts policy. This new emphasis marks a break with long-standing trends in (London-directed) governmental policy in Northern Ireland that sought to introduce fluidity into identity. Instead, the consociational premise that reified identities need to be managed seems to be a driving force behind policy design. The chapter is not solely about identity-based politics, however. Building on the previous chapters on the politics of trauma, the underlying interest pertains to the potential within community-based policies to exacerbate division and exclusion. This is perhaps an example of unintended consequences because, after all, the avowed goals of community-based policy design are to encourage participation within decision making and to cultivate strong, intersecting networks within civil society in a mutually reinforcing fashion. The idea is that a strong, plural civic culture underpins social cohesion. Yet, as Hayward and Komorova point out, in a divided society such as Northern Ireland, where public symbolism retains a high public profile and is seen as politically salient, there remains a tendency to utilize civic culture to bolster intra-bloc cohesion and fuel inter-bloc competition. Referencing Lukes, they point to the danger inherent in that tendency, arguing that 'the shoring up of a sense of social cohesion through ritual occasion by one group can occur at the expense of another – it reflects a broader power tussle'.[4]

Extrapolating to the politics of trauma, the question of balancing power interests becomes, arguably, more intense. Perpetrators, for example, often claim victim status and argue that they were essentially powerless – or at least not fully in control of their actions – within circumstances that were not of their making.[5] The victims of direct (as distinct from structural) political violence also find themselves within a liminal position. As Edkins points out, the key characteristics of that position are feelings of betrayal of trust and inarticulacy. Tackling those problems of power, trust and lack of voice and agency must, I have argued, be central to any conceptualization of peace-building. Yet, I suggest, insofar as the tenor of public policy making in Northern Ireland, which is avowedly peace centred, remains community centred, then the risk remains that these concerns will, at the very least, remain marginal to political developments or at most become exacerbated as resources and attention are steered in other directions. The secondary argument of the chapter is that the political effect of that drift towards community is the creation of a new ethos of responsibility – one that focuses on the needs and concerns that are articulated primarily by community activists and interpreted by community-focused academics and politicians. This nexus of what might be called community entrepreneurs (in the sense that all are focused on similar goals of promoting an explicit or assumed community-based politics) valorizes ideals such as sharing, inclusivity, participation and accountability. The framing that is placed as justifying that project is radically democratic – it is represented as empowering and capacity building, particularly within socio-economic groups and neighbourhoods who have been traditionally been neglected by political leaders and 'the state'. Again, following Rancière, I suggest that this dichotomy between grassroots and elites or top-down and bottom-up policy direction is misleading. Rather, I argue, the new ethics of community responsibility remains as elitist, exclusionary and ethnic as that it purports to replace. The *sotto voce* theme running through this and the next chapter is how that ethics works to displace the most marginal sections of Northern Irish society.

Community and synecdoche

At the start of Joseph Ruane and Jennifer Todd's seminal *Dynamics of Conflict in Northern Ireland: Power, Conflict and Emancipation*,[6] the authors point out that a critical understanding of the concept of community is 'necessary to any analysis of the conflict'. Part of that understanding, they argue, is an appreciation of the fact that the 'stress' on communal division hides the 'multiplicity of communities' in Northern Ireland. In so doing, any intellectual exercise that focuses on the sectarian divide in Northern Ireland risks reproducing and/or reinforcing that division. Because of this, it is sometimes argued that an alternative analytical perspective (addressing, in the first instance, for example, the experience of gender, sexuality, race, class or ideology) can help to broaden and pluralize politics. Such an approach also helps to reinforce the notion that communities are fluid constructs ('emergent entities' in the formulation of Ruane and Todd) in which ideas and practices about self-identification, boundary making and organizational norms (including forms of behaviour and parameters of belief) are more or less open to contestation. Because of this, Ruane and Todd argue, the use of 'community' as an explanatory mechanism is extremely limited:

> Thus conceived, community is neither an essential feature of the social structure nor one which can serve as a general basis of explanation. Nevertheless, at the level of actual social organisation, relations and practices, as well as in public consciousness, communities are very real phenomena.[7]

This chapter suggests that the theoretical balance outlined by Ruane and Todd has become overturned as a result of the bedding down of devolution in Northern Ireland. In other words, community has become in fact an essential feature of the representation of the social structure by government and within strands of academic and journalistic writings. The result is a reification of community at a practical and an abstract level that works to displace the empirical and theoretical reality of fluidity, plurality and contestation. I argue that although 'community' continues to function as a rhetorical trope, it has been steadfastly harnessed to a policy agenda and a philosophical belief in a form of peace-building. Through synecdoche and a misapplication and reinvigoration of communitarian thought, the reality of 'community' in Northern Ireland is no longer delimited by social practices or popular belief; rather, 'community' works to affect the very structuring of society and has become a predominant force governing social relations. I understand synecdoche to refer to *the practice of reading a part as responsible for the whole or reading the whole as responsible for the part;* or, in Roman Jakobson's terms, the juxtaposition of a part with the whole so that the meaning of the part implies the whole.[8] The use of community in contemporary governmental discourse regarding Northern Ireland obscures the realities of divisions between and *within* ethno-religious blocs and instead reads the term into society. This is undoubtedly facilitated not only because, as Ruane and Todd allude, community is such a slippery concept in Northern Ireland, but also because 'society' itself is a highly emotive and contested term: although 'Northern Irish society' enjoys a constitutional and institutional reality, in terms of identity politics, it often serves as a kind of floating signifier that can be ignored or filled with narratives of unrealized nationhood.

As such, I wish to argue that through the use of synecdoche as politics and policy, Northern Ireland is beginning to represent an inversion of Benedict Anderson's classic description of nationhood. Anderson argued that

> . . . [the nation] is an imagined political community – and imagined as both inherently limited and sovereign. It is *imagined* because the members of even the smallest nation will never know most of their fellow-members, meet them, or even hear of them, yet in the minds of each lives the image of their communion.[9]

The conflation of the communal with the societal works to replace the idea of a state or a collective with particularistic and exclusivist forms of identity – particularistic and exclusivist because they are located in relatively rigid and bounded ideologies and geographically situated in specific and often easily identifiable locales, districts and urban neighbourhoods.[10] The process is arguably beginning since it is demonstrably failing, despite the efforts of ethnic entrepreneurs and academic supporters. For example, as Byrne and Topping acknowledge in a recent review of community policing, 'levels of community participation in local initiatives have been inconsistent across Northern Ireland'. They go on to report that '[t]here has been a degree of scepticism at community level as to how much impact the community sector has historically had in relation to community safety and policing issues, especially when set against the influence of elected representatives and service providers'.[11] The point seems to be that despite the best efforts to extend the influence of the 'community sector', the role of the state in providing and legislating resources remains paramount; for it is in the competition over resources that 'elected representatives' are engaged, and although those representatives require the support of their local constituents, there is a limit to the potential for replacing representative democracy with one driven by community activism. Of course, a fundamental and unacknowledged problem is provability – despite over forty references in a seventy-three-page document, Byrne and Topping do not define what they mean by 'community sector'. The import at a discursive and policy level seems to be relatively clear, however – policy does not need to be evidence driven if 'community' is the aim and end goal.

The lack of definition also serves the function – perhaps for the best of intentions of empowering people who have been seen or have claimed to be voiceless – of establishing a rhetoric or discourse that, to paraphrase Deleuze, enables one to speak on behalf of others – the imagined 'community sector'. The valorization of community and the communal involves processes of de-politicization: a draining of significance from the social sphere and a turning of perspective away from the idea of society towards an emphasis on the local and the immediate. The act of de-politicization is the displacement or deferral of difference, multiplicity and plurality within and between Northern Ireland's two main communal/ethno-nationalist blocs (and between those two communities and other modes of identification, including gender or age, for example, and/or belonging to a migrant group). Instead, the focus is placed on the loci of separation involving those communities. The process is, however, double edged and involves not simply a shift in emphasis from the social to the communal – that very shift also creates a new political reality. It does so through a process of *re-politicization*: that is to say, it *re-politicizes* society itself by demanding that notions of responsibility to others who are not primarily or immediately part of our 'group' or local environment be refigured and/or viewed through the lens of 'the community'.

Although synecdoche is prevalent in governmental policy direction and some academic writings on Northern Ireland, it can be troubled by artistic practices or alternative forms of identification and ways in which everyday ethnicity is transgressed, subverted or traversed.[12] Alternative ways of engaging with Northern Irish society, including through sexuality, religion, disability or migration, also work to problematize predominant visions of a community-based society. This chapter focuses on public art policy, not as a means of diverting attention from the important work going on in those areas; but rather, I argue, the fact that artistic practices inevitably work with and through cultural expectations and preferences makes it a key site of contention. The more obvious point is that unlike the politics of the everyday, which often occurs at a 'hidden' or 'private' level, public art is, by its very nature, policy driven and socially situated. Furthermore, the very nature of cultural exchange brings to the fore questions of evaluation and debate in a way that cannot be settled simply with regard to identity – preferences, in other words, have to be justified by reference to some kind of criteria that lie outside of our own personal experiences. The emphasis on community within public art works then to subvert that fundamentally (and thinly) democratic notion of debate and evaluation by imposing a new ethic of progress, society and peace. The key mode of exchange of ideas, therefore, occurs through the prism of community and, in the public sphere, we then relate to each other and to government through the language of what is best for the community. In so doing, something is lost – instead of ideas about civic or societal rights and responsibilities, a vision of community primacy is produced and cultivated.

Community and moral capital

The belated establishment of devolution in Northern Ireland has reinvigorated communitarian thinking. Although this thinking is at times nebulous and hazy – products of its own woolly limitations – it is typically characterized by an unreflexive faith in 'communities' as being, if not the panacea, then certainly the key treatment for Northern Ireland's ills. 'Communities' are extolled by official guardians and promoters of 'cultural heritage',[13] and 'community leaders' are presented within certain segments of academic research as pillars of society who exert a 'moral agency' in the process of conflict transformation.[14] As such, 'community' has become a catch-all term, virtually synonymous with 'peace' and 'society'. It has, as such, become utterly divested of meaning –what it refers to, who it includes and excludes or questions relating to how communities are formed, sustained or transformed are points that are never considered.

An unreflective faith in the value of community lies at the heart of much of the discourse surrounding contemporary efforts to build peace in Northern Ireland. From restorative justice schemes to storytelling initiatives, and from the promotion of cultural heritage to security concerns, Northern Irish political debate is replete with the prioritization of 'community'. One recent example of this is the project by the non-governmental organization Healing Through Remembering to archive the conflict in everyday objects that were transformed by the violence. The exhibition revels in banality: included in the ideas for display are a bin lid used by women as 'a street communication tool and as a means of protest' along with 'a coffee jar explosive, [and] a quilt produced to communicate peace and healing'. It is difficult to ascertain whether that banality is intentional, given the platitudinous rationale for the project:

> It is hoped that once the exhibition is displayed in various locations around Northern Ireland and beyond it will act as a catalyst to help open up a platform

> in which diverse voices and experiences of the conflict can be heard by all members of the public.

As Kate Turner, the director of Healing Through Remembering, explains, the exhibition is decidedly not a 'top-down' approach to dealing with the past. All 'sides', after all, have stories to tell. Yet, within this laudable obligation to inclusivity resides a rather more malign commitment to relativism: for the flip side of the coin is that all stories have the right to be heard. 'Each item has a label written by the organisation or person who owns the item. No label can be vetoed by any other collector'.[15] Because these issues are deferred, 'community' has taken on a dual implication: on the one hand it is increasingly taken as shorthand for progressing the peace process, but, on the other, its very ambiguity has meant it is becoming increasingly unstable: the irony being that this term, which is taken to signifying a shared society, can also be used by champions of closed ideologies who harness it as a way of policing the areas and the modes of thinking from which they originate. The implication, of course, is that rather than creating and fostering a sense of cohesion, mutuality and commonality, the instability surrounding understandings and usages of 'community' can lead to fissures and divisions.

As Byrne and Topping report, policing is a key area in which community-based expectations – or at least the expectations of their respondents – go unfulfilled. Policing, they claim, is often perceived by 'representatives from the community, voluntary and statutory sectors' as lacking in partnership. As such, they argue that the Department of Justice's policy goals of 'creating safer, shared and confident communities' remain hamstrung.[16] The point is underpinned by Quinlan, Spalek and O'Rawe, who distinguish between 'community-targeted' approaches to security, which place the onus on the goal of maintaining security at the level of the nation-state, and 'community-focused' approaches, which emphasize 'building and sustaining trust between state officials and security practitioners and community members'.[17] Within the Northern Irish context, practically speaking, the two approaches seem incommensurable due to the political importance of historical understandings. Thus, writing in the same volume, Rooney and Maskey begin with the assertion that '[t]he uneasy balance between the Protestant and Catholic communities in Northern Ireland, mediated through and impacted by state attitudes and responses to civil unrest, has lasted since the partition of Ireland in 1921'.[18] The writing out of the history of republican (and loyalist) sectarian violence does more than simply place the onus of responsibility for 'unrest' on the state; it clearly posits guilt and a record of de-legitimacy – claims that are not qualified or contextualized throughout the rest of the piece of writing. The implicit solution is that future policy must be devolved from the state and the measurement of accountability for security and safety ought to reside in communities. The point is made clear by another community activist, John Loughran, who argues for a 'new framework for community–police relations' and describes how a 'new social and political space has evolved that is no longer preoccupied with the safety of the nation so much as the safety of communities'[19]. Yet, the displacement of the state as theorized by Quinlan et al is illusionary and misconceived – illusionary because what occurs is not quite a displacement of one approach that is state centred by another that is community focused. Loughran is correct in asserting that the latter is merely an extension, an evolution, of the former as community politics become writ large on the apparatus of governance.[20] The assertion of distinction is shameless in the Deleuzian sense of the problem of speaking for others that is involved in the attempted draining of political significance from the notion of the collective beyond the local.

As the political theorist W. James Booth points out, memory is intrinsically related to justice – and that relation is inherently political: 'What we remember will determine what we become'.[21] To this we can add that we are also shaped by what we forget, for as anthropologist and theorist Marc Augé asserts, '[T]ell me what you forget and I will tell you who you are'.[22] I wish to suggest that the current configuration of the Northern Irish peace process borrows from the worst of both worlds: an impoverished reliance on bland (and ultimately malign) communitarianism married with an ethic of progressivism. More precisely, it is the facticity of the dead that is being forgotten; their memory, which cries out for justice, is placed at the service of an alternative vision of justice that equates right with community and harnesses the language of morality and ethics to garner legitimacy and respectability and, in so doing, defers questions of social responsibility and ethical standards as beyond the pale of consideration.

Northern Ireland and communitarian logics

The substitution of the communal for the collective works in an exclusionary fashion and places control of scrutiny and mechanisms of oversight mainly within the gift of community entrepreneurs. Of course, this does not invalidate Loughran's arguments that 'community people will first relate to an individual before they relate to an institution' or that 'it is important that the police are responsive to community needs and concerns'.[23] Indeed, these points seem to be so obvious that Quinlan et al's development of a two-tiered typology, mentioned earlier, is superfluous. My key point, however, is rather to highlight the potentialities – and dangers – inherent in an exclusionary community focus. This is, of course, emblematized in Loughran's assertion because, presumably, not only 'community people' but most individuals relate to individuals quicker than they do institutions. But the point about danger is often more deeply concealed under what could be described as a soft peddling of the benefits of community. Often this occurs within quite reasonable and benign framings: Maria Power, for instance, has recently highlighted the problem that segregation in Northern Ireland is part of a vicious circle – not only is it perpetuated by a lack of contact across the ethno-religious divide, but it also prevents associational contact. Thus, she argues that 'grassroots peacebuilding has a role to play in encouraging such associational contact by facilitating and mediating communication'.[24] Yet, and at the risk of mixing metaphors, as long as the aim seems to be about 'improving community relationships'[25] the project of peace-building is hostage to a Catch-22: conciliation is targeted by working with the very elaborate cultural, political, social, economic and historical structures (in other words, 'communities') that have played such a large part in frustrating rapprochement. The danger is identifiable by recourse to Rancière's description of what he sees as the central distinction within politics – namely, the gulf between, on the one hand, the *ochlos*, by which he refers to the idea of 'a throng of people' or a 'community obsessed with its own unification',[26] and on the other, those excluded from that effort to create a distribution of the sensible, the *demos,* or 'the people', 'the citizens', 'the commons', 'the plebeians'.

Rancière's point is not to juxtapose two forms of identification or two putative social groups. Instead, he sees 'the people' as supplementary to the police order, as standing outside of the initial 'count' of politics. Whereas the community of the 'throng of people' comprises that first distribution of the sensible, 'the people' remain outwith and demand a redistribution. It is that demand, what Rancière describes as the making visible of a wrong or a claim for equality, that gives rise to political subjectivity, or the creation of a division and a dividing force. 'The people', for Rancière, are, therefore, not pre-constituted or identifiable prior to the claims making, and the division or gulf that lies at the foundation of political subjectivity represents the unmasking of orders of power and sensibility. Rancière's description works to overturn what he sees as established and traditional ways of analyzing politics in which the relationship between the *demos* and the *ochlos* is viewed as competition and regulation – for example, the attempted balancing and institutionalization of conflict between states and social and ethnic groups or between 'the power of the people and the turbulent unification of individual turbulences'.[27] The distinction Rancière makes is to see the *ochlos* not as the 'disordered sum of appetites but the passion' of exclusion. The *demos*, then, he argues

> . . . might well be nothing but the movement whereby the multitude tears itself away from the weighty destiny which seeks to drag it into the corporeal form of the *ochlos*, into the safety of incorporation into the image of the whole. Democracy is neither the consensual self-regulation of the plural passions of the multitude of individuals nor the reign of a collectivity unified by law under the shadow of Declarations of Rights. Democracy exists in a society to the degree that the *demos* exists as the power to divide the *ochlos*.[28]

The relationship between the *demos* and the *ochlos*, therefore, is not simply a matter of one group replacing another – for such a movement would only inscribe another realm of the sensible. Rather, it lies in the emergence of dissensus and division. Extrapolating to Northern Ireland, the movement to balance community with the state is thus a false understanding – the distribution of the sensible remains tied to practices of exclusion and bounding. Despite the ostensible framing by analysts and community activists, the point is not to replace or displace the state with community; it is rather the inscription of a new form of inclusion and exclusion. The apparent limitations of this project to resonate beyond ethno-nationalist entrepreneurs and (self-)appointed community spokespersons works to reveal the gulf between the included and those outwith the 'community sector'. Despite these limitations, the expansion and propagation of communitarian logics represents a discernible discourse within (increasingly prominent) sections of civil society and academia. The turn to a valorization of community entails harnessing language concerning 'peace' and 'progress', 'class' and 'identity', and linking it steadfastly to notions of group. This essentially and overtly descriptive movement is implicitly normative and prescriptive: ironically, the interest in groupism becomes itself a colonizing enterprise, enveloping purportedly affable ideas within its ambiguous catholicity while simultaneously excluding discommodious values.

Although the distinctions between communitarian theory and the practical turn towards communitarianism in Northern Ireland are greater than the similarities, nevertheless the theoretical debate to a certain extent sheds light on the attraction that it holds on Northern Irish political discourse. The rationale is not always the promotion of 'community safety' or 'dialogue' or 'partnership', but rather stems from a concern with the ethnicization of Northern Irish society. Thus, some academics look to civil society as a way of countering ethnic exclusion. Although I do not wish to repudiate these analyses and the proposals that accrue from them, I wish to extend the Rancièrean perspective to suggest that civil society constitutes another form of community and depends on its own exclusionary practices. This is a distinct criticism from that commonly levelled by proponents of consociationalism against a faith in civil society or a civic culture to the effect that it amounts to wishful thinking or paternalistic elitism to expect people to give up nationalist-based identities in favour of liberal cosmopolitan ones.[29]

Yet, this very issue seems to lie at the heart of the use and abuse of the term 'community' in Northern Ireland. For Dominic Bryan, for example, community and culture are intertwined in policy making and everyday discourse in Northern Ireland. 'The idea of "community" seems to be everywhere in Northern Ireland', he argues, yet it remains difficult to define what it actually is or how it is constituted. He asks whether it refers to a set of real or imaginary social relationships, whether it denotes 'an ideal or a practical way of living' and whether it represents 'a conservative control mechanism or a radical opposition to the state'.[30] Bryan goes on to point out that, rather than community being seen as the opposite of society, as a result of the Northern Irish peace process, community becomes a metonym for society and acts to police the political by circumscribing (vague) notions of what constitute peace and progress. Thus, the key document of the peace process, the 1998 Belfast/Good Friday Agreement, enshrines cultural difference as something to be protected. The rhetoric sounds positive – the protection is afforded on the grounds of 'respect' for diversity[31] – but the implication is that difference is not just being protected, but contained: it is something that can perhaps endanger the peace and from which society needs to be sheltered. The dual working of difference (diversity) then becomes entrenched in a conception of deeply rooted identities or traditions. The logic seems to have been that although it may be desirable to leave these antagonistic beliefs in the past, that may either be dangerous or illiberal, so they must be tolerated and governed. In this way, community becomes linked to legislation and is underpinned and justified by recourse to identity. As Bryan explains, '"[c]ulture", "community" and "identity" all emerge as positive things but are clearly also mechanisms of control.

In Northern Ireland culture is sanctified in a "community" that, according to politicians across the political spectrum, needs protecting at all costs'.[32]

Of course, this dynamic in many ways predated the 1998 agreement. Alan Finlayson, for example, has mapped how the policymaking of the Northern Ireland Office (NIO) (the governmental department primarily responsible for administering Northern Ireland) began to change during the 1980s. From an almost singular focus on social policy, increasingly the NIO began to look to culture as a way of promoting a more peaceful and inclusive society. For Finlayson, the emphasis on bringing the 'two communities' together as a way of implementing that policy risked reifying the very ideas that kept the two apart. In addition, it conferred legitimacy to the separatist political aspirations of the Irish nationalist cultural tradition. The problem here is not simply the anomaly of a sovereign government promoting a separatist group despite that group's refusal to recognize the legitimacy of the government, but the fact that the policy also afforded legitimacy to the majority unionist community, which favoured retaining the constitutional link with the rest of the United Kingdom. For Finlayson, an additional problem was one of deferred responsibility. As he explained,

> [A] concentration on cultural questions of tradition and identity is a manifestation of the British government's belief that the problem in Northern Ireland is simply caused by people with deformed world views; that it is "the natives" who are the problem.[33]

Fundamentally, for Finlayson, the issue revolves around the role of politics in reproducing culture; the management of antagonism, in other words, poses serious questions about the depth of democracy. Rather than facilitating cultural exchange, the management of division through communities instead tends to filter competition and debate along pre-established paths.

Novelist and commentator Glenn Patterson discerned similar tendencies in the recommendations arising from the recent consultation on dealing with the legacies of the conflict, parades and public symbolism conducted by American diplomat, Dr Richard Haass and Harvard academic, Professor Meghan O'Sullivan.[34] The emphasis on community there, for Patterson, directly echoes elite discourse on Northern Ireland by tying the word to relations. The movement from 'communities' to the singular 'community', argues Patterson, works to aggregate the divisions between groups. Difference is therefore 'effaced' or sterilized and distinctions are compressed into the rhetoric of 'The Two Communities'.[35] Patterson references Humpty Dumpty in *Alice Through the Looking Glass* by way of explaining this almost post-modern de-anchoring of everyday words: '"When I use a word," Humpty Dumpty said in a rather scornful tone, "it means just what I choose it to mean – neither more, nor less."' Yet the explanation is somewhat less complex. Because what Patterson misses is the (literal) primacy of 'community' in all of this, for the notion of community relations presupposes a singular community. He is correct in stating that this singular depends on a manageable duopoly (the two communities), but that duopoly hangs or depends on the aggregating catchall-ism. Or, to put it more simply, the placing of community is key: community acts to filter and re-envision difference and distinction.

Communitarianism is itself a broad term used to describe reactions to John Rawls' seminal work on liberalism, *A Theory of Justice*.[36] That work precipitated responses from a diverse range of scholars who argued against Rawls' claim that the key function of government is to protect and distribute the liberties and resources to individuals. Although Rawls revisited his theory in later works, the point of departure for his political theory resided in his belief that justice must proceed from a commitment to fairness: regardless of individuals' position in society, all persons are entitled to basic equality within society. Rawls' foundational belief – namely, that individuals do not know their place in society or where they can 'end up' within society – was strongly challenged by theorists such as Amitai Etzioni, Alasdair MacIntyre, Michael Sandel, Charles Taylor, and Michael Walzer. MacIntyre, for example, argued that Rawls' detached, abstract individual owed more to the existential impulse explored by Jean-Paul Sartre before and after the World War II than to historically and socially situated persons:

> [T]he story of my life is always embedded in the story of those communities from which I derive my identity. I am born with a past; and to try to cut myself off from that past, in the individualist mode, is to deform my present relationships . . . What I am, therefore, is in key part what I inherit, a specific past that is present to some degree in the present. I find myself part of history and that is generally to say, whether I like it or not, whether I recognize it or not, one of the bearers of a tradition.[37]

Communitarians also took exception to Rawls' contention that a theory of justice can be universally applicable. Walzer, for instance, argued that although minimal values may be discerned across the globe, it is impossible to arrive at a list of universalizable mores. Walzer goes on to argue that the idea of universalism refracts particular cultural values through a self-designated prism. Instead, he points out that cultural factors influence not only *what* rights are deemed important within societies, but *how* rights themselves are identified and justified. For Walzer, unless these practices are situated historically and socially, any talk of rights is doomed to, at best, either abstract theorizing or, at worst, cultural condescension.[38]

Communitarians argue that communities typically exist along a number of lines: communities based on locale, which should be protected, especially in the era of globalization (examples include urban or rural networks); communities based on collective memory, which tie us to the past and project us into the future (the key example here are national groups) and communities based on socio-psychological ties, namely, personal encounters such as friends and families. For Elizabeth Frazer, political communitarianism exhibits three elements: First, it depends on an emphasis on sharing that holds that 'on virtually every issue there are shared values, meanings and goals that can be appealed to'.[39] Second, an imperative towards participation consisting principally of the elevation of common bonds outside of the auspices of the state; and third, an encouragement towards volunteering and the promotion of localized solutions to problems. For Frazer, then, communitarianism essentially revolves around value politics. The use of the term is redolent of what Frazer and Nicola Lacey, for example, argue is the relationship between community and communitarianism. For them, 'the idea of "community" plays a double role' within communitarianism – 'in generating and grounding moral judgment, and in providing a source of inspiration for at least some forms of value-communitarian commitment'.[40] In this way, communitarian rhetoric gained ground during the Blairite New Labour era (1995–2010) – Sarah Hale notes, for example, that a commitment to 'traditional' family values and the importance of education allowed New Labour to move towards conservative values and adopt policies normally associated with the Right, such as having tough attitudes towards crime. Hale, somewhat unconvincingly and puzzlingly, argues that New Labour's communitarianism was a 'myth' – as if it were merely a rhetorical device that had no constitutive or constructive force in and of itself.[41] Indeed, as feminist scholars such as Frazer and Lacey show, the historical constitution of communities has never been arbitrary and the exclusion of groups based on gender, race, religion, class (or any other category) has been a product of careful construction and maintenance.[42] Frazer and Lacey, for example, criticize communitarianism for its deferral of the 'fundamental importance' between 'club goods' ('those from which it is in fact possible to exclude certain people') and 'genuinely public goods', from which at least within a given space' no one can be excluded'.[43]

Access to goods and resources, then, always involves questions of distribution and redistribution, which, in turn, incorporate issues of group members, political power and, ultimately, justice and communication.[44] The central question that immediately arises from this is the relation of one type of community to another – or one type of community to society in general. In a study of residential communities in America, for example, Daniel Bell pointed to how although particular interests and bonds can break down social isolation and atomization, they can also lead to exclusion and the privatization of responsibility. Despite the virtues of community associations and their challenge to the society of unrelated individuals, Bell posits the unsettling question: 'what if associations in civil society begin to seriously undermine attachment to the polity at large, maybe even to erode the bare minimum of social cohesion and trust needed to promote social injustice and sustain the democratic process?'[45] Taking this idea one step further, Adrian Little points out, even the lens we use to view communities can reveal differing inequalities and abuses:

> There are many practical examples of excluded communities in modern liberal democracies that prove that individuals can be accorded rights and membership of wider political entities such as the state and still face exclusion because of the particular communities that they belong to.[46]

The very idea of community is saturated with political significance. As Anthony Cohen points out, 'community itself and everything within it, conceptual as well as material, has a symbolic dimension', he argues. The idea 'exists as something for people to "think with". The symbols of community are mental constructs: they provide people with the means to make meaning'.[47] If communities are in fact constructs, then the exclusionary ethics that underpin them can also be deconstructed or framed in an alternative fashion. For Gerard Delanty, the types of concerns raised by Bell or Little do not invalidate the idea of community which he explains 'can be exclusive or inclusive'.[48] There are, he points out, many different varieties of communitarian thought – liberal, radical pluralistic, feminism, civic and governmental – but the notion that communitarianism is opposed to 'the state' is inaccurate. Again, as with Little, it depends on perspective: thus he cited Manuel Castells' argument that European integration offers 'many opportunities for local government. "The more national states fade in their role, the more cities emerge as a driving force in the making of a new European society'.[49] As pointed out earlier with regard to the elision of nation and community in Northern Ireland, Delanty is compelling in refusing to separate the state from communities. Yet, arguably, his emphasis on the potential for communities to be not simply exclusionary places works to reproduce the marginalization involved in the framing of Loughran's 'community people'. When placed in the Northern Ireland conflict – and, again, as pointed out earlier – the ideologies that shaped some communities facilitated terror and allowed or compelled individuals within those communities to enable others to perpetuate political violence. There seems, then, to be an incongruity involved in extending community-based initiatives from people and ideologies that inspired or tolerated violence to those who suffered it. One implication may be that incongruity is circumvented by requiring the latter to reconcile themselves with the needs and concerns of the former. Another might be that incongruity can be accommodated through pluralistic institutions and a political culture that values tolerance and dialogue.

This is arguably the sentiment underpinning the Northern Irish political institutions. Yet, the turn towards ethno-nationalist, community-based practices are, in part, a realization of the fears of some critics of the consociational characteristics of the power-sharing assembly. Such sceptics have argued that the devolutionary structures in Belfast promote increased division – incentivizing a dynamic of ethno-religious posturing rather than sustained attempts at inter-bloc cohesion – and, in effect, have 'institutionalised sectarianism'.[50] The importance of the notion of a civic culture is to provide for mediation between political elites and citizens. As Hayward and Komarova argue, '[l]egitimacy and stability are confirred [sic] on any political system by its civic culture'. In Northern Ireland, however, '[c]ultural power works *within* communities' to constrict individuals' capacity to view the world from a range of viewpoints thus working to reinforce segregation and conflict. Hayward and Komarova argue that the response is to tackle the mechanisms that drive the almost path-dependent reproductive dynamics – namely, the investment and interest given over to a struggle and the tacit rules observed by protagonists. However, this seems somewhat self-referencing given that the basis on which to promote alternative imaginings and horizons lies in the belief that discourse can 'legitimize decision-making'.[51] Following from the discussion earlier, this seems only to distribute a new form of the sensible, with the building blocks for the new order being based on perception and belief – that is, on reality as constituted by (elite-driven) discursive construction. In other words, when the ideas of legitimacy, validity or accountability or scrutiny remain fastened to the 'horizons' of ethnic communities, there is no epistemological basis on which to judge whether we are actually viewing the investments and rules accurately or whether any judgement regarding legitimacy is dependent on no more than what 'community' articulates the clearest and most convincing discourse.

Perhaps a more thorough approach to the question of discourse and community conflict in Northern Ireland is found in the work of Shane O'Neill, who adopts a critical theoretical perspective. O'Neill engages with the argument of Walzer that within divided societies, tolerance of the differing and particular historical experiences and ideas about morality among antagonistic communities should be cultivated. This minimal universalism of respect and dialogue is, for O'Neill, given practical substance in Habermas's writings on filtering socio-political conflicts through agreed-upon procedures and institutions. O'Neill argues, for example, that 'if we wish to come to a rational agreement with each other about the justness of a certain norm, then there are legitimate procedural constraints on the arguments that we can make'. [52] And, writing prior to the 1998 settlement, he urged that a 'scenario of a future consensus on a moral principle that respects national differences, and that informs a stable and just constitutional settlement, must be taken to offer a long-term goal'.[53] O'Neill points to the difficulty of importing a Habermasian model to a divided society like Northern Ireland's where the legitimacy of the state itself is questioned.[54] He argues positively for the role of critical theory in identifying 'those structures that have institutionalised social hierarchies historically, so that their explanatory role in causing conflict can be addressed'.[55] However, the outworking of this in terms of policy seems to be a reaffirmation of minimalist legalism (which he argues is embodied in the 1998 agreement).[56]

Taken from a Rancierean perspective, however, neither the O'Neill prescription nor that offered by Hayward and Komorova really seems to circumvent the possibility that incommensurable, zero-sum practices among different groups exist. Or if they do, it is with the redistribution of notions of acceptability and the valorization of alternative forms of community – whether those are in civil society or working with predominant ethno-national blocs. Repeatedly, the question of inclusion and exclusion seems to constitute the basis of policy. I suggest that O'Neill's vision, although concerned with identity politics, can provide a basis for some of the concerns of working through the past and approaching the political implications of trauma. That basis lies in the constructive potential of critique to unmask power relations. But, as I go on to explore in the following chapters, the notion that although a framework of communicative action is possible to accommodate victim and perpetrator stories or facilitate reconciliation is an attractive ideal, the power disparities it seeks to work through may be too extensive – or too early to surmount in the Northern Irish case. As Young points out, the deliberative ideas at the core of such a project are based on 'norms of "articulateness", which must be learned; they are culturally specific, and in actual speaking situations in our society, exhibiting such styles is a sign of social privilege'.[57] In other words, pre-existing power differentials (say between perpetrator and victim) create a context in which imbalance may easily be recycled. Yet, arguably, O'Neill's key insight that constitutionalism can mitigate the divisive effects of identity also retains utility for questions related to working through the past and the politics of trauma – both of which are saturated with issues of identity. The point, which is taken up in the next chapter more fully, seems to revolve around how political and cultural practices work to articulate or disarticulate a set of historical experiences. In Young's framing, these practices depend on a differentiated approach to rights and norms – one that works to reveal oppression and domination and balance injustice with prioritization and affirmation. Within this, the idea of community does not disappear (indeed, it is based on a recognition of the power disparities contained within and containing individuals and communities).Instead the idea is to work to disarticulate and redress community-based imparities by challenging and delimiting rather indulging communal practices.[58]

Re-imagining communities in Northern Ireland

An unreflective faith in the value of community lies at the heart of much of the discourse surrounding contemporary efforts to build peace in Northern Ireland. From restorative justice schemes to storytelling initiatives, and from the promotion of cultural heritage to security concerns, Northern Irish political debate is replete with the prioritization of 'community'.

Now, of course, communities exist in Northern Ireland – the fissures between Catholics and Protestants remain as wide as ever. Although ordinary people constantly negotiate or even transcend sectarian differences of many kinds in their everyday lives, there is little evidence of a thaw in voting practices, and, indeed, the 2010 elections witnessed the two main ethnic tribune parties, Sinn Féin and the Democratic Unionist Party, solidifying their positions.[59] Although the consociational dimensions of power sharing at Stormont – in which ethnic divisions are incentivized and rewarded through quasi-autonomous ministerial positions – have undoubtedly assisted the entrenchment of a dual-party system (what is colloquially known as the 'sectarian headcount'), the idea that the answer lies in the further, unproblematic reification of communities seems a peculiar type of dead-end thinking.

The Arts Council of Northern Ireland (ACNI) has recently launched a scheme to 're-image communities' across the country. The scheme attempts to tackle the reification of culture and community that mars Northern Irish society. It does so by aiming for an almost Gadamerian fusion of horizons – the transcending of sectarian division through socially engaged art. The level of engagement, however, seems determined by relevance in a peculiar fashion. As befitting a publicly funded arts scheme (£3.1 million from various contributors – ACNI itself, the Office of the First and Deputy First Minister, the International Fund for Ireland and the Special EU Programmes Body under the European Union–sponsored

Peace III programme), the outcomes must be socially and politically applicable, but in order to be appreciated, they must engage with social and political realities. The aim is to move beyond these realities, yet the scheme itself seems fundamentally beholden to them – the platitudinous language in which it is couched being unable to approach division in a critical fashion.

The programme is to focus on projects that tick one or more of the following boxes: they should be cross-community, inter-community, inter-cultural, cross-border, urban or rural, targeting young people (under twenty-five) and targeting ethnic minority groups. The objective is laudable – namely, to 'help all communities in both urban and rural settings and the border areas' in focusing 'on positive ways to express who they are and what culture means to them artistically and creatively'.[60] As public and publicly funded art, the programme balances the aesthetic with the social, the cultural with the political. Thus, its fundamental purpose is to foster a shared society in Northern Ireland: 'In order to achieve such a society, communities and agencies need to work together to tackle the physical legacy of segregation and division in towns, villages, rural communities and border areas'. The projects, it is envisaged, will transform the landscape of Northern Ireland artistically, creatively, politically and morally. They will 'enrich communities'; they should be 'locally tailored and community driven'. Success will be measured by the extent to which proposals meet certain 'strategic themes'. For example, a successful project will cultivate 'community cohesion' by working 'with communities to provide opportunities for more stable, safer neighbourhoods and develop strong, positive relations between people from different backgrounds'. By supporting progress towards a 'peaceful, shared and stable society', 'community led [sic] programmes of arts activities' will also help to build that long-sought-after prize – reconciliation. As such, the task for artists and communities should not be underestimated – for grants of between £500 and £50,000 artistic entrepreneurs will become social architects, using their inspiration to create not only pleasing artworks, but also a post-conflict utopia.

As mentioned earlier, these are noble, commendable aims, and ACNI is not acting in bad faith. However, regardless of whatever broad historical narrative one attaches to the origins of the conflict, it is undeniable that, in part at least, the violence proved to be so resilient because of the strength of communal belonging – the gunmen who left 'communities' to kill people from other 'communities' did so because they were driven by beliefs perpetuated at the local level. Partly for that very reason, the idea of 'community' also forms the backdrop over 'legacy issues' – who was justified in doing what they did, whose rights are being acknowledged and whose claims are being ignored. Given that 'community cohesion' was one of the problems behind why the conflict lasted so long and why the peace, at times, seems so shallow, it seems reasonable to expect ACNI to provide some definition of what it means by the term community – for if we don't know what we are creating, the risk is we could end up with some kind of monster on our hands.

What 'community' seems to mean might actually be better expressed as 'communal' – albeit with the distasteful, divisive connotations of religion and/

or ideology removed. This is because on virtually each occasion 'community' is mentioned by ACNI, it seemingly is referring to localities. This brings us to the nub of the problem: what ACNI is actually doing is conflating the broad sense of community with a narrow understanding linked to locality. The result is that the entire population of Northern Ireland becomes in some way responsible for turning these 'community' artworks into something positive. The political effect is twofold: The population is bound to fail in that task because the 'community' element relates not to a whole, but to a part. Second, the failure will serve as evidence that cohesion at the level of the polity is inferior to the cohesion of localities, thereby reinforcing the segregated elite political culture that is inscribed at the heart of governance in Northern Ireland. The failure seems inevitable and may be located in ACNI's brief. For example, its five-year strategic plan (2013–2018) states that '[w]e are living in extraordinary times'; we are also, it avers, 'entering a new age of innovation with people choosing how they consume, share, access and create artistic content'. We are also living, it goes on to state, in 'times of austerity' where economic 'conditions continue to impact upon consumer behaviour, audience spend, corporate sponsorship, as well as limiting access to private finance'.[61]

Like any organization, ACNI needs to balance its books and most likely finds that task difficult in the new 'Age of Austerity'. Yet, more fundamentally, the neo-liberal rhetoric, as found in this programme, reveals that it no longer sees the population of Northern Ireland as citizens, but as consumers. Surreptitiously, government – in the form of ACNI – has transformed the way in which we are supposed to relate to the state. Of course, this is nothing new. It has been happening for the past three decades, if not longer. What is new is that government now seems content to give the people of Northern Ireland what they want – and it has decided that as clients (what ACNI refers to as 'the audience'), they want 'community'. The citizens of Northern Ireland have, in effect, been turned into consumers. It does not matter whether that citizenry desire this change or not, or whether they even recognize it, because the question of choice is being refined through projects like 'Re-imagining Communities'. In other words, whether they want to consume the product of community/communalism is moot: the demand is being created (either by them or the state), and the citizenry will get it and they will like it.

ACNI's project is saturated with politics – and the type of politics it is saturated in, despite the high-flying rhetoric, are the politics of ethnic bloc division, the politics of the consociational settlement at Stormont. It should be noted that the project is also saturated with morality, because it makes the majority of the people culpable for the kind of communalist ideologies that drove terrorists to murder and that continue to inspire hatred and division. Supporters of the programme might reply that it is not about promoting divisive identity; rather, it's about inclusion – inclusion of young people, inclusion of ethnic minorities and the inclusion of marginalized sections of society – in effect, it is the artistic version of affirmative action; besides, there are also (vague) commitments to tackling overt manifestations of hatred, conflict and racism. However, as mentioned earlier, the political reality of ACNI's programme is to elide difference in a relatively homogenized marketplace in which ethno-religious identity is both the currency and the commodity (hence the logic of self-reproduction, self-reinforcement). The paradoxical result is that a broad understanding of community as entailing all the differences that go into making up a polity or a society (age, class, locale, gender, migration) are subsumed within a minimalist understanding that focuses solely on the dominant cleavage in this particular society. Inclusion, then, becomes about recognizing those terms rather than about respect for difference; reconciliation becomes about reconciling difference, justice and ethics to the political dictates of peace. To be clear: ACNI does good work in extremely hostile circumstances – they promote public art not only in an era of cutbacks, but in a deeply divided society. However, even with the best of intentions and deploying the most empowering (yet somehow also asinine language), ACNI may be contributing to the malaise of division that continues to frustrate Northern Ireland.

The ACNI project reflects the limitations of 'socially turned' or 'socially relational' art as outlined by Jen Harvie. Harvie, for example, maps debates regarding the roles and functions of public art as revolving around two poles. On the one hand, relational art promotes immersion – it tends to be large scale and requires audiences to experience it in a 'shared environment' of individuals and art to other individuals. This experience is seen as profoundly democratic – it reveals the political constraints of the 'society of the spectacle and capitalist relations', but simultaneously engenders 'neighbourliness', 'harmony and cohabitation'; in other words, the democratic practice and ethos it cultivates is one of consensus.[62] On the other hand, 'democracy is [seen to be] enacted through art practices that cultivate socially antagonistic and dissonant relations'. Here, the perspective is Mouffian – conflict is seen as an inherent part of democracy, and art's contribution is to enable rather than efface it. Harvie's position lies somewhere between the two approaches: 'participation is not intrinsically politically progressive' (a term that is left ill defined but that seems dialectically related to community reification), but 'pleasurable fun can constructively engage audiences while dissent's bad feeling can risk alienating them'.[63] Participation, then, is associated with context: the relation of art to democracy depends on how art is situated and recognized within society. Again, to echo points made in previous chapters, it is not simply the production of ideas or art that is at stake, but how they are being received in different ways by different groups and individuals. For Harvie, writing principally about the United Kingdom, this context of reception is rendered problematic by a neo-liberal focus on self-interest and its harnessing of art to offset its creation of social inequalities.

The 'public' nature of public art, then, following Harvie, must be set against a broader socio-economic backdrop. It is perhaps more appropriate, therefore, to view participation in terms of engagement and access – artworks/performances are read or engaged in by different audiences and individuals at different levels. This cognitive process is conditioned by a complex web of means and methods by which the public access the artworks and the ideas (purportedly) behind them. This is how Glenn Patterson responded to the ACNI scheme. Writing about his experience with the scheme when contributing to a radio programme, Patterson encountered terms such as 'community worker', 'community practitioner', 'community activist' and 'community gatekeeper'. The tendency, he avers, is to 'turn a blind eye, or at best raise a sardonic eyebrow, to what in certain of these instances the word "community" connotes'.[64] Irony and turning a blind eye may well capture how people in Northern Ireland respond to 'community', but Patterson overlooks the politics of what that response may involve: namely, an apathetic, de-politicizing gesture. This is not surprising, for if community is reconfigured as a form of consumptive togetherness (to paraphrase Tony Judt),[65] then received political wisdom becomes the norm and is reinscribed physically and cognitively on the audience (or, as ACNI terms participants in public art, 'consumers').

A bare sense of political legitimacy is lost in this process. Neither apathy nor irony can mitigate the removal of the conferral that serves as the basis for justifying legitimacy. As David Beetham points out, legitimacy is not simply about belief in the right to govern, but a belief in the justifiability of that right;[66] apathy and irony stand in contrast to that notion and, in fact, work to deepen the de-politicization of governance. In this way, the debates about public art deepening democracy through consensus or dissensus miss the point: the level of engagement or access to public art is fundamentally linked to democracy through the troubling of *belief*. It is presumably not the role of public art to provide rationales for justifying legitimacy; instead, that role may consist in problematizing and helping to deconstruct the ways in which unquestioning belief is tied up and cultivated by power relations. In other words, art draws attention to the loss of power that is involved in de-politicization and the consequent valorization of that loss.

Drawing directly on Rancière, Roland Bleiker supports this point when he argues that art 'acquires political significance when it interferes with, even disrupts . . . commonsensical delineation[s] of what can be seen, said and thought'.[67] He goes on to reference the critical role that Rancière sees art as playing in politics: 'an aesthetic politics always defines itself by a certain recasting of the distribution of the sensible, a reconfiguration of the given perceptual forms'.[68] In a position that is seemingly quite close to Catherine Cole's (cited in the previous chapter), Bleiker argues that such an approach should avoid the Foucauldian trap of a stress on knowledge, given that aesthetic practice and engagement convey more experiences than those which can be conveyed linguistically. However, arguably, in a more pronounced way than Cole, he underscores the dynamics of power that art can also convey and propagate. Art, he argues, works 'like an amplifier. Aesthetics adds a different dimension to our understanding of the political and, by consequence, to the ethical discourses that are central to waging political debates'. If art is indeed a mechanism for working through the legacies of the past and as a way of giving voice to those rendered inarticulate through trauma, then, this chapter has suggested, its potential to remarginalize and reproduce exclusionary ideologies and practices needs to be foregrounded in analysis and policy design.

Conclusion

The concentration on community-based ethics in Northern Ireland, which draw on ideas inherent within communitarianism, often works to draw boundaries and exclude. For example, the problem with applying a communitarian lens when interpreting phenomena such as loyalist alienation and continued violence is that it risks becoming a self-fulfilling prophecy – a version of the advice that the more often one repeats a story, the more it becomes plausible. As actors within the developing, evolving Northern Irish settlement process, both academics and ex-terrorists are constitutive of that process by way of how they articulate it. The resort to 'community' as the key means of articulation establishes a reality that ignores the question of what happens if 'community' conflicts with 'society'. Certainly, the idea of a Northern Irish society is not a settled term, but this chapter has suggested that part of that instability lies in the valorization of community over and above wider and more basic concerns with social responsibility. The secondary problem relates to the closure of debate, for, in the eyes of the aficionados of 'community', community and society are synonymous, and any questioning of that insight is automatically deleterious and dangerous. Yet, the finding of this chapter is that the turn to communities only reinforces the old logics – the alternative being that 'presenting a new way' to make sense in any way must entail waiving the flotsam of 'community' that has served so many vested interests and embarking on a thorough deconstruction and re-imagination of more pluralistic and open-ended ways of articulating identity. The turn towards communitarianism is perhaps an inevitable outworking of the consociational elements of the power-sharing structures at Stormont, but, more than that, it represents a fundamental challenge to how policy makers and ordinary citizens project an idea of Northern Ireland into the future.

Notes

1 Flinders, *Defending Politics*, pp. 71–72.
2 Panagia, '*"Partage"*', p. 98.
3 Jacques Rancière, *On the Shores of Politics*, translated by Liz Heron (London: Verso, 2007 [1992]), p. 32.
4 Katy Hayward and Milena Komarova (2014) 'The Limits of Local Accommodation: Why Contentious Events Remain Prone to Conflict in NI', *Studies in Conflict &* Terrorism, 39(9): 780
5 Rogelio Alonso, *The IRA and Armed Struggle* (Abingdon: Routledge, 2007), pp. 67–101.
6 Ruane and Todd, *Dynamics*.
7 Ibid, p. 9.
8 See Roman Jakobson, 'Two aspects of language and two types of aphasic disturbance'. Available at http://theory.theasintheas.org/wp-content/uploads/2013/02/jakobson_Aphasia.pdf; accessed on 27 July 2014.
9 Benedict *Imagined Communities: Reflections on the Origin and Spread of Nationalism* (London: Verso, 1991 [1983]), p. 6.
10 By 'easily identifiable', I refer to overt signifiers such as murals, painted curb stones and flags, but also to urban and rural areas (city neighbourhoods, towns and villages) that are overwhelmingly constituted by residents from one or the other of the two main ethno-religious factions.
11 Jonny Byrne and John Topping, 'Community Safety: A Decade of Development, Delivery, Challenge and Change in Northern Ireland' (Belfast: Belfast Conflict Resolution Consortium, 2012), p. 2.
12 See McGrattan and Meehan, *Everyday Life*.

13 Sara McDowell (2008) 'Selling Conflict Heritage through Tourism in Peacetime Northern Ireland: Transforming Conflict or Exacerbating Difference?', *International Journal of Heritage Studies*, 14(3): 405–421.
14 Kieran McEvoy and Peter Shirlow (2009) 'Re-imagining DDR: Ex-combatants, Leadership and Moral Agency in Conflict Transformation', *Theoretical Criminology* 13(1): 48.
15 See Turner's response to Brian Rowan's article, 'Playing Politics with the Past' (15 August 2012). Available at http://eamonnmallie.com/2012/08/playing-politics-with-the-past/; accessed on 18 September 2012.
16 Byrne and Topping, 'Community Safety'.
17 Tara Lai Quinlan, Basia Spalek and Mary O'Rawe, 'The sociopolitical contexts affecting police-community engagement in Northern Ireland, Britain, and the United States', in *Preventing Ideological Violence: Communities, Police and Case Studies of 'Success'*, edited by P. Daniel Silk, Basia Spalek and Mary O'Rawe (Basingstoke: Palgrave Macmillan, 2013), p. 37.
18 Noel Rooney and Liam Maskey, 'Communities and policing in transition: The Northern Ireland Experience', in Ibid, p. 91.
19 John Loughran, 'Making sense of models of community-police engagements in North Belfast', in Ibid, pp.106–107.
20 See Cillian McGrattan (2012) '"Moving On": The Creation of a Peaceful Community in Northern Ireland', *Studies in Ethnicity and Nationalism*, 12(1): 172–189.
21 W. J. Booth (2001) 'The Unforgotten: Memories of Justice', *American Political Science Review*, 95(4): 780.
22 Marc Augé (2004) *Oblivion* (London: University of Minnesota Press, p. 18; translated by Marjolin de Jager.
23 Loughran, 'Making sense of models', p. 123.
24 Maria Power, 'Introduction: Peacebuilding in Northern Ireland', in *Building Peace in Northern Ireland*, edited by Maria Power (Liverpool: Liverpool University Press, 2011), p. 8.
25 Ibid.
26 Rockhill, 'Appendix 1', p. 92.
27 Rancière, *Shores*, p. 31.
28 Ibid, p. 32.
29 See Tonge, *Comparative*.
30 Dominic Bryan (2006) 'The Politics of Community', *Critical Review of International Social and Political Thought*', 9(4): 605.
31 The text of the Belfast/Good Friday Agreement can be found at http://cain.ulst.ac.uk/events/peace/docs/agreement.htm.
32 Bryan, 'Politics', p. 615.
33 Alan Finlayson (2007) 'The Problem of "Culture" in Northern Ireland: A Critique of the Cultural Traditions Group', *Irish Review*, Winter/Spring, p.78.
34 For more detail, see Chapter 6.
35 Glenn Patterson, 'Don't mention the C-word', *Irish Times*, 4 January 2014. Available at www.irishtimes.com/news/politics/don-t-mention-the-c-word-1.1643567; accessed 3 March 2014.
36 John Rawls, *A Theory of Justice* (Cambridge, MA: Harvard University Press, 1971).
37 Alasdair MacIntyre, *After Virtue* (Duckworth: London, 1981), pp. 205–206.
38 Michael Walzer, *Thick and Thin: Moral Argument at Home and Abroad* (Notre Dame, IN: University of Notre Dame Press, 1994), p. 8; see also Michael Walzer, *Spheres of Justice* (Oxford: Blackwell, 1983).
39 Elizabeth Frazer, *The Problems of Communitarian Politics: Unity and Conflict* (Oxford: Oxford University Press, 1999), p. 41.
40 Elizabeth Frazer and Nicola Lacey, *The Politics of Community: A Feminist Analysis of the Liberal-Communitarian Debate* (Toronto, Ontario: Harvester Wheatsheaf/University of Toronto Press, 1993), p. 139.

41 Sarah Hale, *Blair's Community: Communitarian Thought and New Labour* (Manchester: Manchester University Press, 2006), p. 4.
42 Will Kymlicka, *Contemporary Political Philosophy: An Introduction* (Oxford: Oxford University Press, 1990), p. 226.
43 Frazer and Lacey, *Politics of Community*, pp. 140–141.
44 Iris Marion Young, *Justice and the Politics of Difference* (Princeton, NJ: Princeton University Press, 1990).
45 Daniel A. Bell, 'Residential community associations: Community or disunity?', in *The Essential Communitarian Reader*, edited by Amitai Etzioni (Oxford: Rowman & Littlefield Publishers, 1998), p. 168.
46 Adrian Little, *The Politics of Community: Theory and Practice* (Edinburgh: Edinburgh University Press, 2002), p. 47.
47 Anthony P. Cohen, *Symbolic Construction of Community* (London: Routledge, 1989), p. 19.
48 Gerard Delanty, *Community* (London: Routledge, 2003), p. 12
49 Ibid, p. 63.
50 See, for example, Paul Dixon (2012) 'The Politics of Conflict: A Constructivist Critique of Consociational and Civil Society Theories', *Nations and Nationalism*, 18(1): 8–121; Edwards and McGrattan, *The Northern Ireland Conflict*; Robin Wilson, *The Northern Ireland Experience of Conflict and Agreement: A Model for Export?* (Manchester: Manchester University Press, 2010).
51 Hayward and Komarova, 'The Limits of Local Accommodation'.
52 Shane O'Neill, *Impartiality in Context: Grounding Justice in a Pluralist World* (Albany, NY: State University of New York Press, 1997), p. 190.
53 Ibid, p. 198
54 Ibid; see also Shane O'Neill (2003) 'Are National Conflicts Reconciliable? Discourse Theory and Political Accommodation in Northern Ireland', *Constellations*, 10(1): 76.
55 Shane O'Neill (2007) 'Critical Theory and Ethno-National Conflict: Assessing Northern Ireland's Peace Process as Model of Conflict Resolution, *Irish Political* Studies, 22(4): 423.
56 O'Neill, 'Are National Conflicts Reconciliable?', p. 91.
57 Iris Marion Young, 'Communication and the Other: Beyond Deliberative Democracy', in *Democracy and Difference: Contesting the Boundaries of the Political*, edited by Seyla Benhabib (Chichester: Princeton University Press, 1996), p. 124.
58 See also Delanty, *Community*.
59 See McGrattan and Meehan, *Everyday Life*; Cillian McGrattan (2011) 'The 2010 Westminster General Election in Northern Ireland', *Irish Political Studies*, 26(2): 265–275.
60 See www.artscouncil-ni.org/award/re-imaging_communities.htm.
61 See Arts Council Northern Ireland, 'Consultation draft: Ambitions for the arts: A five-year strategic plan for the arts in Northern Ireland, 2013–2018', available at www.artscouncil-ni.org/documents/research/equality/equalityimpactassessment/draft_five_year_strategy.pdf, accessed on 16 May 2015.
62 Nicholas Bourriard, cited in Jen Harvie, *Fair Play: Art, Performance and Neoliberalism* (Basingstoke: Palgrave Macmillan, 2013), p. 7.
63 Ibid, p. 10
64 Patterson, 'Don't mention'.
65 Tony Judt, *The Memory Chalet* (London: Vintage, 2011), p. 32.
66 David Beetham, *The Legitimation of Power* (Basingstoke: Palgrave Macmillan, 2013).
67 Roland Bleiker, *Aesthetics and World Politics* (Basingstoke: Palgrave Macmillan, 2012).
68 Jacques Rancière, *The Politics of Aesthetics*, p. 59.

4 Drawing on the past: ideology, reconciliation and nationalism in Northern Ireland

This chapter explores the conceptualization of 'reconciliation' within modern Northern Irish nationalist discourse. Although it may be expected that nationalist ideology will inevitably harness reconciliation to its own policy ends, I argue that, in Northern Ireland, this results in a foreclosure of the radical potential of the concept. The chapter traces how this tendency is implicit within framings of reconciliation and how it becomes operational in Northern Ireland, despite a language of pluralism and openness. I wish to suggest that this is a result of the outworking of dynamics described in Chapter 3: namely, the displacement of the whole for the part, or, to put it more concretely, the substitution of the community for the nation, or the communal for the social. The rhetoric that is used to frame and justify that movement actually revolves around ideas about openness, accountability and sharing; however, the reality of community-based politics (as it plays out in Northern Ireland, at least) is a tendency towards foreclosure. This chapter maps the intersection of discourses and policies about 'reconciliation' with community-based politics. Primarily, reconciliatory policies are framed within the language of peace, but that language also often overlaps with the kind of terminology that is characteristic of community-based politics. It is perhaps helpful to view this mixing of rhetoric as a spectrum or Venn diagram in which 'peace' and 'democracy' are the two keywords. This is because the language of peace is, arguably, often framed within notions of democratization. This 'positive' or 'maximalist' idea of peace implies institutional reform and societal harmony. Yet, I suggest, that promise is belied by its anchorage in the politics of community. The chapter concludes by beginning to sketch an alternative framing of reconciliation that may work to undercut the particularizing tendencies of the nationalist conceptualization of the term.

The focus of the chapter is on Northern Irish nationalist use and articulation of reconciliation. The fundamental ideological aim of nationalism is to end partition by transcending the current constitutional settlement. The notion of community is key to this project: as Todd points out, Northern nationalism centres around and is built on ideas of community and interlocking and reinforcing community networks that consist of cultural and religious organizations.[1] The idea of a community apart maintains these links through the articulation of a narrative of injustice, discrimination and eschatological triumph: the injustice of partition, the discrimination of exclusion and marginalization within the Northern state between 1920 and 1972 and the end goal of the manifestation of a self-determining community that encompasses the island of Ireland. 'Reconciliation' is a recurring trope within this ideology: for example, the idea of an 'agreed Ireland' that would embrace Catholics and Protestants was a constant refrain in the speeches of the nationalist leader, John Hume, through the Troubles and has since become a key element within Sinn Féin's peace-making rhetoric. The focus on Northern Irish nationalism therefore reveals the congruence that occurs between reconciliation and community – the intertwining of community-based politics with concerns about sharing, restitution, rebuilding and moving forward from political violence. As I point out, the exclusionary nature of community-based politics works to fence off and constrain 'reconciliation' within an ideological frame and maintain the exclusion of wider society in general and those who suffered and continue to suffer from the aftermath of trauma in particular.

The case of Northern Irish nationalism is instructive of these two points due to the way it is constructed and articulated within a framework that is putatively internationalist, pluralist and universalist. Northern nationalists hold that the state is illegitimate because of constrained democracy – the island of Ireland is ultimately the unit in which questions of self-determination and societal progress should be decided. Northern Irish nationalism is represented by two political parties. Sinn Féin, the largest grouping, has in the past supported armed resistance to ending Irish partition and promotes a strong defence of Irish cultural values north and south of the border; Martin McGuinness is the deputy first minister of Northern Ireland and was in the early 1970s the leader of the Provisional Irish Republican Army – a terror group responsible for almost 60 percent of the 3,700 deaths in the conflict – in Derry, the province's second largest city. The Social Democratic and Labour Party (SDLP) is a more moderate grouping, traditionally linked closely to the Catholic middle class; the SDLP was seen as a key architect of the peace process, but has lost ground electorally to Sinn Féin following the ceasefires of the 1990s.

Of course, reconciliation is always open to ideological manipulation,[2] and it may be expected that when it is harnessed to such a 'slippery and self-referential' ideology as nationalism[3] that inconsistencies and politically expedient framings will be the norm. This is confirmed in the analysis later; but, instead, the main objective of the chapter is to outline or begin to map how this is occurring in relation to Northern Irish nationalism. As such, the chapter aims to address the questions of what the relationship of Northern Irish nationalism and reconciliation looks like and how reconciliation is informing the articulation of nationalist discourses in and about Northern Ireland. The secondary, and more fundamental, aim is to reflect on the framing and shape of reconciliation within Northern Irish nationalism. I argue that Northern Irish nationalist appropriation and utilization of 'reconciliation' works to foreclose debate and to defer consideration of the differences of opinion, experience and aspiration that precipitate thoughts and calls for reconciliation. Reconciliation is often seen as restorative and as providing the basis for building institutions that will cultivate more harmonious future relations (see, for example, the framing of South Africa's transition by Archbishop Desmond Tutu),[4] or else it can be conceived as the beginnings (to put it crudely) of the political – the process by which conflictual politics can be filtered through agonistic understandings and practices.[5] The elision of nationalism and reconciliation in Northern Ireland, on the other hand, embraces a teleological and tautological vision, a barely concealed question regarding what constitutes the actual object of the reconciliation – in other words, the question of to what end reconciliation is directed and who it is that is doing the reconciling. In a way, then, arguably, reconciliation in the Northern Irish nationalist understanding is less related to a verb and more to a direct object. The effect is to undercut the relationship of reconciliation to the stated aims of peace-building.

Ideology, reconciliation and dealing with the past

Andrew Rigby defines reconciliation against forgiveness as two distinct processes to deal or come to terms with difficult, violent or divided pasts. Forgiveness, he argues, is a personal act that does not necessarily require the knowledge of those who (were perceived as having) inflicted the wrong that has occurred. Reconciliation, on the other hand,

> . . . refers to the future and requires the active participation of those who were divided by enmity. At the core of any reconciliation process is the preparedness of people to anticipate a shared future. For this to occur they are required not to forget but to forgive the past, and thus be in a position to move forward together.[6]

Reconciliation, then, is a political and a social act; when related to societies that are moving beyond contentious and violent pasts, it can be seen as forming part of the policy framework for facilitating peaceful and stable transitions. The panoply of measures to work through the past is varied (ranging from juridical prosecutions to restorative storytelling measures), and can be seen as falling within transitional justice studies as a subfield of peace research.[7] Indeed, the United Nations holds that building peace requires not only the reintegration of ex-combatants into society, but that a 'right' to the truth about violent pasts exists.[8] The UN acknowledges, however, that there are 'practicable' limits to this right, for example, the need to balance truth retrieval with states' legal systems and abilities to provide full disclosure. Added to this is, of course, the 'Faustian bargain' outlined by Weber in the aftermath of World War I:[9] Do states concentrate their resources on working through and forensically examining the actions and strategies that caused unrest, and perhaps bring those accountable to justice; or do they avoid the potential instability that uncovering old wounds can create and the time and resources it requires to implement judicial redress and compensation to victims and, instead, build towards future prosperity? Within these considerations, reconciliation is seen as future oriented, a political intervention (or, perhaps more likely, a series of interventions), that emphasizes reparation and progress rather than reworking and reliving traumatic histories. Michael Humphrey distinguishes 'thick' from 'thin' practices of reconciliation. 'Thick reconciliation', he argues, 'includes accountability, acknowledgement of responsibility, victim recognition, compensation, apology and forgiveness'. Thin reconciliation, on the other hand, 'is restricted by a political agreement based on degrees of amnesty and amnesia in which victims are marginalized'.[10]

The public and political nature of reconciliation as an idea that informs peace-building must, Ernesto Verdeja contends, have a firm, empirical basis. Reconciliation, he states, 'rests on the possibility of discussion [and] deliberation . . . it falls short of deep acceptance, or wilful [sic] embrace of the "other" '. It seemingly is capable of embracing agonist and deliberative conceptions of democracy and provides for a 'contentious coexistence' of former antagonists.[11] Some kind of fundamental empirical understanding about the nature and broad causes of historic division and/or violence seems to be necessary to this approach, along with a basic agreement on key societal values and a respect for the rule of law. This may be difficult to establish; hence, Verdeja argues for flexibility in deliberation. Flexibility, he believes, 'moves us toward achieving *respect* among citizens, since open deliberation is fundamentally inclusive of everyone who could potentially be affected by the outcome, and at the very least accepts their claims to participation'.[12] A cohesive civil society seems to be key to this vision: the argument seems to be that the kind of flexible and responsive political institutions for dealing with the past and promoting reconciliation can only be built on a solid bedrock of an engaged and open framework of quasi-political organizations and voluntary groups. In addition, the role of political elites must be carefully managed because through their words and actions they 'shape political culture' and 'signal to the population what kinds of behaviour are proper in democratic society'.[13]

Verdeja's reading of reconciliation as occurring within an institutional framework echoes that of Claire Moon, whose work on the South African Truth and Reconciliation Commission (TRC) describes how 'reconciliation is constructed and not inherent – that is to say that it is grounded in particular social, political and historical conditions and emerges at particular junctures in time'. Moon rejects the idea that reconciliation is a strictly moral or normative practice, but instead argues that it is saturated with politics – and, as such, it 'is put in the service of new power elites with the primary purpose of underpinning state-making and political legitimacy' within new, transitional regimes.[14] She therefore situates the TRC within a narrative framing, seeing it as an intrinsic part of the historiographical representation of South Africa. In her reading, the TRC constituted this history and authorized what can be said about it and who is deemed authoritative to speak about it. Because of the movement of that narrative – from apartheid oppression to national unity[15] – the TRC's practical outworking focused on perpetrators and amnesty, despite pledges to give voice and reparation to victims. This was facilitated through and in Tutu's emphasis on *Ubuntu* – a Xhosa term denoting restorative justice, 'reparation and rehabilitation of victims, and forgiveness rather than punishment, of perpetrators',[16] but perhaps more so (at least in my reading of Moon), in the focus away from victims and towards perpetrators by the introduction of a political, historical and moral relativism involved in the introduction of the notion of multiple truths – or, more specifically, the 'recognition' that a 'unified truth about the past' would be unpalatable to all.[17]

The writings of political theorist Andrew Schaap arguably represent an attempt to distinguish reconciliation from the potential towards impunity, relativism and equivalence. I wish to suggest, however, that the question of counterfactualism remains. Although it is not explicitly part of Schaap's concerns, which I outline later, I wish to suggest that the possibilities recommended by counterfactual reasoning are inextricably linked to any reading of reconciliation within deeply divided societies such as Northern Ireland's and also when filtered through the politics of trauma. In his monograph *Political Reconciliation*,[18] Schaap advocates a critical approach to the ideological implications involved in conceptualizing reconciliation. His approach is to move reconciliation from ideology and towards what he sees as a more 'positive account of reconciliation as *politics*'.[19] What he means by this is linked to his definition of reconciliation, which he maintains, must remain political:

> [I]t must be understood as a striving for a sense of commonness that might be disclosed from the clash of perspectives we bring to bear on the world in our historical relation to each other. As such, would not be about transcending the conflicts of the past by striving for social harmony. Rather, reconciliation would condition the possibility of politics by framing a potentially agonistic clash of world views within the context of a community that is 'not yet'.[20]

For Schaap the politics of reconciliation mean overturning the urge to resolve, repair and settle; rather, they inspire an opening up, an injection of dissensus and agonism, and an ethic of hope that difference gives way to plurality and democracy (broadly conceived) rather than the propagation of fear and suspicion and the imposition of violence and injustice. It is for this reason that Schaap is critical of the tendency within liberal thought to avert violence through institution building. This approach to peace-building is suspicious of individual's and group's motivations in this worldview and paternalistic in its attempts to mitigate the possibility of a recurrence of violence. Instead, tolerance for difference is framed as a positive societal aspiration, but one which retains a policing or containment purpose – primordial forces lie beyond the limits of tolerance, the logic seems to imply, and to go there is to put oneself outside of the borders, protections and indulgence of agreed-upon politics. Reconciliation, in a way, becomes securitized: it is framed as a societal imperative with the implicit existential threat being that beyond it lies anarchy. Notions of tolerance and respect, therefore, work to shut down and limit the kinds of politics that 'would enable citizens to call into question (and so potentially discover reasons) why they should want collectively to secure the conditions that make society possible between them in the first place'.[21]

Schaap frames reconciliation as a radical politics. He views reconciliation as ideology as falling within what Rancière calls 'the police', which is usually linked to his account of the norms and logics that are constitutive of communities. This account stresses the notion of *le partage du sensible*, namely, the 'distribution/partition of the sensible' or of the sensitive or the responsive, the discernible. 'Policing', then, as Samuel Chambers explains, 'is a way of dividing up and linking up, of making visible and making invisible, the various parts of the social order'.[22] 'Policing', Schaap explains, is intrinsically and intimately ideological – the world is interpreted and subsumed within a pre-existing order. Schaap argues that reconciliation can be viewed as a 'mode of activity that is "antagonistic to policing"', if ideology is juxtaposed with the political.[23] The politics of reconciliation involve a revelation and a representation of the police order, which counts and delimits the groups and the norms and the ideas that constitute what is sensible and acceptable.

Rancière's emphasis on what might be called the ephemeral nature of the political allows Schaap to distinguish a radical politics of reconciliation from reconciliation-as-ideology. The latter occurs because the 'concept' of reconciliation is operationalized, or given meaning by and through political contestation – that is, in the arguments over how the past is worked through, how the aftermath of political violence is dealt with and how justice is dispensed and the injured and dead remembered and commemorated. 'If reconciliation depends on a population within a state coming to think of itself as a people, then a particular conception of reconciliation cannot be determined in advance but must be worked out politically by those who would get together to reconcile in the first place'.[24] A radical politics of reconciliation, on the other hand, reveals the 'order of the sayable of the ideology of reconciliation' because the political 'always calls into question a social order by demonstrating the fundamental equality that it implicitly presupposes'.[25] This is because, despite their differences, antagonists 'possess the same faculty of understanding'. The politics of reconciliation is then framed around the Rancièrean description of subjectivization: the enunciation of a claim or wrong that stands outwith the existing distribution of the sensible. Reconciliation, in this view, is an approach to politics, the 'processing of the wrong on which political community is founded'.[26]

The importance of Schaap's critique is to clarify how, despite laudable intentions, reconciliation can become quickly conflated with compromise and take on an imperative of groups or individuals reconciling themselves to a particular ideological project. Thus, as he argues, viewed as ideology, reconciliation risks complicity 'in the exercise of various forms of structural violence in its appeal to an idea of commonality to legitimate a social hierarchy'.[27] Schaap, arguably, sidesteps the problem identified by Rancière's treatment of the distribution of the sensible, because although reconciliation may work to draw attention to the distribution of what Schaap sees as ideological, the politics of distribution, as Rancière points out, is to reinstitute another realm of what is sayable.[28] The counterfactual arises immediately that the agonistic realm that Schaap identifies as 'political' may be another distribution of exclusionary practices. This seems pertinent when dealing with the politics of trauma, which are, in part, defined by inarticulacy. In other words, the politics of trauma draws attention to its own silence; the agonistic idea that the recognition of contention and division can mitigate violent conflict seems almost superfluous. In other words, the politics of agonism are revealed as yet another ideological sphere (if ideology is read as a counting, or a police realm), because the marginalized remain marginal. A worse counterfactual lies in the possibility that agonism may reproduce the terms of oppression by placing the onus of recognition on individuals and liminal groups who suffered political violence and terror. As such, it imagines an equilibrium that, historically or chronologically, does not exist, given the gulf between victims and perpetrators. Even when perpetrators are also, to a degree, victims (where the oppressed become oppressors), the agonistic faith in understandability (or reason) works to throw the onus of responsibility on vulnerable subjects.

Ethnicity adds a complicating layer to this process of radical or agonistic reconciliation. Rancière's conceptualization of the distribution of the sensible gives way to two formulations of community – the throng of the people, the community obsessed with its own unification (*ochlos*) and the part-without-part, those excluded from that division (*demos*).[29] The creation of a community divided within the agonistic approach to democracy works to replicate that fundamental exclusionary dynamic described by Rancière. The process of reconciliation of community, therefore, works in an exclusionary fashion. As both Rancière and Schaap point out, this is not necessarily a bad thing in and of itself. However, it is difficult to work from what might be described as an essentially normative framing to either the politics of trauma or ethnic politics. Whereas the latter is in many ways concerned with the part-without-part, the latter is concerned with the community obsessed with its own unification. The limitations of the agonistic approach to institute an open-ended politics is based on the gulf between these forms of community, but nonetheless works to reveal the constraining influence of ethnic- or community-based politics in dealing with divided histories and traumatic experiences. The counterfactual then relates essentially to what kind of community results from the reconciliation process. If the distribution of the sensible 'represents the taken-for-granted configuration of perception and meaning that allow a community to recognize itself and defines the conditions in which arguments can be made, recognized as such, and engaged',[30] it is possible that the type(s) of recognition, engagement and argumentation that ensue from the reconciliation process may only reinforce the community-based perceptions and meanings that inspired division in the first place. In other words, the understandability that is inherent to reconciliation may work to replicate the exclusions that ethnicity depends on. I wish to suggest in the following section that that gulf lies at the heart of efforts to apply reconciliation discourses to Northern Ireland.

Reconciliation and Northern Ireland

Reconciliation has become something of a term of art in discourse on and about Northern Ireland's post-conflict transition; as with the way that reconciliation is conceptualized ideologically in general, the use of the term in Northern Ireland is slippery and fluid in import and difficult to pin down and define. Often, politicians and spokespersons for non-governmental organizations or community groups view reconciliation as intrinsic to peace. In this understanding, reconciliation is either the first step or the culmination of a peace process.

Adrian Guelke has argued that one of the reasons why the idea of reconciliation, and in particular the TRC model, became so attractive to Northern Ireland was because of perceived political stasis during the period immediately subsequent to the 1998 agreement. The coincidence of the Northern Irish and the South African transitions also lent the TRC process a certain degree of public profile within Northern Ireland. Arguably, this was inspired, not by party political leaders, who were given legislative roles in the new assembly, but by civic society and community-based organizations and spokespersons. Again, arguably, part of the motivation for the upsurge in interest in South Africa and the TRC was the development of the kind of reconciliation industry described by Moon: a self-sustaining policy field or network of transitional justice academics, faith-based groups and civil society/community-based activists who constituted a community of 'expert reconcilers' through mutual recognition.[31] This nexus was sustained through government cultivation of 'grassroots' initiatives that presented alternatives to paramilitarism in loyalist- and republican-controlled areas[32] and, to a greater extent, through European Union–driven funding (the PEACE programmes) along with grants from philanthropic organizations.[33]

Arguably, the nexus also worked to shield political leaders from decision making. This has been facilitated by the running of consultation processes and a series of proposals to set up further commissions and public bodies to promote reconciliation and deal with aspects of the legacies of the past. The British government, for example, established the Consultative Group on the Past in Northern Ireland (CGPNI). This group, which reported in 2009, advocated a 'Legacy Commission' that would 'combine processes of reconciliation, justice and information recovery' together with a 'Reconciliation Forum' that would be run jointly by the Legacy Commission and the already existing Commission for Victims and Survivors for Northern Ireland.[34] These proposals were seemingly placed to the side by the British government following controversy inspired by the group's proposal to grant a one-off 'recognition' payment to all families who suffered bereavement, regardless of the circumstances of death. Yet, closer inspection seems to point to a certain vagueness in even the basic framework that the group advocated.

After several failed attempts to produce an agreed-upon vision of Northern Ireland's future (including the publication of two rival visions of a shared future in September by the Democratic Unionist Party [DUP] and Sinn Féin), in 2013 the devolved executive published a policy paper entitled *Together: Building a Better Community*. The underpinning idea seemed to be to defer consideration of critically divisive issues by handing consultation and consideration over to other bodies. Thus, the paper pledged that the executive 'will establish an All-Party Group, with an independent chair to consider parades and protests; flags, symbols and emblems and related matters; and the past'. The paper aimed at providing mechanisms that would '[b]ring our shared vision to a reality in people's everyday lives'. The outcome was the commissioning of the American diplomat, Dr Richard Haass, and the Harvard international relations scholar, Professor Meghan

O'Sullivan, to conduct a consultation and negotiation process in the autumn of 2013. Interestingly, the Haass/O'Sullivan paper does not so much define 'reconciliation' as posit it as an end goal. 'A civic vision is needed', they suggested, 'we will need a sense of common purpose – an agreed rationale'. 'It is clear', they asserted, 'that the vast majority of citizens and communities wish to live free of the division and enmity that has too often defined this society'. That vision and objective, they argue, are what characterize reconciliation: it is at the 'heart of the challenge of reconciliation – the transition from a divided society to one that is whole, from a wounded society to one that is healed'.[35]

The reason for the Haass/O'Sullivan call for a civic vision is, in part, because words like reconciliation are conceptualized and mobilized ideologically within and between different constituencies and communities within Northern Ireland. It is useful to focus on one of these – Northern Irish nationalism – for a number of reasons. First, the peace process itself is often viewed as having originated within Northern Irish nationalism,[36] and the ideology itself has been viewed as a highly complex framework whose strategic emphases or hierarchies are constantly shifting between a set of core ideas to do with territory, community and justice: namely, the cultural and geographical unity of the island of Ireland, the organic interrelationship between Catholic and Gaelic networks and modes of belonging; and the commonality of perceived injustice at British imperialism, colonialization and the imposition of partition.[37] I also wish to concentrate on the case of Northern Irish nationalist politics because it is there that the fluidity in definitions can be found most clearly; for within the nationalist imagination, ideas about reconciliation are filtered through an ideological lens, lending them transitional qualities. In the process, the Janus-faced dimensions of reconciliation (looking to the past as well as the future)[38] become drained and reformulated: reconciliation then takes on a meaning of transcending cultural and political division. 'Reconciliation' then becomes harnessed to a political vision that in the end seems to mean constitutional change. In other words, as understood and as used by Northern Irish nationalism, reconciliation seemingly will require Ulster unionists to give up their constitutional allegiances to Britain. This section aims to try to tease out how reconciliation becomes synonymous with a demand for political resignation – in other words a resignation to inevitable constitutional change.

Before this, however, it may be helpful to situate or contextualize the broad conceptualization of reconciliation in Northern Ireland. Although (and to paraphrase Dominic Bryan) 'reconciliation' seems to be everywhere, part of the reason for the Northern Ireland executive commissioning Haass and O'Sullivan to facilitate a report is because of the fact that in policy terms, the debate over dealing with the past in Northern Ireland seems to have stalled – there is no political consensus on establishing a truth and reconciliation commission. Although the British government's favoured position seems to be a commission of historical clarification, this has not proceeded; although a dedicated commission and a forum for victims and survivors have been established, recent legislative changes have seen a medicalization of victimhood and trauma care, the establishment of a new victims' service and, arguably, an attempt to remove it as a live issue in the public realm. In reality, a drip-drip effect has been created by the concatenation of a series of high-profile juridical and coroner cases together with a chain of stories about collusion and the investigation of murders by the police's Historical Enquiries Team. Whether these trends are seen as piecemeal or as an intrinsic part of contemporary politics, the result is more of the same. This stasis may be either guillotined by sweeping legislative changes by the British government that would undercut the victims' industry (the assorted non-governmental organizations and the legal processes), or it may be ameliorated by the fostering of a new political culture in Northern Ireland. Certainly, this seemed to have been the aim in 1998. For example, the Belfast/Good Friday Agreement includes reconciliation as a key aim. However, as with Haass/O'Sullivan, reconciliation is not really defined in any other way than as a vague aspiration; it is something to be enacted through 'rapprochement within the framework of democratic and agreed arrangements', but also something that will facilitate that rapprochement. Perhaps it is because of this latter sense that the parties to the agreement pledged 'their continuing support to such organisations and will positively examine the case for enhanced financial assistance for the work of reconciliation'.[39]

What then might reconciliation look like if it is so hazily defined by the Belfast/Good Friday Agreement and it becomes untidily linked with ideas about the past and the future in political parties' understandings? In a much-cited report, Brandon Hamber and Gráinne Kelly set out a typology of reconciliation.[40] Their 'working definition' involves five elements: First, reconciliation, the authors argue, requires the 'development of a vision of a shared future' involving 'the whole society'. More specifically, this does not mean individuals or groups giving up their opinions or beliefs; rather, it entails 'the articulation of a common vision of an interdependent, just, equitable, open and diverse society'. Second, reconciliation involves 'acknowledging and dealing with the past'. This includes an institutional focus in the form of establishing mechanisms for dealing with 'justice, healing, restitution or reparation, and restoration'. Third, relationship building is seen as essential: this includes the fostering of trust and acceptance of difference, as well as the breaking down of prejudice and intolerance. Fourth, 'significant cultural and attitudinal change' is required. This consists in the opening up of space 'in which people can hear and be heard' and seems to imply a commitment to empathy, along with popular participation in society. Finally, reconciliation entails steps towards a conception of positive peace that involves 'substantial social, economic and political change'.

Hamber and Kelly's 'working definition' was created for the social and economic development programme PEACE II.[41] However, the authors were critical of the way in which the programme was implemented with applicants having to promise to do three of the five elements. Hamber and Kelly saw this as a compartmentalization of reconciliation and stated that instead they 'envisaged the five strands of reconciliation as being deeply interdependent and any reconciliation process should consider how it furthers reconciliation holistically and not based on a selection of strands'.[42] The problems with the Hamber/Kelly model of reconciliation, however, go deeper and the 'tick-box' exercise as they saw it is, arguably, emblematic of their inherently mechanistic approach. These problems relate to the authors' suggestion that the five strands are 'interwoven' and imply that none is necessarily more important than the others. It also implies that there is no causal chain and because of this, the model can potentially be more harmful than is intended. In short, unless the first point is satisfied, it (and arguably points three, four and five) can be undermined by the second. In other words, it may be easily possible to espouse beliefs in pluralism, equity, openness and diversity while still holding particularistic views on the past. The logic is as follows: Violence occurred because we were denied equity, openness, fairness; now that we've proved our point, we will continue to ensure that such denials never happen again; and we will allay ourselves with other human rights activists across the world because a threat to liberty anywhere is a threat to liberty everywhere. Quite what this means to other citizens who believe that although society was or is not ideal, the resort to violence needs to meet strong criteria before it can be justified,[43] is a critical question that is not resolved by a simple evocation of pluralism – pluralism in this case might be seen to work against social cohesion and operate to marginalize voices who might also favour a fair and shared society. As Schaap explains, reconciliation depends on shared understandings of what actually occurred or, rather, where the grievance happened. It is the agreement on facts that allows a meeting of minds over explanations. As such, Schaap may be seen as adopting a straightforward but lucid empirical standpoint on which to base his theory – namely, that 'reconciliatory politics requires respect for factual truth, of that which is simply because it was not otherwise'.[44] By sidestepping the logical inclusion of notions of accountability and responsibility for past crimes within their definitional framework, Hamber and Kelly underpin the ideological apparatus that links reconciliation to empathy and acknowledgement. This is undoubtedly an unintended consequence of their theorizing, but it nonetheless points to the fact that the Lederachian approach of substantial socio-economic change that they advocate is politically ineffectual when it comes to counteracting the nationalizing tendencies towards ideologically based historical selectivity.[45] In other words, while attempting to work through the politicization of the past through the construction of a comprehensive and workable definition of reconciliation, the latter elements offset the problematic relationship of reconciliation to accountability and the key question of whether too much accountability can forestall reconciliation.

Reconciliation within Northern Irish nationalism

The case of Northern Irish nationalism demonstrates the limitations of the Hamber/Kelly model and reveals that even though reconciliation is figured and represented as transformative and pluralistic, in reality, when it becomes quickly serviceable to ideological ends, any purported democratic, dissenting and radically political potential of reconciliation – the potential that undoubtedly Hamber and Kelly seek to unlock – becomes foreclosed. I suggest that this is an inevitable threat posed by nationalism to any conceptualization of reconciliation. Just as liberal institution building works to constrain and police reconciliation through the imposition of norms of tolerance and restorative justice,[46] nationalism works to circumvent and defer the unresolvable and revelatory dimensions of reconciliation. I argue that it accomplishes this through a dual and related movement of teleology and tautology. On the one hand, teleology because nationalism tends to work towards some kind of eschatological vision whether that is avowedly political, constitutional and institutional (for example, the self-determination claims pursued by the Scottish National Party) or the rectification of historic grievances (see, for example, the commemorative activities of migrant groups).[47] The approach is one of advocacy – namely, to reconcile oneself to a political project. On the other hand, tautology because nationalism tends to work in a subsuming fashion similar to the Rancièrean 'police' where a range of goals (social change, gender equality, conflict transformation) may rise and fall on the list of priorities but the fundamental objective has, to an extent, already been achieved – namely, group cohesion.[48] The approach in this case is that reconciliation is imposed ideologically – it is not only the answer to nationalist aspirations, but it is already intrinsic to the nationalist worldview where difference is not mutually exclusive with pluralism, or, as alluded to earlier, where particularistic, ideologically inspired beliefs about the past can co-exist with an openness to others even if they are logically and empirically contradictory. Here, it is perhaps more useful to see the emphasis on culture rather than politics, as reconciliation is harnessed to pre-existing ideals of cultural cohesiveness. Of course, the division of nationalism into teleology and tautology is neither new nor distinct – the two concepts, rather, work as poles on a continuum and hold in common a vision of reconciliation that is saturated with ideological import.

Sinn Féin's mobilization of the past is a necessary part of its political project; linked to the main paramilitary organization in the conflict, the party's policy agenda has also taken on characteristics of path dependency: accrue gains through political leverage (with the appeal that they are necessary for sustaining peace and the representation of this strategy to its supporters that the peace strategy is the new and necessary phase of the project) and move forward from the concessions that are 'banked'.[49] The 'path' then established is one of ethnic particularism, for not to win concessions would mean facing up to historical responsibilities, and facing up to those responsibilities would mean conceding ground to the inter-bloc 'others' (namely, Ulster unionism). The zero-sum dynamic is therefore self-reinforcing and can only be escaped by a reframing of the answer as to whom ethnic political parties are responsible.

The interesting element of Sinn Féin's attempt to answer that question is that the language of inclusivity and pluralism, of democracy and accountability, and of acknowledgement and responsibility, is placed at the service of a particularistic, ethnic agenda. Thus, party spokesperson on reconciliation and the past, Declan Kearney's rhetoric is based around catch-all terms: 'There is a shared obligation to ensure that future generations grow up in a better place than we did. Discussion is needed now on how to do that. There is no alternative to dialogue'. The rhetoric is transformative: '[we must] accept who we are, and where we are now, and focus on the future and new possibilities', which are contained in ideas such as 'generosity, compromise and forgiveness'. The idea of acknowledgement works to circumvent specificities (such as the question of why adopt a peace strategy after so many years of violence, or why was such a long-armed campaign necessary). It does so by reference to a recognition of the 'truth' of everyone's experiences and the related notions of the multiplicity of narratives and plurality of possible stories (or histories) that should and ought to be told. As such, Kearney and Sinn Féin have sought to deliberately 'decouple' truth from reconciliation.[50]

The discursive construction of reconciliation is buttressed by a performative ritual that is perhaps consciously designed to fend off attack from its critics within 'dissident' republicanism – namely, those radical or extremist groups who perceive that Sinn Féin have 'sold out' and who continue through either political mobilization or violence campaigns to repudiate what they see as the illegitimacy of a British presence on the island of Ireland. The Sinn Féin choreography is based around what might be termed a 'bad cop–good cop' routine. This typically takes the form of perceived 'hard men' such as the former prisoner Gerry Kelly making statements espousing 'traditional' republican values regarding the justification of the 'war' or the sacrifices made by Irish Republican Army (IRA) volunteers at commemorative events where the 'primary audience' consists of Sinn Féin supporters. The 'secondary audience' may be seen as the Ulster unionist constituency whose abhorrence for such statements works to confirm Sinn Féin's credentials as the standard bearers of the republican flame.[51] The 'good cop' then follows up to present a more flexible approach – typically, this is either Declan Kearney or the deputy first minister of Northern Ireland, Martin McGuinness, whose preferred framings centre around the rhetoric of acknowledgement, generosity and responsibility.[52]

The SDLP's idea of an ethical approach is also logically ambiguous but ideologically sound. The party's most recent document explicitly rejects what it sees as the equivalency involved in 'acknowledgement processes' and calls instead for 'robust mechanisms of truth'.[53] The SDLP's document places the onus of responsibility for reconciliation on the London and Dublin governments and calls for them to institute a 'comprehensive truth process'. The document goes on to claim that there

> . . . is a singular test for Sinn Féin and the IRA – will they endorse a comprehensive truth process, support robust mechanisms of accountability and agree that those who were in command and control of the IRA have a higher and a particular responsibility to account for IRA actions.

Reconciliation and dealing with the past seem to be about more than just acknowledgement of multiple experiences, which, arguably, the SDLP view as not 'robust' enough. The issue at stake in its vision of working through the past and achieving reconciliation is, rather, one of accountability. However, the conceptualization of accountability, and its linking to the notion of reconciliation and dealing with the past, arguably mirrors Sinn Féin, for the question immediately arises with regard to who is to adjudicate over accountability, or, to put it another way, who is accountable and for what?

Reconciliation as accountability or reconciliation as acknowledgement work as different sides of the same coin: the ideological mediation of the concept of reconciliation contained in both is suggestive of a foreclosing of debate and a circumscribing of what constitutes 'the past' that is in need of being reconciled. The ideological nature of the answer to that question is rarely concealed, perhaps simply because the SDLP has a clear vision of what it means when it talks about the past. The response might be that historiography is ideological, which is, of course, the case, but if historiography is ideological and nothing more – if it is *only* ideological – then it may be impossible to distinguish it from conspiracy theorizing. For example, as perhaps part of the party's own political choreography, key figures in the SDLP have chosen to focus on drawing out the links between loyalist and republican terror groups and British state agents/agencies. Although collusion between government operators and Northern Irish terror groups undoubtedly existed and created a poisonous, treacherous and sinister atmosphere in Northern Ireland, the SDLP has self-consciously promoted the narrative that this was systemic and directed from the top-down. Such conspiracy theorizing tends to point towards conclusions that, in the absence of causal facts, works to harness suspicion and doubt. As one prominent SDLP politician stated, '[j]ust how deep and how high collusion ran in the security forces has for too long been a dirty secret'. Again, the solution to this problem is, as she goes on to explain, acknowledgement 'by people at the highest level of government if necessary' the pain and anguish caused by collusion and a 'robust and comprehensive mechanism' to which politicians should commit.[54] The critical importance of contextualization and corroborative evidence that are the hallmarks of historical and political science inquiry (among those of other cognate disciplines such as criminology and law) are, in this way, sidelined in preference to acknowledgement. This is not to say, of course, that acknowledgement is exclusive of such work or that it contradicts robust approaches to the past; rather, it is to suggest that the ushering in of acknowledgement for groups and individuals who were not directly responsible for crimes depends on the same logic as requiring innocent victims to reconcile themselves with the changed dispensation brought about by the decision by perpetrators to opt for a peace strategy. The political effect of this logic is to replace responsiveness and responsibility with imperatives for recognition of a new reality and reconciliation based on a compromise with that. In other words, the result is to reaffirm communal, ethnic or nationalist truths at the expense of questions of broader societal ethics.

Drawing on reconciliation

If the nationalist conception of reconciliation involves a drawing-on process – a drawing on of history and a drawing on of that history onto contemporary politics – does this necessarily mean that the radical potential of reconciliation is inevitably forestalled in deeply divided and/or ethno-centric places like Northern

Ireland? By way of moving towards a conclusion, I wish to provide a negative answer and to sketch an alternative conceptualization that itself draws on the language of nationalist ideology but that points towards a less constrained and limited agenda. In so doing I wish to suggest that Iris Marion Young's intellectual journey offers insights (and perhaps even metaphoric parallels) that can be drawn with the nationalist conceptualization of reconciliation. This may be seen in the way that Young's last, posthumously published book works through ideas that she developed in her early groundbreaking work on the politics of difference.[55] In that final work she begins to elaborate a theory of how difference gives way to fundamental and foundational ideas about societal responsibility. One way of articulating this within the previous considerations of this chapter is that Young's arguments complement, but also definitively break from and build a different structure on, the idea of a civic vision. The aspiration is less restrictive and more radical, involving consideration and recognition, not simply of rights but also their implications. In her text, Young carefully distinguishes between responsibility and guilt at a conceptual level: there are things for which we are, by dint of our participation in society, responsible – we have a duty, for example, to try to tackle injustice where we can identify it occurring; however, there are other events for which individuals, by either act or omission, are culpable – for these we may not be liable, directly or indirectly, unless we contribute in some way to their perpetuation by our negligence or lack of interest. Guilt is, in this framework, linked to blameworthiness and the principle of 'but for' – that is, but for what I did (or omitted to do), the resulting harm would not have taken place or would not have occurred to the extent it did.[56] As Young explains:

> To the extent that we participate in the ongoing operations of a society in which injustice occurs, we ought to be held responsible. This does not, however, make us guilty or blameworthy or directly liable for paying compensation to victims of harm.[57]

Collective responsibility, therefore, does not exist and, in fact, ends by draining the idea of responsibility of all meaning – for if everyone is responsible, no one is culpable. It becomes meaningless to talk of victims' experiences or trauma because if everyone is complicit, no one truly is guilty; if everyone is a victim of conflict, then no one is really a perpetrator: we are, in short, all victims of a system. (Intent becomes important in differentiating between degrees of culpability, and understanding is essential to ascribing responsibility, which, of course, is attenuated in instances of limited knowledge.) Young outlines what she calls a 'social connection model of responsibility' in which she argues responsibility can be ascribed to individuals for 'social injustice because they contribute by their actions to the processes that produce unjust outcomes'.[58] She goes on to define responsibility as deriving

> . . . from belonging together with others in a system of interdependent processes of cooperation and competition through which we seek benefits and

> aim to realize projects . . . All who dwell within the structures must take responsibility for remedying injustices they cause, though none is specifically liable for the harm in a legal sense.

Thus, in Young's understanding, responsibility derives not simply from living in a society; rather, it comes from 'participating in the diverse institutional processes that produce structural injustice'. As such, responsibility is not collective; rather, it is 'shared' and, as such, it can be 'discharged only through collective action'.[59]

Young contrasts her social responsibility model with liability and describes five features that distinguish the kind of structural bonds that concern her from concerns about legal culpability. The first condition, she identifies, is the need to avoid isolating individuals from their broader societal contexts, which can work, she argues, to absolve others 'whose actions contribute to the outcomes from bearing responsibility in a different way'.[60] Second, she argues that to ascribe responsibility means paying attention to the background conditions in which injustice occurs; in so doing, it will be possible to evaluate harm over and above 'normal and acceptable' hurts. Third, she argues, responsibility is forward looking. Unlike guilt, which is focused on the past, social responsibility is centred on the imperative of ending injustice and establishing a better society. Fourth, she argues, responsibility is shared within society: every person 'is personally responsible for the outcome in a partial way, since he or she alone does not produce the outcomes';[61] since culpability cannot be isolated (as distinct from a more legal understanding of liability), responsibility is to an extent shared. Finally, the promotion of social justice must be predicated on collective action – it is not simply the duty of the state or particular organizations or agencies to remedy injustices; instead, these bodies should be viewed as 'mediated instruments for the coordinated action of those who share responsibility for structures, rather than as actors independent of us'.[62]

Young's ideas about social justice arguably help to clarify the terms of debate surrounding reconciliation and acknowledgement in an ethnically divided, post-conflict society such as Northern Ireland's. Extrapolating from her distinction between guilt and responsibility, for example, helps to demarcate more exactly who was culpable for violence. The focus on the shared nature of responsibility meanwhile contains an imperative to not let victims be remarginalized for political and/or societal expediencies. Her commitment to asserting culpability and blameworthiness, and her conceptual distinction of guilt from responsibility, meanwhile, opens up space for some kind of shared understanding about what actually occurred. As such, Young's ideas prepare the ground for the kind of reconciliatory politics theorized by Schaap and desired by Hamber and Kelly.

Conclusion

This chapter has suggested that conceptionalizations of reconciliation that sidestep questions of accountability and responsibility can work to mobilize community-based exclusions and nationalistic selectivity; furthermore, they can potentially end by reinforcing ethnic boundaries and established power relations.

The potential of reconciliation to promote political change can, therefore, be foreclosed through the harnessing of it to ideological articulation. The case of Northern Irish nationalism suggests some reasons how this occurs: the subjects of reconciliation (namely, both the past *and* the future) become conflated for strategic reasons in order to push forward a particular, ideologically inspired view of history, or the relation of the past to the present in terms of grievance and juridical redress is filtered through present-centred ideological criteria. The result is an avowed interest in working through the legacies of the past that require redress or an ostensible concern for (and probably at some level genuinely held belief in) interpersonal and societal reconciliation. The decoupling of truth and reconciliation within the Sinn Féin approach is consistent with this ideological trajectory – not only for callous, consequentialist purposes (many of the 'truths' about republicans' pasts may appear contradictory with their current situation of being a party of government in Northern Ireland and aspiring to a similar goal in the Irish Republic). In other words, the decoupling is not only about political manoeuvring; it also speaks to and from the tautological and teleological aspects of the nationalist project: reconciliation is both meaningless (as it is assumed and evidenced through the maintenance of a group identity) and the ultimate aspiration (the future nationalist polity will be defined by reconciled viewpoints). It is for these reasons that foreclosure can be couched in pluralistic, generalized and almost universalist language.

The movement to foreclose reconciliation goes beyond party politics, and I have suggested that despite the impact at a national and supra-national level, the limitations of academic interventions such as Hamber and Kelly's to tackle the (inevitable) ideological conceptualization of reconciliation in a deeply divided society such as Northern Ireland are clear: that is, despite the avowed aim of challenging division, the modular approach, if it can be so described, ends by facilitating a reproduction of the terms of division, the framework that the reconciliation process aims to break down. Extrapolating from Iris Marion Young's ideas about how societal responsibility is an emergent and fragile element of difference, I have tried to sketch an alternative path. Just as nationalist politics articulates reconciliation through specific ideological frames, my alternative is to inject a language of societal responsibility into nationalist rhetoric. This may be criticized as untenable and idealist, but I have tried to convey that such a movement would not require nationalists to become apostates but instead would cultivate a minimal step towards recognizing the implications of their aspirations beyond the confines of their putative group. As such, I have tried to suggest that a radical politics of resistance to the ideological conceptualization of reconciliation may begin within situations of deep societal division by reinvesting nationalist articulation of reconciliation with the ethos of social responsibility.

Notes

1 Jennifer Todd (1990) 'Northern Irish Nationalist Political Culture'. *Irish Political Studies*, 5: 31–44

2 Andrew Schaap (2008) 'Reconciliation as Ideology and Politics', *Constellations*, 15(2): 249–264.

3 Danielle Conversi (2012) 'Modernism and Nationalism', *Journal of Political Ideologies*, 17(1): 14.
4 Desmond Tutu, *No Future without Forgiveness* (London: Rider, 1999).
5 See, for example, Andrew Rigby, *Justice and Reconciliation: After Violence* (London: Lynne Rienner Publishers, 2001); Andrew Schaap, *Political Reconciliation* (London: Routledge, 2005); Ernesto Verdeja, *Unchopping a Tree: Reconciliation in the Aftermath of Political Violence* (Philadelphia PA: Temple University Press, 2009).
6 Rigby, *Justice and Reconciliation*, p. 12.
7 For a recent appraisal of the policy implications of transitional justice see Tricia D. Olsen, Leigh A. Payne, and Andrew G. Reiter, *Transitional Justice in Balance: Comparing Processes, Weighing Efficacy* (Washington, DC: United States Institute for Peace, 2010).
8 UN Human Rights Council, Resolution 9/11. Right to the Truth. Available at http://ap.ohchr.org/documents/E/HRC/resolutions/A_HRC_RES_9_11.pdf; accessed on 9 March 2014.
9 Steve J. Stern, *Remembering Pinochet's Chile: On the Eve of London 1998, Book One of the Trilogy: The Memory Box of Pinochet's Chile* (Durham and London: Duke University Press, 2004), p. xxvii.
10 Michael Humphrey 'Marginalizing 'victims' and 'terrorists': modes of exclusion in the reconciliation process', in *Reconciliation after Terrorism: Strategy, Possibility, or Absurdity?* Edited by Judith Renner and Alexander Spencer (Abingdon: Routledge, 2012), p. 54.
11 Leigh A. Payne, *Unsettling Accounts: Neither Truth nor Reconciliation in Confessions of State Violence* (London: Duke University Press, 2008), p. 10.
12 Verdeja, *Unchopping*, p. 148. See also Verdeja's argument that '[t]ruth is fundamental for reconciliation. Societies need a basic understanding of past events to assign responsibility and resist impunity' (op. cit., p. 40).
13 Ibid, p. 71.
14 Claire Moon, *Narrating Political Reconciliation: South Africa's Truth and Reconciliation Commission* (Plymouth: Lexington Books, 2008), p. 6.
15 Ibid, p. 37.
16 Ibid, p. 35
17 Ibid, p. 39.
18 Schaap, *Political Reconciliation.*
19 Schaap, 'Reconciliation', p. 249; original emphasis.
20 Schaap, *Political Reconciliation*, p. 4.
21 Schaap, *Political Reconciliation*, p. 35.
22 Chambers, *Lessons*.
23 Schaap, 'Reconciliation', p. 260.
24 Ibid, p. 251.
25 Ibid, p. 260.
26 Ibid, p. 261.
27 Ibid, p. 259.
28 Rancière, *The Politics of Aesthetics*.
29 See Rancière, *Shores*.
30 Derek Ruez (2012) '"Partitioning the Sensible" at Park 51: Rancière, Islamophobia, and Common Politics', *Antipode*, 45(2): 1129.
31 Moon, *Narrating*, p. 2.
32 Richard Needham, *Battling for Peace: Northern Ireland's Longest Serving British Minister* (Belfast: Blackstaff Press, 1998).
33 See, for example, Sandra Buchanan, *Transforming Conflict through Social and Economic Development: Practical Lessons from Northern Ireland and the Border Counties* (Manchester: Manchester University Press, 2014).

34 McGrattan, *Northern Ireland*, pp. 176–178.
35 'Proposed agreement, 31 December 2013: An agreement among the parties of the Northern Ireland Executive on parades, select commemorations, and related protests; flags and emblems; and contending with the past'. Available at www.northernireland.gov.uk/haass.pdf; accessed on 11 March 2014.
36 See, for example, Christopher Farrington, *Ulster Unionism and the Peace Process in Northern Ireland* (Basingstoke: Palgrave Macmillan, 2006).
37 See Todd, 'Northern Irish Nationalist Political Culture'; or P. J. McLoughlin, *John Hume and the Revision of Irish Nationalism* (Manchester: Manchester University Press, 2012).
38 Schaap, *Political Reconciliation*.
39 'The Agreement'.
40 Brandon Hamber and Grainne Kelly, 'Reconciliation: A working definition' (Belfast: Democratic Dialogue, 2004). Available at http://cain.ulst.ac.uk/dd/papers/dd04recondef.pdf; accessed on 5 May 2013.
41 The programme was part of a series of conflict transformation initiatives in Northern Ireland and the border counties of the Irish Republic that have spent approximately €2.95 billion since 1986. The initiatives drew on funds from Ireland, the United Kingdom, the European Union, Canada, the United States, Australia and New Zealand. See Sandra Buchanan, 'Examining the peacebuilding policy framework of the Irish and British governments', in *Building Peace in Northern Ireland*, edited by Maria Power (Liverpool: Liverpool University Press, 2011), pp. 172–190. See also 'PEACE III: EU Programme for Peace and Reconciliation, 2007–2013: Northern Ireland and the Border Region of Ireland. Operational Programme', p. 29. Available at www.dfpni.gov.uk/peace_iii_programme_2007–2013; accessed on 12 March 2014.
42 Cited in Buchanan, 'Examining', p. 181.
43 Timothy Shanahan, *The Provisional Irish Republican Army and the Morality of Terrorism* (Edinburgh: Edinburgh University Press, 2008).
44 Schaap, *Political Reconciliation*, p. 8.
45 Historical selectivity may, of course, be primarily ideological, particularly in Ireland (as per the argument in Eva Gkotzaridis, *Trials of Irish History: Genesis and Evolution of a Reappraisal, 1938–2000* (Abingdon: Routledge, 2006)); but it can also be seen as intrinsic to the principally narrative-based approach of historiography (as per the argument of Alun Munslow, *Narrative and History* (Basingstoke: Palgrave Macmillan, 2007)) or influenced by broad post-modern or late capitalist currents (for two differing views, see, for example, David Cannadine, *The Undivided Pasts: History Beyond Our Differences* (London: Allen Lane, 2013) and Martin L. Davies, *Imprisoned by History: Aspects of Historicized Life* (Abingdon: Routledge, 2010)).
46 Schaap, *Political Reconciliation*.
47 See, for example, Timothy Kubal, *Cultural Movements and Collective Memory: Christopher Columbus and the Rewriting of the National Origin Myth* (Basingstoke: Palgrave Macmillan, 2009).
48 Thus, Rogers Brubaker's work, for example, emphasizes the importance of 'ethnic commonsense' or 'everyday ethnicity' in maintaining group boundaries; see, for example, Rogers Brubaker, *Ethnicity Without Groups* (Cambridge: Cambridge University Press, 2004).
49 See, for example, Anthony McIntyre, *Good Friday: The Death of Irish Republicanism* (Dublin: Ausubo, 2008).
50 The quotations are taken from Declan Kearney's address to Sinn Féin's 2013 annual convention (*ard fheis*), 'Reconciliation and Legacy'. Author copy.
51 See, for example, Martina Purdy, 'Castlederg parade a defining moment in difficult summer', BBC Online, 19 September 2013. Available at www.bbc.co.uk/news/uk-northern-ireland-24169334; accessed on 5 November 2013.

52 One example is McGuinness's attempt to deflect criticism of the party leader's (Gerry Adams') alleged involvement in the disappearance of a mother of ten, Jean McConville, in 1971, by the assertion that such tactics were 'wrong' and 'unjustified'. See, M. McHugh, 'IRA's burial of "informers" unjustified: McGuinness', *Irish Independent*, 5 November 2013. Available at, www.irishexaminer.com/ireland/iras-burial-of-informers-unjustified-mcguinness-248499.html; accessed on 5 November 2013.
53 SDLP 'Addressing the Past: A Comprehensive Truth Process and the Ethical Way Forward' (N.P., 2012). Author copy.
54 Dolores Kelly, 'Collusion'. Available at http://blogs.qub.ac.uk/compromiseafterconflict/; accessed on 5 November 2013.
55 Young, *Responsibility*.
56 Ibid, p. 101.
57 Ibid., p. 104.
58 Ibid., p. 105.
59 Ibid. p. 105.
60 Ibid. p. 106.
61 Ibid. p. 110.
62 Ibid, p. 111.

5 Historical accountability and the democratization of memory

The previous chapters have considered the issues and problems associated with community-based and ideological framings in relation to ideas about dealing with the traumatic legacies of Northern Ireland's past – and, by extrapolation, of the perils associated with the framing of peace-building in terms of the community or grassroots level and the limitations and opportunities inherent in the ideological harnessing of peace. The final chapters of this book will address some alternatives to those restrictions and incongruities. They aim to join a narrative arc from the introductory considerations regarding the inarticulacy and facticity of trauma, while keeping in mind the Deleuzian advice (see Chapter 1) to not put words into the mouths of the voiceless. The emphasis, then, in these concluding reflections is on history and policy, and I wish to take as a point of departure the idea that in contrast to comparative examples of processes of truth recovery and dealing with the past, historians and political scientists have been conspicuously absent in contributing to similar initiatives in Northern Ireland.[1]

This absence is pronounced when one takes into account the idea that dealing with violent pasts in post-conflict societies is especially problematic in ethnically divided polities where ideas about historical events are inextricably bound up with ideas about identity, community and nation. In such cases 'the past' often becomes a key issue on which to contest long-standing grievances and justify particularistic visions of the future. Elazar Barkan, for example, argues that the centrality of history to politics in such cases provides opportunities for historians to contribute to ongoing debates: 'Because group identity is shaped by historical perspectives', he writes, 'historical narratives have an explicit and direct impact on national identities. Thus, by playing an adjudicatory role in the creation of such narratives and ensuring adherence to ethical norms, historians can contribute to reconciliation among nations'.[2] For Barkan, this role is intrinsic to the historian's methodology – namely, a concern with impartiality, source criticism, the maintenance of credibility through peer review and attention to the importance of the chronology of cause and effect, together with the understanding that 'the construction of history continuously shapes our world'.[3]

Barkan's arguments are substantiated in a comparative survey of the methodologies and political effects of truth commissions in South Africa, Haiti and Guatemala.[4] The latter argue that '[a]t the end of the day, it is far easier to clarify history than to find and promote reconciliation through public hearings'.[5] In an echo of Michael Ignatieff's comment that the most that truth commissions can achieve is to limit the number of permissible lies,[6] Chapman and Ball argue that 'truth commissions "shape" or socially construct rather than "find" the truth'. For example, they describe how the South African Truth and Reconciliation Commission choose to focus on significant incidents, or 'window cases', that seemed to shed light on a particular aspect of violence.[7] The mediation of these cases, then, becomes critical with regard to how they are received by the general public. As Steve Stern points out in relation to Chile, for instance, silence over certain aspects of the country's authoritarian past does not necessarily denote amnesia; rather, he argues, Chileans understand and interpret the past in different ways depending on a number of different, reinforcing and overlapping filters such as class position, proximity to violence and gender.[8]

This chapter explores these issues through the primary filter of the politics of trauma. As pointed out earlier, the nebulous nature and enforced inarticulacy associated with trauma lends another layer to the ambiguities associated with history and memory. In particular, the import of betrayal and rupture troubles superficial ideas that memory operates in a pluralistic arena – one that is fostered by the superimposition of ideas about globalized tourism, multifaceted technologies and the decoupling of territory and identity onto sites of memory, commemoration and representation of the past.[9] I suggest that, in conjunction with judicial procedures, post-conflict societies might best foster fragile settlement processes by fencing in or framing historical narratives about the past. Utilizing Rancière's notion of 'literarity', I argue that one approach away from a dead-end aestheticization of trauma (trauma merely as inarticulacy or a policy response based around artistic forms of representing trauma) is through a naming strategy or methodology. For Rancière, the idea of 'literarity' denotes the 'excess of words' that transcends attempts to exclude people or groups from civic life or that attempts to render them without voice. Literarity, he explains, 'disrupts the relation between an order of discourse and its social functions'.[10] In other words, even those people left outwith the (dominant) social order, or who are deemed to be outside of the distribution of the sensible, have access to words and writing. As Alison Ross points out, it 'is because words exceed their function of naming that the distribution or positioning of things in social space is always provisional'.[11] Again, the question of reception (and responsibility for reception) enters into considerations precisely because it is that very excessive quality of speech that goes beyond the political logic of demarcating what is perceptible and what ought to be ignored. In order to explicate these ideas, I borrow the notion of 'framing' from social movement theory to argue for the importance of perspective. The framing of the past involves a repositioning of historical events in relation to the present and involves not simply a rewriting of the historical record but its re-presentation through discursive tropes. Although that process is intrinsic to ethnic mobilization, I argue that it can be counterproductive to cultivating peace and consolidating democracy. Alternatively, I argue that the recognition of framing processes with regard to dealing with the past is the beginning of 'politics' – as characterized by dissensus and debate – which is the opposite of the stultifying tendency to superimpose ethnically inflected received wisdoms. That recognition can give way to alternative frames that speak to broader concerns about peace-building through democratic consolidation.

Dealing with the past in ethnically divided societies

Recent debates in post-conflict Northern Ireland and the countries of the former Yugoslavia have increasingly centred on the issue of to what extent perpetrators of war crimes and human rights abuses can be held accountable for their actions.[12] Policing the past remains a real and immediate problem in societies that are seeking to move beyond violent conflicts. Indeed, the question lies at the heart of the issue of how societies move beyond division and towards stability. It captures the paradox between what has been described, perhaps most famously by Theodor Adorno in relation to the post-war German case, as 'coming to terms with' and/or 'mastering' (*Vergangenheitsbewältigung*) the past: justice is seen to be done through prosecutions; but prosecutions are never enough to heal the psychic and emotional wounds that violence inflicts.[13] Primo Levy poignantly articulated this dilemma in what was to be his final (and posthumously published) book, in which he described how the wounds that victims suffer take on the character of traumatic recurrence: 'the injury cannot be healed: it extends through time, and the Furies, in whose existence we are forced to believe, not only wrack the tormentor (if they do wrack him, assisted or not by human punishment), but they perpetuate the tormentor's work by denying peace to the tormented'.[14]

Trauma can be doubly exacerbated in ethnically divided, post-conflict societies. First, such societies face the perennial problems of pursuing prosecutions and punishment in the midst of limited budgets and a dwindling public appetite to be constantly reminded of events from a longed-to-be-forgotten period. Second, that dwindling appetite may be a product of the dynamic within ethnically divided societies to mobilize the past for particularistic, nationalistic ends. In other words, in ethnically divided societies, willful blindness, forced amnesia or outright denial may not simply be psychological coping strategies; they may also be the product of the communal identification with specific narratives about the past. Stanley Cohen has, in this regard, spoken of how 'memory wars' can erupt in the aftermath of conflicts, which pit 'those trying to suppress versus those trying to resurrect what has been or what potentially might be forgotten'.[15]

'Memory wars', then, are part and parcel of the way that societies and political groupings frame and re/present the past and the methods for how we use the past to project our goals onto the future. The pursuit of justice in these cases is not simply about the revelation of 'truth' about the past or the prosecution of terrorist acts; rather, the pursuit of justice becomes intertwined with debates over how that past and those acts are explained and understood in the present. Victims of violence, then, are at risk from suffering under the presumption that a line can be drawn under the past or from pressure to conform to the societal imperative to 'move on' for the sake of stability in the present and prosperity in the future.

They also suffer from what might be described as a process of re-victimization: those who suffered violence are re-silenced, re-marginalized and displaced from political discourse.

The reframing of the past is, probably, inevitable, but in order for those risks to be avoided or offset, as an alternative to particularistic, ethnically focused narratives, basic common or shared historical narratives could possibly be fenced in and promoted. Fencing in involves the identification of common elements and the subsequent warding off of others. Of course, we mould our divided and troubled pasts into manageable shapes, but fencing in involves the recognition that that should not be incompatible with manageable futures. Following Hannah Arendt, Andrew Schaap argues that such a shared basis is central to political plurality since 'we depend upon sharing how the world opens up uniquely to each of us in order to experience meaning'.[16] The paradox between shared experience and individual recounting is fundamental to any conception of politics and, as such, incorporates the diversity and division over historical representation that helps to define nationality and ethnicity.[17] Whereas the 'memory wars' that erupt over these differing representations involve the reframing and repositioning of the past in relation to the present, I contend that the problem resides at a deeper level concerning how we articulate our identities. Furthermore, that articulation poses serious questions for democratic consolidation, not only in terms of issues to do with accountability or justice for victims, but also in terms of the values, norms and understandings we wish to pass on to future generations. In other words, the very concept of 'peace' is under contestation because in post-conflict situations, the articulation of historical memories can lead to the deferral of unwelcome, obtrusive and disruptive elements into our narratival self-understandings and hence perpetuate the divisive relationships that encouraged violence in the first place.

The framing of the past involves a construction of historical narratives – not simply a re-writing of history, but rather, a form of history making: lessons are selected and shared, events are inscribed with salience and meaning and episodes and actions (and omissions) are repositioned in relation to the present. This construction is both backwards *and* forwards looking: we look to the past to bolster our agenda and justify our concerns in the present; but the past is not entirely malleable – ideas and stories, scripts and narratives carry moral and institutional weight in and of themselves and create a potent force that influences, if not determines, the values and options of future generations. Although both Northern Ireland and Bosnia have to a large extent moved beyond violent ethnic conflict, there has been no 'Year Zero', and the promises of peace seem to be increasingly held to ransom by cynical forces (both within the government and terrorist spoilers outside the democratic process) who draw inspiration from those ideas that plunged both societies into killings and mayhem. Methodologies and approaches for engaging victims into a process require careful consideration of amnesty, truth, justice and public openness. In both Bosnia and Northern Ireland the state remains a contested concept, and the attempt by competing groups to inscribe it with ethnicized memories is a key characteristic of political dynamics. I argue that the recognition of those strategies is the beginning of a deeper conception of peace insofar as it makes visible the political dynamics that seek to defer and displace awkward questions. For this to occur, however, it is important to delineate how the central issue of dealing with the past is being framed and, subsequently, what counter-frames are implicitly or explicitly also underpinning the discourse.

Framing the past

At the end of his 1968 essay on the relationship of historiography to social and political institutions, J.G.A. Pocock remarked that '[d]isinterested historiography is possible only in stable societies, where the present is fortified by means other than the writing of histories'.[18] In other words, history making becomes drained of political significance when the ideas and narratives that it is concerned with no longer have any purchase on the contemporary political imagination. For the historian J. H. Plumb, writing around the same time, historiography itself played a crucial role in that process insofar as it hollowed out the past – or, rather, beliefs about the past – thereby undercutting the foundations of tradition itself.[19] In Plumb's radical vision, historiography digs its own grave; yet, in deeply divided societies (and to borrow from Plumb's title), 'the death of the past' can work in what might be seen as the opposite direction. In those societies, in other words, the past is reduced to a truly foreign country by virtue of it being filtered through the lens of communal politics. What Stanley Cohen calls 'cultures of denial' can, in such cases, quickly take root and can involve quite conscious decision making. For instance, he argues that 'social control' over the past does not just involve confronting historical legacies, but it can also involve processes of obliteration. Often these occur simultaneously as 'regimes of continuity' seek to eliminate certain elements of the past while preserving others.[20] Cohen's own radical and deeply unsettling vision is that denial of historical facts is more common and the question we should be asking is why it fails to occur rather than why it does.[21] Indeed, Cohen's insight is shown again and again in historical revisionist controversies from Ireland, France, Poland and numerous other countries – an almost totalizing consensus descends as subjects and narratives become taboo.[22]

Work on framing and framing processes that have been developed within social movement theory help to elucidate the ways in which this history making is both agential and limited – namely how it influences and is also shaped by broader political and discursive structures. David A. Snow, who was instrumental in developing framing theory in the 1980s, relates that frames help to explain political events: they function as 'articulation mechanisms in the sense of tying together the various punctuated elements of the scene so that one set of meanings rather than another is conveyed, or . . . one story rather than another is told'.[23] They do so by encapsulating 'truths' about an issue and highlighting them by holding them within a recognizable, coherent structure *and* by providing content and a network of support to those ideas – in other words, frames encase but they also act as basic structure on which to build.[24] The static and dynamic nature of the concept is important and captures the fact that how we speak about issues inevitably involves political elements in terms of what is included, what is left unsaid, what is amplified and what is muted. As such, it is difficult to separate completely the meanings of the verb (framing) and the noun (frame) without diluting their effect.

In other words the interpretative, descriptive 'frame' also involves an active intervention that is implicitly political.[25]

Frames are instrumental in mobilization: they diagnose problems and provide prognoses. Although linking frames explicitly to collective action outcomes is methodologically and theoretically difficult,[26] the idea that frames have a dual function of both articulating grievances *and* offering solutions is intuitively attractive and, more so, speaks to the time and effort that political actors place in trying to shape public debates. Thus, as Ferree et al point out, even though policy processes may not be driven primarily by ideas, political actors who 'do badly' in the public discourse become vulnerable when it comes to 'pursuing policy interests'.[27] The importance of framing, then, is not only related to mobilization or the articulation of identity narratives; it also involves influencing the types of questions that are asked in the public sphere and shaping the contours of political debate. Frames can create footholds, or 'cleaves',[28] in the public sphere – ideas and articulations of concepts that take hold and 'resonate' in political discourse.[29] Although, again, frame 'resonance' can really only successfully be judged after the fact,[30] the idea speaks to the potential for certain messages to align with certain constituencies, seemingly capturing grievances and providing optimism for change and redress.[31] There are many reasons why this occurs – from the 'moral shocks' that suddenly provide new ways for people to view the world and become politically involved to the slow accumulation of influence and voice by proponents of ideas.[32] However, what it essentially involves is the accenting of 'events, issues, and beliefs or ideas' in contrast to others, 'with the result that they become more salient in an array or hierarchy of group-relevant issues, perhaps coming to function as significant coordinating symbols or mechanisms'.[33]

In order for this to occur, frames need to rise to prominence within the broad public sphere. And just as political actors attempt to gain footholds within governance structures, so, too, do ideas and frames battle for space within the political discourse. The 'discursive opportunity structure' refers to 'all of the institutional and cultural access points that actors can seize upon to attempt to bring their claims into the political forum',[34] but for ideas or themes to find purchase and resonance within that discursive field, they often need to have recognizable elements that correspond to broadly held stories and understandings.[35] Although certain framings resonate deeply with popular culture, their impact is seldom totalizing. As William A. Gamson argues, implicit within each frame is a counter-frame: 'whenever one is invoked, the other is always present in latent form, ready to be activated with the proper cue'.[36] Gamson's insight has profound implications for the study of ethnic politics: groups not only frame issues and mobilize around grievance claims, but do so often in zero-sum terms – yet, underpinning those terms is an unarticulated acknowledgement of alternative visions of belonging. Timothy Kubal has traced this process in the United States and linked it to the cultivation of collective memory, arguing that

> . . . [g]roups strategically construct collective memory through negotiation and conflict; competing groups seek to institutionalize their partisan memory

of the past and the outcome of that competition is collective memory – partisan stories about the past that are shared across space and time.[37]

The partisan memories that become collectivized, suggests Kubal, are those that successfully mobilize state resources, those that construct a community of recruits by convincing individuals they share a common history and purpose and those who communicate their ideas about the past and the future successfully and create plausible, recognizable schemes or frames. To this we might add groups who successfully mobilize emotions – though, as Kubal also suggests, as groups gain resources and influence, they 'tend to abandon memory protest' and 'turn from easy targets like cultural symbols to more tangible targets like jobs, housing, and wealth.[38] Although Kubal's 'political opportunity structure' approach reveals the links between the state and political groupings, the suggestion of an eventual break between culture and politico-economic strategies seems to have little purchase in post-conflict divided societies such as the former Yugoslavia or Northern Ireland where those very 'tangible targets' are deeply contested primarily due to conflicting ideas about identity and, ultimately, the past. When upward mobility is inextricable from questions of constitutionality and the very form of the state, then memory mobilization will continue to play a forceful and decisive role in contemporary politics. The inextricable linkage between memory and identity within ethnic politics in turn points to the reasons as to why certain ideas and frames resonate rather than others. Theorists have argued that the resilience of such frames relate directly to the persistence of conflict. Daniel Bar Tal, for instance, has argued that collective memory consists of societal beliefs that are 'developed and disseminated' by individuals and organized into what he calls 'thematic clusters'.[39] Using somewhat complementary logic, historical institutionalists have claimed that ideas within those 'clusters' become salient because people become attracted to them and in so doing, they develop a potency of their own – in effect, they become assimilated into communal consciousness and become very difficult to argue against, reproducing themselves across generations.[40]

In Northern Ireland, such dynamics are clearly seen in the self-exculpatory stance of former loyalist paramilitaries who, in admitting to acts of violence against innocent Catholics, insert the justification that anyone wishing to defend their community against attack would have done the same.[41] The concern within the international community to avoid scapegoating the Serbs speaks to a similar logic: for example, during the North Atlantic Treaty Organization's (NATO's) Kosovo campaign in 1999, the *Guardian* newspaper in the United Kingdom warned that as a result of the intervention, Serbia would have a 'huge new motive for bitterness and victimhood' and implored NATO governments to placate it by 'drop[ping] the argument that Serbia will get no reconstruction aid as long as [Slobodan] Milosevic stays in power'.[42] Again, the particular reluctance of Croatian society to negotiate the ethical dilemmas inherent in the Operation Storm offensive of 1995 illustrates the intimate ties between memory and nationality. In this instance, stalling of cooperation with the International Criminal Tribunal for the former Yugoslavia (ICTY) and the eulogizing of war criminals is tied not simply to economic improvement (though, of course, it was the 'carrot' of European Union [EU] accession that undoubtedly led to authorities beginning to work with the ICTY), but rather, to self-pitying ideas about self-designated victimhood.[43] Journalistic and academic analyses have highlighted the practical and ethical problems that ensued from the international community's acceptance and indulgence of such claims: in a recent coruscating critique, journalist Ed Vulliamy, for instance, attacked what he called the doctrine of 'equivalence' – namely, that in the ethnic conflicts of the 1990s in the Balkans, all sides were equally culpable and should, in effect, be left to settle their differences between themselves. Equivalence, he argued, effectively leads to erasure: empirical, historical facts are ignored at the time of violence, and victims' experiences and stories are concealed in the aftermath.[44]

The ethnic state and democracy

The problems associated with the erasure and the representations of historical experiences are central to Rancière's concept of literarity, which, he suggests, is related to a process of naming and revealing – or rather, a making visible of that which may otherwise be left unperceived or rendered imperceptible or mute. There is a link in this regard to the concern of some social movement theorists with the normative underpinning of framing theory, which is seen as involving questions relating to the 'quality' of public debate as measured by such criteria as inclusiveness or civility.[45] In post-conflict, ethnically divided societies such as in Northern Ireland or the Balkans, such questions crystallize around issues concerning whose voices are being heard and whose stories are represented in the public sphere. In such instances, framing works to denote what is acceptable and what is taboo – or, in Rancièrean terms, what is 'sensible' and what is 'inaudible'. As pointed out in previous chapters, for Rancière, 'the distribution of the sensible' (*le partage du sensible*) is a means of establishing a system of inclusions and exclusions, of political voice and silence. The system involves a shutting down of voice and debate, and, he argues, represents the end of politics: it pertains, ultimately, to an imperative to contain what constitutes acceptable behaviours and beliefs:

> Consensus is the 'end of politics': in other words, not the accomplishment of the ends of politics but simply a return to the normal state of things – the non-existence of politics'. The 'end of politics' is the ever-present shore of politics (*le bord de la politique*), itself an activity that is always of the moment and provisional.[46]

The reason that Rancière views consensus as the end of politics concerns its imposition of uniformity:

> What consensus means . . . is not people's agreement amongst themselves but the matching of sense with sense: the accord made between a sensory regime of the presentation of things and a mode of interpretation of their meaning.

> The consensus governing us is a machine of power insofar as it is a machine of vision.[47]

As pointed out in previous chapters, Rancière contrasts politics with what he terms the 'police' – that is, the realm of the 'sensible'. Importantly, he argues, that realm is not simply constituted through force: '[t]he essence of the police lies neither in repression nor even in control over the living. Its essence lies in a certain way of dividing up the sensible'.[48] 'Politics', on the other hand 'is an intervention of the visible and the sayable'.[49] Whereas the realm of the police resides in delimiting, democracy is about broadening the 'political stage'[50] and about making it visible. The naming of a wrong marks, for Rancière, the beginning of politics; it gives way to a form of counting, but, as Chambers points out, this is not necessarily a circular process of relativistic claims making. Instead, the naming of the wrong and the incipient and linked enunciation of subject status can resist a demand of inclusion in the centre or a move from the margins. Chambers, for instance, argues that this politics of resistance characterizes the Queer Nation chant, 'We're here, we're queer, get used to it'.[51] I would suggest that a similar parallel might be seen in the demands of trauma victims for recognition and acknowledgement – the demands that resist an easy and troublesome reconciliation as much as they trouble shallow political and economic 'answers'. This is because the concept of literarity – of writing and speaking – establishes speech acts without reference to a settled authority; or, rather, by their very nature, they work to re-form what can be perceived and received by society. Literarity, then, in this reading, denotes a politics of interruption, based on the drawing of attention to the very act of interruption.

Interruption, however, can give way to iteration within the operation of the (re)distribution of the sensible. Ethno-nationalism, for Rancière, works in this way, because, as he argues, 'there will never be a shortage of appropriate classifications'.[52] This is the opposite of democracy, which

> . . . consists above all in the act of revoking the law of birth and that of wealth; in affirming the pure contingency whereby individuals and populations come to find themselves in this or that place; in the attempt to build a common world on the basis of contingency.[53]

Of course, that very contingency gives rise to classification and violence through the ordering of what is perceptible and sayable. But the importance of history in building that commonality is key to the giving of voice or revealing the stories and experiences of those marginalized, traumatized and muted by violence and oppression:

> The status of history depends on the treatment of this twofold absence of the 'thing itself' that is *no longer there* – that is in the past; and that never was – because it never was *such as it was told*. Historical affect is bound to the personal absence of what the names name.[54]

However, the movement is paradoxical; the historian, he writes, 'can't stop effacing the line of death, but also can't stop tracing it anew'.[55] It is this revelation of knowledge and experience through narrative and imitation that encapsulates the historical method for Rancière. And, as such, the excess of words that is produced by the tension between the two modes that links historiography to politics and democracy by broadening what is perceptible and admissible within civic discourse.

Rancière's ideas are echoed in literature on collective memory and its links with processes of democratization. Nancy Bermeo, for example, has argued that '[u]nless the range of negotiable issues expands, the divisions that produced the breakdown of democracy in the first place will simply emerge again'. It is for this reason, she claims, that 'the change of mind intrinsic to political learning is so important'.[56] However, collective learning is a complex issue, and, as Paloma Aguilar outlines:

> When a political decision is successful, the costs of that decision are rarely considered, nor is any consideration given to whether a different decision might have been able to produce better results. This means that, in many cases, few lessons are learned when the outcome is successful, given that nobody ever inquires into whether this outcome has really been achieved as a result of a political decision or whether, on the contrary, it has been achieved in spite of that decision.[57]

For Aguilar, these lessons are 'deposited' in socio-political institutions that essentially act as archives for collective memories. People absorb these beliefs, she argues, when they first become politicized.[58] As such, it is possible to distinguish between 'dominant memories', which enjoy broad means of dissemination, and 'hegemonic' ones, which 'predominate' state ideologies.[59] Although the two are often similar in democracies, they can differ radically in totalitarian regimes. They can, we might add, explain why certain tropes and narratives seem to be prioritized or take on prominence within ethnic ideologies. In Northern Ireland, for example, a process of underbidding can be said to have occurred within both electoral blocs: the once-radical Sinn Féin has overtaken the more moderate Social Democratic and Labour Party without the latter 'hardening' its ethno-nationalist agenda, whereas the Democratic Unionist Party comfortably saw off an incipient challenge from more hardline elements within the unionist constituency.[60]

The implications for framing and for the fostering of collective memory are far-reaching if framing is seen as principally consisting in the creation of taboo, the cultivation of the unsayable and the rendering of the invisible. Yet, as Gamson points out, that rendering always depends on counter-themes and counter-frames, albeit implicitly.[61] The revelation of both frame and counter-frame marks a radical normative point of departure for assessing democracy. The concept of democracy itself becomes part and parcel of ethnic contestation; or, in other words, democracy itself becomes interlinked with the very articulation of the state in those areas where ethnic contention is most pronounced. The attempt to inscribe the state with ethnic understandings characterizes much of what constitutes 'politics' in post-conflict Northern Ireland and Bosnia.

The state, in these cases, is not a monolith to be defended or besieged; rather, it is a relational construct: 'the strategic site of organisation of the dominant class in its relationship to the dominated classes'.[62] In other words, the state is the arena where confrontations over resources are fought out; but it is also the source, inspiration and fuel for these confrontations insofar as it enables groups to realize their ambitions and, in so doing, it may equally restrict or prohibit others. The inscription of ethnicized and nationalistic politics in the very fabric of the Northern Irish state provides a lens through which to view political struggle and also a filter for political intervention. This inscription typically harnesses communal or ethno-national rewards and aspirations over alternative issues – typically, ideas about class, gender, age or geography are sidelined, elided or put to the active service of matters of ethnic or national interest. Effectively, the apparatus of the state then begins to operate in the function of what Nicos Poulantzas termed 'relay screens', which protect the state and its nodes of power through intermediation rather than exclusion.[63] In other words, groups are brought within the state or given access to its resources – conflict, of course, exists, but it exists within the parameters of the state and not along the lines of state versus society. The idea of the state as a network of interlocking and interrelated series of nodal power points has a series of further implications: first, it explains how state power enmeshes and envelops contradictory forces by offering access to resources. Second, it locates power as a fact – some individuals and groups hold sway over others. Third, it highlights the importance not only of decision making but of non–decision making and the power of ideology to set political and socio-economic agendas, meaning that certain voices are amplified over others, that certain questions are asked rather than others or that debates are framed in a particular way.[64] Finally, it locates resistance to dominant ideologies within a strategic setting and raises a problem of resistance – namely, that placing oneself outside of the logics of state ideology may leave the ground open for a take-over by proponents of that ideology, or it may result in a quietist retreat.[65]

The framing of the state in ethnic terms is, in the first instance, an inevitable though unintended consequence of the politico-legal agreements that provide the constitutional structure in each case. For example, the 1995 Dayton Accords ended the Bosnian conflict, but also cut the territory in two – the Republika Srpska (RS) (Bosnian Serb Republic) and the Federation of Bosnia and Herzegovina (BH). Although the short-term aim was to reduce conflict and separate the warring sides, the longer-term aim was 'more ambitious' and focused on 'engender[ing] cooperation between the parties to the conflict'.[66] Yet, in devolving all the trappings of statehood, including control of policing and military, Dayton effectively ratified the population displacement and ethnic cleansing that had occurred in the previous three years.[67] As Robin Wilson has pointed out in a comparative study of both regions, '[t]he old ethnic parties were duly returned to power'. He goes on to warn that while

> . . . BH might seem a more successful power-sharing case than Northern Ireland, in as much as the State institutions, however dysfunctional, have . . .

> [existed] ever since the Dayton accords. But the weakness of the State by comparison with the ethnically defined entities is debilitating.[68]

Wilson's scepticism echoes that of David Chandler who has been among the most scathing of analysts of the Bosnian settlement, describing it, for example, as a 'parody of democratisation'.[69] In a similar vein, recent work by Andy Aitchison has also pointed to the tendency of political parties within RS and BH to deploy the rhetoric of criminalization to mask other political realities. The Office of the High Representative (OHR) has, Aitchison points out, also been 'opportunistic' in resorting to questions of crime to defer consideration of questions of democratic legitimacy.[70] Indeed, the intervention of the OHR – particularly in the court system – has been seen to have resulted in a situation where '[f]ar from planting the seed of democratic politics in Bosnia's postcommunist political culture . . . [it] implicitly teaches that technocratic rule at arm's length from the people is perfectly good governance after all'.[71] Of course, this damning verdict overlooks the sweeping intervention into the debate over dealing with the past by Paddy Ashdown who, in 2003, ordered RS to hold a commission into the massacre at Srebrenica. Ashdown dismissed the denials in the subsequent report as 'a scandalous indictment' of RS and ordered the commission to sit again. As Vulliamy points out, '[o]n this occasion, in June 2004, the Bosnian Serbs for the first and only time seriously faced and admitted to their own recent past'.[72]

In Northern Ireland, meanwhile, despite the hopes of consociational theorists, the 1998 power-sharing agreement divided power proportionally between the two main ethno-national blocs (Ulster unionists and Irish nationalists) and institutionalized the sectarian divisions that characterized the 'Troubles'. As Henry Patterson has observed, the 1998 accord

> . . . was an elite-brokered settlement that balanced precariously on deep reserves of communal distrust and antagonism. The fact that political elites North and South have been prepared to take risks for a historic compromise, rather than indulge populist ethnic agendas, represents not the 'end of history' but the opening of a new phase, where northern sectarianisms lack the legitimisation given to them for much of the twentieth century by the states and dominant parties in Belfast and Dublin.[73]

In both instances, the articulation of the state is seen as a way of furthering ethnic standing; or, put another way, having been already articulated on ethnic lines, the only question that remains concerns with what kind of accent will that articulation be heard. Thus, under the new dispensations in each region, ethnic competition is maintained but the ethnicized nature of this political dynamic is never questioned; rather, the zero-sum conflict maintains itself because of the consensus that that type of politics is acceptable and necessary. Indeed, even to broach an alternative is to introduce profound instability into the system – for a politician to do so would amount to career suicide since she or he would be seen as effectively handing a trump card to the 'other side'.

If democracy and peace are framed ethnically, then in the logic of Poulantzas, power in society will be reflected in the capacity of one group or class of people to maximize their interests and to minimize the capacity of others to do likewise.[74] Viewing power as capacity rather than simply inherent in an individual or social group allows us to recognize the importance of ideology in determining not only outcomes and decision making, but the very process by which people work through decision making and implementation. Power, therefore, constructs our identities: it influences how and who we see ourselves as being and who we identify as 'others', it shapes what we consider to be worthwhile and it colours our beliefs about where we came from and our aspirations about where we wish to go in the future.

Policing the present

In both Northern Ireland and Bosnia, the ethnicization of politics and the battle for control over the articulation of the state is made possible to a large extent by processes of silencing, deferral or displacement. The process is paradoxical: ethnic markers are at once recognized but placed to the side. In both cases, this paradox plays out on a number of levels: for example, at the level of elite politics or party political interaction, elite contention mirrors everyday segregation; at the level of the everyday, people's lived experiences meet, infuse with and are influenced by elite discord through the cross-currents within political discourse that serve to cultivate collective memory.[75] The processes of silencing occur therefore due to an unstable mixture of pressure from international norms and, from below, as it were, from resilient ethnic understandings. The mixture is unstable not so much from a conflict between the two sets of forces, but rather because of the imperative within both to articulate ethnicity as a way of deferring it and to signpost the bloodied past as a way of displacing it. In turn, that instability jars against the very ideas of moving forward, sharing, cooperation and inclusivity insofar as it serves to marginalize victims of violent conflict and reduce their experiences to political utility.

As alluded to in Chapter 2, a key feature of transitional justice is that the ambiguity of the term and its constituent quasi-legal, quasi-theological and quasi-psychological practices of storytelling, juridical inquiry and confessions lend themselves to different interpretations and a plethora of institutional recommendations.[76] Thus, transitional justice balances uneasily between several ideals. In the case of the former Yugoslavia, the ideal of truth recovery jarred with workings of the politico-legal institution of the ICTY, which had been established by Resolution 827 of the United Nations Security Council in May 1993. The ICTY has been criticized on numerous grounds – particularly for failing to educate citizens in the Balkans about its remit and role leading to a lack of accountability and transparency. These in turn led to a tendency to treat the ICTY almost as a panacea that did not require any engagement with the past by politicians, militias and individuals in the region, or, on the other hand, an attempt to use it to score points off perceived ethnic rivals.[77] Jelena Subotić has recently traced how this has played out in the Balkans, arguing that the application of transitional justice mechanisms in effect 'streamlined justice' in certain instances, working as a quick-fix to show compliance with international norms.[78] In other cases, the goals of the ICTY in prosecuting the perpetrators of historical atrocities and war criminals were reprioritized when placed in the light of other structural and economic issues in the EU's preparation of Croatia and Serbia for membership.[79] Subotić goes on to argue that although transitional justice was harnessed to the rhetoric of the international community for the purpose of peace-building, it was quickly 'hijacked' by domestic concerns within the Balkans. Subotić explains that the language of transitional justice works at an international and supra-national level to create a normative paradigm – namely, 'a set of expectations for state behaviour during democratic transitions'.[80] In order to become a part of the liberal democratic 'club', transitional states must adhere to those expectations and be seen to implement and oversee those norms. Yet this top-down model does not speak to the ethnic dynamics of mobilizing groups based on perceptions of 'truth' and 'grievance', 'retribution' and 'justice' for particularistic ends.[81] Subotić argues that that 'hijacking' 'reduces the effectiveness of transitional justice projects, jeopardizes their legitimacy, and does not bring about the profound social transformation that countries coming out of violent conflict require'.[82]

As Jelena Obradović-Wochnik points out, the transitional juridical emphasis on institutions and procedures renders it blind to 'individuals whose engagement with war crimes is not one of public discussion but of silent knowing'.[83] The focus on procedures seems, to Leigh Payne, premised on the 'hope' that confessions lead to reconciliation, which, she argues, is founded on the incommensurability between perpetrator and victim.[84] Even where confessions do occur, they may only serve to highlight that something should not have happened rather than go into any detail as to the moral or ethical reasons as to why. The example of the victims' rights campaigner Willie Frazer in Northern Ireland underlines this point: Frazer recently admitted to receiving apologies from some of the IRA men who were responsible for his father's murder in 1975. However, the apologies, at least in Frazer's retelling, do not seem to have contained expressions of atonement for killing an unarmed man.[85] For Obradović-Wochnik, an alternative is to look to those otherwise hidden or subterranean ways in which people live with violent pasts. For instance, she highlights the importance of resistance strategies, including the resort to conspiracy theorizing, that are deployed as ways of constructing plausible deniability – or a sort of bad faith with regard to the past.[86]

This idea of framing and positioning the past in relation to the present lies at the heart of Vamik Volkan's thesis about the transgenerational transfer of trauma in which violent pasts may adversely affect younger generations who did not experience conflict directly or who may not be totally conscious or who deliberately choose to ignore recent history. The idea that received wisdoms about the past colour attitudes and beliefs in the present is, in some ways, an obvious point. But it is also, paradoxically, somewhat insubstantial: history by itself cannot mould identities; rather, a prime political function is to lend legitimacy and authority. What is perhaps more consequential, though, again in subterranean ways, is the fact that trauma, politically speaking, can be constructed strategically. Volkan, for example, speaks to this idea in his description of 'chosen trauma' – namely, the adoption of traumatic language and perception through the selection of particular historical reference points or interpretations. For Volkan, chosen trauma works itself out in a number of ways – division, victimization, guilt, shame, humiliation, helplessness – and, he argues, it can become particularly problematic when it becomes taken for granted; that is, when historical events become mythologized and psychologized to an extent that the perception and representation of events become more important than what actually happened.[87]

The idea surfaces in studies of everyday life in the former Yugoslavia. Stef Jansen, for example, has described how framing and articulating stories about the past can be empowering at a personal level: '[b]y embedding those [references to the past] in authoritative discourses of nationalism, people exerted control over their version of history and thereby over their own personal narrative'.[88] Although this allows people to make sense of a violent, disparate past and give meaning to their lives in the aftermath of traumatic events, the danger is that it can also mark a retreat into a privatized world, devoid of social responsibility or awareness. This reveals itself in a reluctance to face up to the past in any shape or form beyond ambiguities – calling to mind the Northern Irish aphoristic dictate, 'whatever you say, you say nothing'.[89] As Jansen argues: '[v]agueness . . . [became] a crucial instrument in self-protection'.[90] It absolved speakers of the need to confront their individual pasts or their ethnic group's historic actions, and it allowed them to cast blame on their perceived antagonists.

The fact that transitional politics in ethnic conflict situations are not simply about manipulation but rather involve complicated framing battles is supported by research into everyday nationalism in Bosnia by Torsten Kolind. With echoes of Rancière's notion about the interruptive nature of the political, Kolind explains that Muslim Bosnians use the term *politika* as a derogation of the cynicism of ethnic power politics. Yet, the term goes beyond disgust at craven political entrepreneurs; instead, as Kolind explains, '[u]sing the term *politika* as an explanatory device is a withdrawal from using ethnic stereotypes and as such resists the dominance of ethnic identities created by war-related violence and the post-war political situation'.[91] It also represents, he argues, a kind of coping mechanism – in other words, it was nationalist discourse and the 'politicians' that were to blame for the violence, not the people you meet on the street every day. Of course, this is only an echo of Rancière. It not only represents a re-invasion of the realm of the 'police' or the separating out of the sensible into the strategies of everyday existence; but it is also representative of a move to, if not subvert ethnicized understandings, at least to negotiate or even transcend them.

Again, the Northern Irish case sheds light on the simultaneous silencing and revealing that underpins transitional ethnic politics. The development of a heritage industry has occurred within a peculiar framework in which 'the past' is always clearly signposted, but the signposts do not point to any kind of recognizable history. These signposts are not simply physical markers or performative rituals such as murals, gaols, memorials and marches – which have been extensively documented[92] – they also encompass deeper trends concerned with discursive understandings about 'history'. Laura McAtackney, for instance, has deployed an archaeological approach to assessing how the peace process has affected space in Northern Ireland. Under the heading of 'regeneration' the policy of disposing of conflict-related edifices (such as police and army barracks) has been half-hearted – disposal occurs, certainly, but 'regeneration' often takes the form of these zones becoming sites of contestation or outright ethnic ownership. Regeneration Zone' signage becomes overwritten with sectarian and racist/anti-immigrant slogans and symbols. As McAtackney argues, this 'move to normalisation' has had deleterious consequences: 'derelict lots pepper urban working class areas highlighting the past conflict through absences – not transformations'.[93] As McAtackney's work reveals, framing is inevitable in post-conflict societies such as Northern Ireland's and, by extension, other sites such as Bosnia where the state remains subject to ethnic contestation. The past is interwoven with that contestation and provides rationales for claims making in the present. However, the way that it is made present – the way that it is re-presented – involves framing strategies that cumulatively pose major problems for sustainable peace or a deep, consolidated democracy.

Several scholars have pointed to the Spanish case as illustrating these tendencies. Georgina Blakely, for example, has explored how the issue of disinterring remains from the civil war period has largely been driven by judicial but also grassroots pressure.[94] Likewise, the groundbreaking work of Paloma Aguilar has mapped how 'lessons' from the Spanish past were articulated through ideological frameworks to become instrumental in shaping modern Spanish democracy and visions of the nation.[95] Following Aguilar's lead, Vincent Druliolle has recently argued that the 'amnesiac' lessons that underpinned the *pacto de olvido* (pact of silence), which were seen as vital for preventing another civil war, not only established a 'veil of ignorance' but 'became one of the main nodal points around which democracy, the empty signifier *par excellence*, was given meaning and constructed'.[96] For Aguilar, this dynamic lies behind the very different historical trajectory of the Basque region in Spain where nationalist elites articulated memories of the civil war that reflected alternative views of democracy, community and nation than those espoused by right and left wing leaders in Madrid.[97]

The transitional justice approach purports to tackle those gaps. Certainly, the juridical pursuit of terrorists and war criminals is necessary if any semblance of justice and state functioning is to be upheld in transitional societies, but as pointed out by Obradović-Wochnik and others, transitional justice is not enough: ideas about truth and justice are often harnessed by ethnic entrepreneurs and citizens at an everyday level and are framed in order to either attempt to make political capital or just to make sense of the aftermath of trauma. In Rancière's terms, the policing of society begins at that point – taboos are inscribed on collective memory and alternative versions of the past and dissenting ideas about the future are written out of debate. Policing the past then becomes a way of ensuring authority in the present. The recent example of state-sponsored denial by the new Serbian president Tomislav Nikolic underlines this point. In direct contradiction of the ICTY, Nikolic asserted that '[t]here was no genocide in Srebrenica, grave war crimes were committed by some Serbs who should be found, prosecuted and punished. It is very difficult to indict someone and prove before a court that an event qualifies as genocide'.[98] Nikolic's logic and his strategic hope depends on cultivating what Cohen calls a culture of denial: '[d]on't always ask the Serbian president if he is going to [the annual commemoration in Srebrenica', he complained, '[m]y predecessor was there and paid tribute. Why should every president do the same?'[99] The only response to this is that of Ashdown: rather than debate the point with genocide deniers, frameworks must be adhered to. Such a position should not be conflated with a liberal faith in progress and rationality in the face of the inevitable attempts by Serbian nationalists to deny what occurred at Srebrenica. Neither is it a form of democratic quietism that suggests that it 'seems better not to impose but to give free reign to memory contestation'.[100] Rather it is a reaffirmation of faith in basic historical and empirical facts and an assertion that, contrary to the wishes of the perpetrators of political violence and terror, these facts remain.

Conclusion

Rancière speaks of the interruptive force of politics as dissensus: as a return of the repressed and an acknowledgment of silencing. Framing theory speaks to how this is possible – within every frame there are counter-frames, and recognizing the potency of each reveals the extent to which political debate revolves around issues not only of representation but also re-presentation. In this view, the transition to a new politico-historical dispensation therefore involves issues that go beyond the methodological and disciplinary boundaries of either 'politics' or 'history' – narrowly conceived – and are saturated with ethical concerns. In other words, they are imbued with assumptions about what Rancière has called a 'poetics of knowledge' – namely, framework or discourse based upon a structure of rules which define how 'truth' is arrived at and how it is (re)presented and (re)produced.[101]

Of course, there can never be one past in any society, not least ethnically divided ones. However, unless the past is articulated in such a way that the connection of events and experiences are integrated in a real and meaningful way, the 'truths' which drove conflict will continue to be reproduced. The problem with this, naturally, is that 'real and meaningful' are in themselves social constructs; as Chapman and Ball, among others, point out, one of the political effects of truth recovery processes is to give weight to that construction. This chapter has sought to build on the concern of previous chapters that in that process of truth construction, the empirical elements of traumatic historical experience are downplayed or deferred in favour of transitional juridical, (communally) restorative or aestheticized visions of 'truth'.

The idea goes back to Rancière's extrapolation of the difficulty and necessity of historical analysis. For Rancière, history is essentially a naming exercise, but that very naming is called into question through the narrative mode that is traditionally deployed. 'Things would be too simple if one could say of any history, as the expression goes, that it is only a story', he writes. 'The distinctive feature of a history [is] that it may always be either a story or not a story'. Historians, in

Rancière's depiction, come face to face with the distribution of the sensible: their subjects are silent, apart, that is from the evidence or historical trace that they leave, but through that silence historians render them visible. In Rancière's formulation: 'The question of the poetic form according to which history can be written is then strictly tied to that of the mode of historicity according to which its objects are thinkable'.[102] The 'fragility'[103] of historiography, then, lies in its association with its subject. The factual basis, as such, of the history of the Northern Irish conflict has its beginnings and basis in the memories of victims and others who lived through the violent past; they are recorded in newspapers, governmental and party political archives and in the marked and unmarked graves across places such as Northern Ireland and the Balkans. Fencing in narratives about the past means paying attention to those links and excluding through reasoned argument and documentary evidence those ethnicized understandings that try to suggest otherwise.

Notes

1 Cillian McGrattan (2009) '"Order Out of Chaos": The Politics of Transitional Justice', *Politicism*, 29(3): 164–172; Cillian McGrattan (March 2011) 'Historians in Post-Conflict Societies: Northern Ireland after the Troubles', *History & Policy*. Available at www.historyandpolicy.org/policy-papers/papers/historians-in-post-conflict-societies-northern-ireland-after-the-troubles; accessed 9 April, 2015.
2 Elazar Barkan (2009) 'Historians and Historical Reconciliation', *American Historical Review*, 114(4): 900.
3 Ibid, p. 907.
4 Audrey R. Chapman and Patrick Ball (2001) 'The Truth of Truth Commissions: Comparative Lessons from Haiti, South Africa, and Guatemala, *Human Rights Quarterly*, 23(1): 1–43.
5 Ibid, p. 33.
6 Michael Ignatieff, *Warrior's Honor: Ethnic War and the Modern Conscience* (London: Vintage, 1999), p. 171.
7 Chapman and Ball, p. 8.
8 Stern, *Remembering*; see also Kristin Sorensen, 'Chilean historical memory, media, and discourses of human rights', in *Global Memoryscapes: Contesting Remembrance in a Transnational Age*, edited by Kendall R. Phillips and G. Mitchell Reyes (Tuscaloosa, AL: The University of Alabama Press, 2011), pp. 159–172.
9 See, for example, Sara McDowell and Máire Braniff, *Commemoration as Conflict: Space, Memory and Identity in Peace Processes* (Basingstoke: Palgrave Macmillan, 2014); Sharon Macdonald, *Memorylands: Heritage and Identity in Europe Today* (Abingdon: Routledge, 2013).
10 Jacques Rancière (2000) 'Dissenting Words: A Conversation with Jacques Rancière', *Diacritics*, 30(2): 115.
11 Alison Ross, 'Expressivity, literarity, mute speech', in *Jacques Rancière: Key Concepts*, edited by Jean-Philippe Deranty (Durham: Acumen, 2010), p. 137.
12 The appointment of a former Irish Republican Army member – and, at one time, one of the 'most wanted' persons in the United Kingdom – to a new victims' liaison body, for example, was the cause of much controversy in Northern Ireland (Alex Kane, 'Who are the real victims of the troubles?', *Newsletter*, 11 June 2012. Available at www.newsletter.co.uk/community/columnists/alex-kane-who-are-real-victims-of-troubles-1–3936688; accessed on 26 June 2012). In Croatia, meanwhile, authorities remain inundated with cases relating to the violence of the 1990s; although the State Prosecutor's Office revised its procedures for dealing with such cases – reviewing,

for example, cases in which undue importance may have been given to ethnicity, it has continued to be the subject of criticism from human rights agencies (Máire Braniff and Cillian McGrattan. 'Dealing with the past in post-conflict societies'. Available at www.opendemocracy.net/maire-braniff-cillian-mcgrattan/dealing-with-past-in-post-conflict-societies; accessed on 26 June 2012). Again, in Bosnia, the multinational company ArcelorMittal remains the subject of lobbying by victims' groups who wish it to build a monument acknowledging the human rights abuses and murders carried out at the Omarska detention centre, whose land it now owns (see Ed Vuillimy, *The War Is Dead, Long Live the War, Bosnia: The Reckoning* (London: The Bodley Head, 2012), pp., 143–145). ArcelorMittal's reluctance to do so echoes the British government's position on the question of a truth commission for Northern Ireland: namely, that any decision would be impossible due to the lack of public consensus (Marie Breen-Smyth, *Truth Recovery and Justice after Conflict: Managing Violent Pasts*. London: Routledge, 2007), p. 139.

13 See, for example, Theodor Adorno, 'The meaning of working through the past', in *Can One Live after Auschwitz? A Philosophical Reader*, edited by Rolf Tiedermann (Stanford: Stanford University Press, 2003), pp. 3–18.

14 Primo Levi, *The Drowned and the Saved* (London: Abacus, 2010), p. 12.

15 Stanley Cohen, *States of Denial: Knowing about Atrocities and Suffering* (Cambridge: Polity Press, 2008), p. 241.

16 Schaap, *Political Reconciliation*, 61.

17 Anthony D. Smith, *National Identity* (Penguin: Harmondsworth, 1991) pp. 14, 21.

18 J.G.A. Pocock, 'Time, institutions and action: an essay on traditions and their understanding', in *Political Thought and History: Essays on Theory and Method* (Cambridge: Cambridge University Press, 2009) p. 126.

19 J. H. Plumb, *The Death of the Past* (Basingstoke: Palgrave Macmillan, 2004 [1969]).

20 Cohen, *States*, p. 243.

21 Ibid., 249.

22 See Tony Judt, *Postwar: A History of Europe Since 1945* (London: William Heinemann, 2005), pp. 803–31.

23 David A. Snow, 'Framing processes, ideology, and discursive fields', in *The Blackwell Companion to Social Movements* (Oxford: Blackwell, 2004), pp. 384.

24 See Myra Marx Ferree, William Anthony Gamson, Jürgen Gerhards and Dieter Rucht, *Shaping Abortion Discourse: Democracy and the Public Sphere in Germany and the United States* (Cambridge: Cambridge University Press, 2002).

25 Hank Johnston, 'Verification and proof in frame and discourse analysis', in *Methods of Social Movement Research*, edited by Bert Klandermans and Suzanne Stagenborg (Minneapolis: University of Minnesota Press, 2002) p. 66.

26 See, for example, Karl-Dieter Opp, *Theories of Political Protest and Social Movements: A Multidisciplinary Introduction, Critique, and Synthesis.* (Abingdon: Routledge, 2009) pp. 234–303.

27 Ferree et al, *Shaping Abortion*, p. 15.

28 James M. Jasper (2004) 'A Strategic Approach to Collective Action: Looking for Agency in Social-Movement Choices', *Mobilization: An International Journal*, 9(1): 1–16.

29 See David A. Snow, E. Burke Rocheford, Jr., Steven K. Worden and Robert D. Benford (1986) 'Frame Alignment Processes, Micromobilization, and Movement Participation', *American Sociological Review*, 51: 464–481.

30 John A. Noakes and Hank Johnston, 'Frames of Protest: A Road Map to a Perspective' in *Frames of Protest: Social Movements and the Framing Perspective*, edited by Noakes and Johnston (Oxford: Rowman & Littlefield, 2005), p 15.

31 Doug McAdam, *Political Process and the Development of Black Insurgency, 1930–1970* (London: University of Chicago Press, 1999).

32 James M. Jasper, *The Art of Moral Protest* (Chicago: University of Chicago Press, 1997).

33 Snow, 'Framing processes, ideology, and discursive fields', p. 400.
34 Ferree et al, *Shaping Discourse*, p. 62.
35 David A. Snow and Robert D. Benford (1988) 'Ideology, Frame Resonance, and Participation Mobilization', *International Social Movement Research*, 1: 197–217.
36 William A. Gamson, *Talking Politics* (Cambridge: Cambridge University Press, 1992), p 135.
37 Kubal, p. 3.
38 Ibid, pp. 170–171.
39 Daniel Bar Tal, 'Collective memory of physical violence: Its contribution to the culture of violence', in *The Role of Memory in Ethnic Conflict* (Basingstoke: Palgrave Macmillan, 2003), pp. 78, 85.
40 McGrattan, *Northern Ireland.*
41 Cillian McGrattan, " 'Order" '.
42 Jonathan Steele, 'Break the cycle of abuse', *Guardian*, 14 June 2009. Available at www.guardian.co.uk/world/1999/jun/14/balkans11; accessed on 26 June 2012.
43 Ivana Sekularac, 'Warcrimes court jails ex-Croatian general for 24 years'. *Reuters*, 15 April 2011. Available at www.reuters.com/article/2011/04/15/us-warcrimes-gotovina-idUSTRE73E3W820110415, accessed on 26 June 2012.
44 Ed Vulliamy, *The War Is Dead, Long Live the War, Bosnia: The Reckoning*. See also Valère P. Gagnon, *The Myth of Ethnic War: Serbia and Croatia in the 1990s* (London: Cornell University Press, 2004).
45 See, for example, Ferree et al, *Shaping Abortion*, pp. 205–231.
46 Jacques Rancière, 'Ten theses on politics', in *Dissensus*, pp. 42–43.
47 Rancière, *Chronicles*, p. viii.
48 Ibid, p. 36.
49 Ibid, p. 37.
50 Jacques Rancière, 'Does democracy mean something?' in *Dissensus: On Politics and Aesthetics* (London: Continuum, 2010), p. 54.
51 Chambers, *Lessons*, p. 160.
52 Rancière, *Chronicles*, p. 7.
53 Ibid, p. 6.
54 Jacques Rancière, *The Names of History: On the Poetics of Knowledge* (London: University of Minnesota Press, 1994), p. 63.
55 Ibid, p. 75.
56 Nancy Bermeo (1992) 'Democracy and the Lessons of Dictatorship'. *Comparative Politics*, 24(3): 277.
57 Paloma Aguilar, *Memory and Amnesia: The Role of the Spanish Civil War in the Transition to Democracy* (Oxford: Berghahn Books, 2002), p. 21.
58 See also Lorenzo Cañás Bottos and Nathalie Rougier (2006) 'Generations on the Border: Changes in Ethno-National Identity in the Irish Border Area', *Nationalism and Ethnic Politics*, 12: 617–642.
59 Aguilar, *Memory and Amnesia.*
60 McGrattan, 'The 2010 Westminster General Election'.
61 Gamson, *Talking Politics.*
62 Nicos Poulantzas, *State, Power, Socialism* (London: Verso, 2000), p. 148.
63 Ibid, p. 152.
64 Steven Lukes, *Power: A Radical View* (Basingstoke: Macmillan, 2005).
65 Poulantzas, *State*, p. 153.
66 Máire Braniff, *Integrating the Balkans, Conflict Resolution and the Impact of EU Expansion* (London: I. B. Tauris, 2011), p. 60.
67 Jelena Subotić, *Hijacked Justice: Dealing with the Past in the Balkans* (Ithaca, New York: Cornell University Press, 2009), p. 124.
68 Robin Wilson, *The Northern Ireland Experience of Conflict and Agreement: A Model for Export?* (Manchester: Manchester University Press, 2010), p. 64.

69 David Chandler, *Bosnia: Faking Democracy after Dayton* (London: Pluto. 2000), p. 204.
70 Andy Aitchison (2012) 'Governing Through Crime Internationally? Bosnia and Herzegovina', *British Journal of Politics and International Relations* (iFirst, 2012), p. 14.
71 Gerald Knaus and Felix Martin (2003) 'Lessons from Bosnia and Herzegovina: Travails of the European Raj', *Journal of Democracy*, 14(3): 70.
72 Vulliamy, *The War Is Dead*, p. 173.
73 Henry Patterson, *Ireland Since 1939: The Persistence of Conflict.* (Oxford: Oxford University Press, 2002), pp. 342–343.
74 Poulantzas, *State*.
75 Of course, people continue to traverse and subvert ethnic boundaries at an everyday level in both regions, where daily existence means not only recognizing but also not recognizing or transcending those barriers; see, for example, Cillian McGrattan and Elizabeth Meehan, 'Introduction: The politics of everyday life', in McGrattan and Meehan, *Everyday Life*, pp. 3–29.
76 Olsen et al, *Transitional Justice;* see also Jon Elster, *Closing the Books: Transitional Justice in Historical Perspective* (Cambridge: Cambridge University Press, 2003).
77 See, for example, David Marshall and Shelley Inglis (2003) 'The Disempowerment of Human Rights-Based Justice in the United Nations Mission in Kosovo', *Harvard Human Rights Journal,* 16: pp. 95–146.
78 Subotić, *Hijacked Justice,* p. 5.
79 Braniff, pp. 177–178.
80 Subotić, *Hijacked Justice,* p. 26.
81 See also on this point, Patrick Pinkerton (2012) 'Resisting Memory: The Politics of Memorialisation in Post-Conflict Northern Ireland', *British Journal of Politics and International Relations,* 14(1): 131–152.
82 Subotić, *Hijacked Justice*, p. 6.
83 Obradović-Wochnik 'The Dilemma', p. 339.
84 Payne, *Unsettling Accounts*, p. 2.
85 *Newsletter*, 'Local IRA men apologise for Frazer father murder', 19 June 2012. Available at www.newsletter.co.uk/news/local/ira-men-apologise-for-frazer-father-s-murder-1–3965445; accessed on 26 July 2012.
86 Obradović-Wochnik, *Ethnic Conflict.*
87 For Volkan, a clear example of 'chosen trauma' was Slobodan Milosevic's conjuring of the ghosts of the Battle of Kosovo to mobilize Serbian nationalism. See www.vamikvolkan.com/Chosen-Trauma,-the-Political-Ideology-of-Entitlement-and-Violence.php; accessed on 25 September 2012.
88 Stef Jansen (2002) 'The Violence of Memories: Local Narratives of the Past after Ethnic Cleansing in Croatia', *Local History,* 6(1): 79.
89 Seamus Heaney, 'Whatever you say say nothing', in *New Selected Poems, 1966–1987* (London: Faber and Faber, 1990), pp. 78–80.
90 Jansen, 'Violence', p. 85.
91 Torsten Kolind, 'In search of "decent people": Resistance to the ethnicization of everyday life among the Muslims of Stolac', in *The New Bosnian Mosaic: Identities, Memories, and Moral Claims in a Post-War Society*, edited by Xavier Bougarel, Elissa Helms and Ger Duijzings (Aldershot: Ashgate, 2007) p. 126.
92 See, for example, Neil Jarman, *Material Conflicts: Parades and Visual Displays in Northern Ireland* (Oxford: Berg, 1997).
93 Laura McAtackney, 'Sectarianism', in *The Oxford Handbook of the Archaeology of the Contemporary Past*, edited by Paul Graves-Brown, Rodney Harrison and Angela Piccini (Oxford: Oxford University Press, 2013), p. 237.
94 Georgina Blakely (2005) 'Digging up Spain's Past: Consequences of Truth and Reconciliation'. *Democratization*, 12(1): 44–59.
95 Aguilar, *Memory and Amnesia.*

96 Vincent Druliolle (2008) 'Democracy Captured by Its Imaginary: The Transition as Memory and Discourses of Constitutionalism in Spain', *Social and Legal Studies*, 17(75): 81.
97 Paloma Aguilar (1998) 'The Memory of the Civil War in the Transition to Democracy: The Peculiarity of the Basque Case'. *West European Politics*, 21(4): 5–25.
98 *The Guardian*, 'Serbian president denies Srebrenica genocide', 2 June 2012. Available at www.guardian.co.uk/world/2012/jun/02/serbian-president-denies-srebrenica-genocide; accessed on 27 June 2012.
99 Ibid.
100 Ger Duijzings, Ger. 'Commemorating Srebrenica: Histories of violence and the politics of memory in Eastern Bosnia' in *The New Bosnian Mosaic: Identities, Memories and Moral Claims in a Post-War Society*, edited by Xavier Bougarel, Elissa Helms and Ger Duijzings (Aldershot: Ashgate, 2007), pp. 142–166.
101 Rancière, *The Names of History*, p. 8.
102 Ibid, p. 101.
103 Ibid, p. 103.

6 Literarity and historical responsibility

This chapter returns to Iris Marion Young's formulation of justice as intrinsically linked with responsibility and to her emphasis on the historically situated nature of that relationship. The aim is to tease out themes that were mentioned in the previous chapters regarding the politics of trauma and its implications for community, responsibility and memory, with an analysis of how those issues are currently working themselves out in Northern Ireland. The argument develops the closing ideas of the previous chapter – namely, that the collation and construction of ethnicized histories represents a parcelling out of difference that can be deleterious to notions of peace and democracy. The argument is, of course, ostensibly obvious; but what I wish to stress is that the collation and construction of those histories is facilitated by the policy design, orientation and direction of transitional justice initiatives. The core of my argument follows from this: namely, that transitional justice is responsive to the distribution of communal or ethnic sensibilities precisely at the cost of societal responsibility. Building on ideas about the fencing in of historical narratives in the previous chapter, I sketch an alternative vision: one that draws essentially from the relationship between lustration and/or affirmative action–type policies and transitional democratization.

Responsibility for history

Arguably, for Young, historical responsibility means responsibility in history, as in a specific time, place and socio-economic setting. For example, as pointed out earlier, her decoupling of guilt from responsibility can be seen as having a certain pragmatic attraction in that it places the emphasis on moving forward, based, that is, on a proper or accurate accounting of injustice or wrong-doing. Thus, her 'social connection model' seems to link guilt with blame, in contrast to the responsibility–empowerment nexus. Following Arendt, she points out that many people can 'share responsibility without being guilty' for a historic crime.[1] As the work of Jansen, described in the previous chapter, exemplifies, Young's corollary of this is that assertions of blame can work to defer responsibility and set aside or ignore culpability for wrong-doing.

What does responsibility actually look like for Young? It is primarily to do with scrutiny, it seems. Thus she argues that

> . . . because we dwell on the stage of history, and not simply in our houses, we cannot avoid the imperative to have a relationship with actions and events performed by institutions of our society, often in our name, and with our passive or active support. The imperative of political responsibility consists in watching these institutions, monitoring their effects to make sure that where such watching and monitoring can occur and citizens can speak publicly and support one another in their efforts to prevent suffering. To the extent that we fail in this, we fail in our responsibility, even though we have committed no crime and should not be blamed.[2]

The tethering of political responsibility to scrutiny, then, involves ascertaining the capability of agent(s) to make a positive change to improve unjust circumstances. In other words, it brings to the fore questions of power and resource mobilization. It is this tethering which gives way to the separation of guilt from responsibility – for, if wrong-doing can be pinpointed, then the imperative seems to be to move forward by correcting the injustice. Yet, as Martha Nussbaum points out in her foreword to Young's book, the decoupling can have problematic implications. One of which, for instance, concerns what might be described as chronology: 'it is really very difficult', Nussbaum argues, 'to maintain the retrospective/prospective portion of the distinction, guilt being appropriate to past acts only, and responsibility to future acts only, for the simple reason that time marches on'.[3] In other words, it is not enough to say that an agent ought to have shouldered responsibility for an action at a certain point in time – if that responsibility is shirked, then the debt or guilt remains. Again, for Nussbaum, although the 'accent should always lie on the future, which can be changed, rather than the past, which cannot', unless blame for an action (or set of actions) is identified, it is difficult to know what might be done differently the next time – learning, as such, seems to depend on identifying such alternatives.[4] Nussbaum goes on to point out that blame need not distract from background conditions as Young avers – indeed, getting blame 'right' depends on an accurate assessment of why certain actions rather than others were taken, which involves a certain historical reimagining. As has been pointed out earlier, although the causality of blame/evasion may hold in a number of cases, guilt may also provide an incentive towards inspiring or precipitating change: 'when the appeal to guilt is coupled in the right way with respect for the person, or even love, it can produce such motivations even more powerfully'.[5]

The pragmatic decoupling of guilt from responsibility, then, may, in fact, work in a counterproductive fashion. In other words, the breaking of the guilt/debt relationship militates against the implication that Nietzsche saw as following from it: namely, recompense or restitution. As he pointed out, the German *die Schuld* denotes blame, guilt *and* debt (which is itself closely linked to *schulden*, to owe), which, by definition, can be paid off (*Wiedergutmachung*, or 'making good'). In this perspective, historical responsibility is located in history – that is, responsibility for a wrong that actually occurred and whose ramifications may still be resonant. As Duncan Ivision contends although corrective justice for a past wrong may be analyzed separately from distributive justice to tackle ongoing or future problems, the two are never completely independent: 'both corrective and distributive justice presuppose that people can be held responsible in various ways, in the sense that they can be held blameworthy'.[6] The point may, as Ivision goes on to demonstrate, give way to debates about the primacy of reparations over reconciliation or vice versa. However, that seems to miss the centrality of the responsive/responsibility pairing that, I argue, colours how history is filtered through and into the public realm in transitional societies.

As Bernhard Schlink has pointed out, the idea of mastering the past (*Vergangenheitsbewältigung*) is, in a way, a response to history based on a curtailment of ongoing responsibility – if the past can be worked through, the historical trauma or wrong-doing can come to an end, or, in other words, the debt can be paid off.[7] Paradoxically, perhaps, Dominick LaCapra has identified a similar politics in Schlink's novel *The Reader* (*Der Voresler*). LaCapra argues that the novel emblematizes a response to history that he characterizes as a discernible body of opinion (if not quite a coherent school of thought) that looks to the idea of a 'machinery-of-destruction': a system or ideological framework or a technological *Gestell* that facilitated the industrial horrors of genocide. For LaCapra, the Schlink novel reduces otherwise extraordinary actions into an 'indiscriminately empathic, "it-could-happen-to-anyone"' feeling.

The book circles around a dilemma: Michael, the narrator, who has a university degree in law, comes into contact with the trial of a woman, Hanna, with whom he had had an affair as a teenager, who stood accused of crimes relating to her time as a guard at Auschwitz; at the time of the affair she was in her late thirties and had disappeared unexpectedly and without trace. During the trial, the narrator becomes aware that she is unable to fully comprehend the charges against her due to her inability to read. Turning to his father for advice on how or whether he should intervene, he is informed that:

> No, your problem has no appealing solution. Of course one must act if the situation as you describe it is one of accrued or inherited responsibility. If one knows what is good for another person who in turn is blind to it, then one must try to open his eyes. One has to leave him the last word, but one must talk to him – to him and not to someone else behind his back.

The artifice of Schlink's text lies in part in Michael emblematizing the plight of post-war Germany in terms of uncertain, partial recognition of the past and a reaction by younger generations against the actions and omissions of their parents. Refusing to intervene, Michael embodies the existential discomfort of that predicament:

> How could it be a comfort that the pain I went through because of my love for Hanna was, in a way, the fate of my generation, a German fate, and that

> it was only more difficult for me to evade, more difficult for me to manage than for others?

LaCapra's assessment that the book represents the notion of a banality of evil lies in the passivity of the main protagonists – almost devoid of agency, they seem to sleepwalk into their fates, Hanna 'falls' into her job as a camp guard; Michael is able to face his own victimhood by reading books into a Dictaphone to Hanna in gaol.[8]

Although LaCapra is correct in his reading of the political effect of the book, it is not the only possible reading. The book also exists as a kind of thematic history, giving voice to the (historical) theme of perpetrator victimhood. This is made clear in Michael's reading of Hanna's motivation:

> [A]t the trial Hanna did not weigh exposure as an illiterate against exposure as a criminal. She did not calculate and she did not manoeuvre. She accepted that she would be called to account, and simply did not wish to endure further exposure. She was not pursuing her own interests, but fight for her own truth, her own justice. Because she always had to dissimulate somewhat, and could never be completely candid, it was a pitiful truth and a pitiful justice, but it was hers, and the struggle for it was her struggle.[9]

The distinction between historical clarification and artistic truth lies here: the pursuit of individual (solipsistic) 'truth' in a novel can happen because the 'facts' pertain to the text – they are or will be or may be established in relation to that text. The distinction is important, but, arguably, not absolute. On the one hand, historical texts (primary evidence, or traces of the past, and historiography) can be self-referential – the cabinet conclusions of the UK government, for example, follow relatively rigid formats that are presumably designed to facilitate institutional learning. On the other hand, as Rancière points out, historiography can never completely detach itself from the tension between story and history.[10] As pointed out in the conclusion of the previous chapter, the representation of the past through narrative gives rise to what Rancière terms a 'poetics of knowledge'; namely, 'a study of the set of literary procedures by which a discourse escapes literature, gives itself the status of a science, and signifies this status . . . [It] has an interest in the rules according to which knowledge is written and read, [and] is constituted as a specific genre of discourse'.[11] Seemingly, this 'poetics of knowledge' draws attention away from itself as a 'discourse' – the genre of historiography, in other words, works to complement narrative with documentary fact by placing specific pieces of evidence in context with each other. Rancière thus argues that 'history is, in the final analysis, susceptible to only one type of architecture, always the same one – a series of events happens to such and such a subject'.[12] However, what happens when these events are barely articulate, when violence and betrayal implode into private and public life, leaving behind little sense of meaning?

I wish to suggest that Rancière's treatment of history as embodying an 'excess of words' helps to move trauma from the aestheticization and silence that is created by the conceptualization of Caruth, among others. This claim lies in Rancière's identification of history as being founded in the appropriation of others' words. As Hayden White points out in the foreword to Rancière's key text on historiography, the original title was the 'Words of History', with *Les Mots* changed to *Les Noms* for the second French edition and English translation. As White explains, 'By "les mots" Rancière designates all the "words" that comprise the documentary evidence on which historians base their accounts of the past and also all the "words" that have been written by historians in those accounts'.[13] Rancière's interest in historiography revolves around the concern of what historians' words do to the words of history – to the accounts and traces of the past left behind by others. As such, it calls to mind the injunction regarding speaking for others, but, I would argue, paradoxically, the emphasis on words and representation can allow historians to mitigate the effects of indignity and appropriation implied by Deleuze. The paradox lies in the incidence that not only do historians write 'hidden histories' of those rendered voiceless by historic political forces, but, rather, that in cases of traumatic experience, there is both a surfeit and deficit of words to account for what occurred. Rancière moves beyond this paradox by stressing the 'literariness' of historiography. Literariness is distinct but related to the concept of literarity, which, as Chambers argues, represents 'the countervailing force to "police", it denotes a political or politicised response to 'counting'.[14] 'For Rancière, literarity defines both 'the fundamental condition of the human animal, but also constitutes the fundamentally political nature of that animal'.[15] As Chambers goes on to explain, literarity 'makes disagreement possible; it serves as the condition of possibility for disidentification'.[16]

Although Rancière writes in terms of the literariness of historiography in *The Names of History* (with the concept of literarity becoming more defined in his later thought), and although he does not specifically write about trauma or traumatic histories, his identification of historiography as embedded in an 'excess of words' provides a bridge between history and the politics of trauma. For just as trauma is commonly linked with a deficit of speech and the removal of the means to master and move beyond a violent experience, Rancière links history writing with those rendered speechless or left at the margins of historico-political power. Thus, his chapter in *The Names of History*, 'The Excess of Words', develops a close reading of Tacitus's account of the revolt of the legionary Percennius. The revolt took place from 'a void', a period of enforced idleness for the army during an interregnum in which Augustus has died and Tiberius has not yet taken control. As Rancière points out, not only has Percennius, a former theatrical troupe leader and common soldier, 'no place to speak', but that, for Tacitus, his revolt was essentially meaningless; it was to be overtaken by events and be made wholly illegitimate. Despite this, 'Tacitus makes him speak. And his speech is ordered, precise, convincing'.[17] Rancière goes on to note that we cannot be sure at all about Percennius's speech:

> [W]ho knows what Percennius could really have said? Surely Tacitus has no information on this topic. And it is without importance. Restating this

> discourse is not a matter of documentation but of invention, of knowing what a personage of this sort could have said in such a situation.[18]

Rancière's point is not to do with the invention of fact or the manipulation of history. Certainly, as he argues, an 'appropriation' has taken place, but more than an appropriation because Tacitus has given a form of historical and political reality to Percennius and his revolt. Tacitus, writes Rancière, 'creates a model of subversive eloquence for the orators and simple soldiers of the future'.[19] The subversive nature of Tacitus' representation and appropriation stems from the fact that Percennius is thus afforded rights that he did not have: his speech works to transcend the boundaries of propriety. The 'reversal' of the appropriation, then, lies in the subversive power of speech and writing to transcend socio-political boundaries – in other words, by 'signify[ing] differently' forms of exclusion and inclusion.[20] This reversal is significant, because it does not simply institute another regime of the sensible. In other words, it is not simply a matter of subversion of a dominant order or a critical deconstruction of existing power relations and the substitution of a new order or understanding. As Chambers argues, what might be called the Rancièrean methodology or intervention is based on the assumption and then verification of equality – an equality that is vouchsafed by language. That assumption does not simply demand an unveiling of the otherwise hidden structures or discourses of power that create unjust situations because such an unveiling can give way to an inversion of power through the substitution of one set of understandings with another.

The Rancièrean intervention points towards not only this inversion – which is, of course, the achievement of critical theory – but also to a more ambiguous result. As he argues with regard to Percennius and Tacitus, '[w]hat remains 'is the gathering power of language and of the play that it authorizes, the power of a discourse that is always susceptible of allowing entry into its community of those excluded when its circle is drawn'.[21] That is to say, the excess of words gives way to a new political disposition. In this way, Rancière provides an answer to the Spivakian question regarding how marginal or subaltern groups can claim and assert agency, because it is in the assumption of equality – founded in literarity – that subversion and claims making can begin.[22] The emergence of barely articulate traumatic experiences into history and historiography begins with that sensibility – namely, the suspicion that something untoward has occurred or, more accurately, the sense that a betrayal has happened and the assumption that that has been unjust. I would argue that with regard to the politics of trauma (and perhaps political struggles for equality in a more general sense), the process is not one of easy causality – assumption leading to verification – because, as Das points out (cited earlier), trauma is a hurt that calls for acknowledgement.

In post-conflict situations such as Northern Ireland's, the beginning of any effort or policy initiative to deal with the legacies of violence ought to be found at that point. Responsibility for history in such situations, in other words, proceeds from the recognition of the part-without-part, namely, the 'hidden' histories of victims of political violence. This gives way to no specific policy programme – as the Spanish case demonstrates, institutional amnesia can promote peace and democracy in the absence of transitional justice-type measures.[23] But it resists the tautological imposition of such measures onto the memories of victims and the historical legacies created by violence and terror. Although the notion on which the Belfast/Good Friday Agreement was premised – that the best way to 'honour the dead' was to build a political culture of peace, tolerance and respect for human rights – is rhetorically sensible – in other words, justifying a peace by invoking the memory of the victims of violence – it arguably confused what that peace was about. For the Belfast/Good Friday Agreement was not primarily about dealing with the past, but about establishing workable power-sharing institutions and cross-border cooperation – testified in the structure of the text and the amount of space given over to these imperatives. Given the long process of negotiation that preceded (and proceeded) it, it is surely nonsensical to criticize subsequent efforts as piecemeal, as Christine Bell has written.[24] This is because implicit in the 'piecemeal' assertion is a counterfactual that something else could have been done differently, together with an elitist assumption that dealing with the past can somehow be extracted or abstracted from ongoing political realities. As pointed out earlier, this essential tautology is intrinsic to the transitional justice paradigm, and the confusion it creates works to mask its redundancy and condescension. Viewing Northern Ireland's struggle to come to terms with its past can, of course, proceed from a Year Zero–type understanding: a new disposition was instituted by law in 1998 and a line can be drawn. Yet, even within that understanding, the politics of the past remain embedded within the politics of the present – residues, as previously argued, carry over and continue to be drawn upon. What the politics of trauma gives way to, therefore, is this understanding: namely, that a new openness is possible that can work to subvert the established ethnic order that operated in both the past and the present. Chronology is important, but, following Rancière, the point is not simply about perspective, but rather the meaning given to perspective. In other words, the assumption of the kind of difference Bell implies cannot be verified and gives way to redundancy and a silencing effect. A perspective that begins with the acknowledgement of the facticity of suffering and is distinguished from the theodicy of the notion that conflict can be cherry-picked to aid peace (or in a more recent work by Bell, that traumatic experience can be utilized to further (or sensationalize) academic research).[25] Responsibility for history and moving beyond violent pasts thus lies in the advice of Deleuze, but also in the intervention of Rancière: traumatic experience cannot be mobilized, but neither can it be left in a de-politicized, legalized and/or aestheticized realm.

History as commemoration and interruption

The point can be illustrated in the interjection of the high-profile Irish historian, Professor Diarmaid Ferriter, into recent debates concerning the legacy and remembrance of Ireland's violent past. Taking aim, for example, at the belief of the former Taoiseach, John Bruton, that Ireland had been given a similar opportunity to peacefully win political independence a century ago as more 'about wishing something else happened, not honestly assessing what happened and why'.[26] Ferriter bases his argument on Richard J. Evans' recent exploration of counterfactual history. Ferriter seems acutely aware of the potential for the history of the 1910s to become politicized in contemporary Ireland and has spearheaded a viewpoint that prioritizes historical accuracy within state-sponsored commemorations. In deconstructing Bruton's counterfactual, however, Ferriter seems to have missed a rather crucial qualification raised by Evans (via Aviezer Tucker) that any counterfactual scenario can 'always be got around by anyone determined enough to assert the validity of teleology in the long term'.[27] The idea of 'plausibility' does the logical work for Ferriter – in other words, 'Ireland', as he sees it, is a reified and, hence, inevitable and necessary entity. It just so happens that the nationalist emphasis within the content and sensibility of that entity is one with which Ferriter is at ease. Thus, he criticizes Bruton for using catch-allisms such as 'we' or the 'Irish' when referring to constitutional nationalist politics before the 1916 Rising, but refuses to qualify similar terms when it suits his own argument (see, for example, his assertion that Bruton ignores 'Britain's imperial priorities, its governments' inept and dishonest Irish policy, a refusal to contemplate or tolerate Irish nationalist self-determination, and the militancy and militarisation of the era'). Ferriter's position is, therefore, superficial; as journalist Brian Walker points out: '[h]is argument to Bruton is basically simple – look, the Rising had the obvious effect of radicalising nationalist Ireland. It happened, get over it, stop regretting it'.[28] The political implications are, however, troubling because it is easy to get over something when you are at ease with the consequences. And it is precisely at that point that plausibility works to obfuscate and conceal because an insult, injury or injustice may be mitigated by reason and inevitability but never completely negated.

In other words, the logic of plausibility is saturated with political assumptions, and concealment and silencing occur when those go underarticulated or deployed as double standards. Yet, as Judith Butler argues, there is a paradox within this movement because the concealment and silencing can never be complete. She writes:

> If violence is done against those who are unreal . . . then, from the perspective of violence, it fails to injure or negate those lives since those lives are already negated. But they have a strange way of remaining animated and so must be negated again (and again).[29]

To revert to the Irish case: the teleology of nationalism requires constant reaffirmation. In this regard, it is not surprising that Ferriter avoids engaging directly with Evans' point about counterfactual history being more about the present than the past because to do so would be to admit that the type of history that Ferriter is seemingly prioritizing within the political culture of commemoration is one that is closely aligned with the foundational myths of the Irish state. Bruton's point was, arguably, to draw attention to the resonance that those myths have to contemporary nationalism, and, in particular, to party political agendas that valorize the necessity of violence.

Although debates over the meaning and remembrance of World War I continue to dominate historical and political debate in the United Kingdom, the island of Ireland has been working through what has become known as the 'decade of commemorations' (or decade of centenaries to evoke a rather more restrictive terminology). For example, the commemoration of the centenary of the Ulster Covenant (1912) occurred mainly, and probably unsurprisingly, within the Northern Irish Ulster unionist community. In contrast, the anniversary of the 1916 Easter Rising seems to be a particular concern to the political establishment in Dublin. So, for example, the Irish government has established an advisory group to try to ensure that the commemorative programme will 'set a tone that is inclusive and non-triumphalist, ensuring authenticity, proportionality and openness'. The programme aims to 'encourage original research at local and national level, at all times acknowledging the multiple identities and traditions which are part of the historic story of the island of Ireland'. [30]The historians themselves have been in no doubt about the fundamentally political implications of their appointments. They see their role as advising how commemorations 'should reflect or explore history with a true integrity, without recrimination, of a shared history'.[31] Although the group has deflected the idea that historians should write and research towards specific political ends, they are also aware of the political implications of their work. Ferriter, who is part of the group, complained that it was excluded from discussions over whether to invite the queen to the Easter Rising commemorations. The invite was extended by the Taoiseach Enda Kenny and, arguably, reflected the wariness among the Irish political class that the fiftieth anniversary of the Easter Rising had provided something of a catalyst for the insurgent nationalism that inspired the subsequent Northern Irish conflict.[32] Ferriter argued that historically informed commemorative events and activities can be obscured by political interventions (such as extending an official invite to the queen):

> I'm on the side of evidence. There was no evidence that Britain was prepared to settle its Irish question until it was forced to do it. We don't need to abandon our critical faculties because of the warm haze after the Queen's [2012] visit.

The role of public history, he infers, is democratic, educative and pluralistic. 'The State doesn't own the legacy of 1916. Nobody does except the people. We are trying to organise public consultations to get people's views'.[33] It is difficult to ascertain what Ferriter's central argument against the idea actually is since public consultation seems to have little to do with historical debate over the evidence for or against 'Britain's' role in Ireland in the early part of the twentieth century. The central point, however, is that the very obscurity of his comments has the political effect of raising barriers to pluralism or inclusive commemoration. For example, by juxtaposing 'Britain' with 'Ireland', Ferriter's comments work to silence the pro-union 'British' presence on the island (historically and contemporaneously). Yet the politics of Ferriter's intervention (inadvertently) reveal what seems to be a basic lesson with regard to historical commemoration: whether commemorations are multiple or plural is not really the point; within a national setting, a commemoration 'celebrating multiple identities' will always exclude. Of course, historians should not try to 'reignite old tensions' – as the Taoiseach's panel points out – nor should they tailor their writings to promote political ideas or concepts such as 'reconciliation'. Instead, historians can play a positive role by taking history out of politics. In other words, the democratic potential of historical research can be slightly widened by an awareness of plurality and education; but more fundamentally, it lies in the ability to divest the politics of historical arguments of their salience and emotion through recourse to evidence and context.

If there is a danger of prescribing relevance for historians, commemorations also provide an opportunity for raising awareness of historical problems. The public nature of this awareness lies in the tendency for these problems to extend beyond questions of evidence and context to affect contemporary society. The idea then becomes to use history as a lens to throw light on actual political problems in the present day. The fortieth anniversary of the first experiment in democratic power sharing in Northern Ireland (1973–1974) provides one opportunity to explore how these issues work themselves out. For example, at a recent conference on that anniversary, political commentator Malachi O'Doherty remarked how the fortnight-long Ulster Workers' Council Strike, which precipitated the collapse of the 'Sunningdale executive' was a period when the spectrum of opinion became monochrome. In other words, despite the complexity of what was unfolding historically, the contemporaneous interpretation and representation of that period was coloured simplistically – that is, according to received ethno-nationalist and governmental wisdom(s). Nationalists, for example, focused on what they perceived as Ulster unionist obduracy and reluctance to share power; unionists, on the other hand, looked to what they saw as British perfidy and nationalist hollowing out of the union; political elites in London, meanwhile, concluded that everyone was as bad as each other and that the British government were there to just 'referee the fight'.[34] Although, as Alvin Jackson has pointed out, the virulence of these disparate historical understandings creates a kind of blame-game that presents difficulties for anyone analyzing the period;[35] the critical point is that many of these 'historical' perspectives continue to reside at the heart of contemporary Northern Irish politics. Treating them as historical residues may, I argue, help to drain them of some of their emotional and symbolic resonance; in other words, by detaching the historically informed ideas and narratives from a central role in contemporary politics, by handing the past back to historical analysis, the ground may be (slightly) cleared for consensual appreciations of what occurred and for political debates that are not shaped and dominated by (presentist) understandings of history.

The 'Sunningdale' assembly and executive were established by a communiqué signed in Berkshire in December 1973; they sat from January 1974 before collapsing in the midst of a general strike that was spearheaded by a shadowy group of loyalist militants, the Ulster Workers' Council, in May of the same year. The communiqué provided for devolved government in Northern Ireland – control of the administration of the province had been assumed by London following the prorogation of the majoritarian-based government in March 1972 – and a Council of Ireland that would bring together ministers from Belfast and Dublin to 'harmonize' laws. The experiment had been under threat from the start: rejectionists in the form of unionist politicians such as Ian Paisley and extremist nationalist paramilitaries in the Irish Republican Army (IRA) continued to mobilize against the arrangements. The Irish government was unable to offer any kind of support in terms of trying to ameliorate unionist suspicions due to a legal objection regarding the communiqué's constitutionality that had been lodged in the High Court by a hard-line republican politician. And when the strike began, it was felt by executive politicians that the recently elected Labour government did not have the same loyalty as the conservatives who had negotiated the agreement.[36]

There is no question that the history of Sunningdale can be dealt with in a prescriptive way, and it seems impossible to recuperate the Sunningdale period through thematic or empirical analysis: the year 1974 witnessed 303 conflict-related killings.[37] Nor can the idea that the disparate conclusions of participants be seen as support for historical relativism – indeed, a certain historical consensus is forming around the idea that Sunningdale was not really a 'missed opportunity' but was rather more simply indicative of the inability of the political class to 'make the compromises necessary to make such a political settlement work'.[38] Embracing the problem of allocating responsibility for the collapse of power sharing means exploring Sunningdale's monochromatic tendencies with an eye to their complexity – in other words, instead of reaching for certainty with regard to the allotment of blame, Sunningdale might instead be read as an exercise in democracy. Seen in this way, the Sunningdale initiative can still be demarcated from the violent and extremist opponents of a political way forward at the time. What it also allows is for the period to be seen as a kind of interruptive history. As Bonnie Honig explains, 'Interruption, which aborts another's speech, may be a deliberate speech act . . . but sometimes interruption just happens as a side effect or a by-product of other doings'.[39] Honig proposes a radical rereading of *Antigone*, in effect, contending that to view Sophocles' heroine as an individual acting against the state (a frame of feminine/maternal fragility) works to depoliticize lamentation and mourning. It is not a matter of merely interpreting *Antigone*, Honig argues; rather, we should approach the play and the dilemma of individual mourning versus the (changing, ambiguous and totalizing) demands of the state. In other words, in approaching the conflict between Antigone, who wishes to bury her brother, and Creon, the ruler who wishes to present him as a traitor, we ought to be aware of the nature of that very approach. Honig's argument reverses the traditional political science problem of interpretation to reframe it as one of reception. Part of the effect of interruption then, is to draw attention to the idea that the meaning of a work such as *Antigone* or a political intervention or historical event lies in how it relates to our context and circumstances. The resonance of *Antigone*, for Honig, is, in part, to draw attention to the 'debt' that we owe to Sophocles, who invites us 'to look hard at the myriad ways in which we silence the grief that in our politics we yet do so much to generate'.[40]

An interruptive history, as such, cannot be pre-arranged according to established historical narratives; rather, it works to undercut and trouble such notions.

Viewing Sunningdale as an interruptive history means paying attention to the democratic themes that constitute the interruption: themes such as differing beliefs in legitimacy and the inability of the institutions to cultivate a belief in the justifiability of their legitimacy (which are two different things); themes concerning voice and voicelessness and the perception of powerlessness engendered by the feeling that history is running away from you; themes also of violence and the tendency of protest and street politics to take on meanings and lives of their own. Of course, many of these themes resonate in Northern Ireland today and belie the notion that any remembrance of Sunningdale could be authentic or shared. Perhaps the best that could be hoped for is that by embracing the democratic potential of interrupted history, its potential for colonizing contemporary politics may be offset.

Narrating the Northern Ireland conflict

The Haass/O'Sullivan policy paper (see Chapter 4) was structured around the areas set out by the Northern Ireland Executive: namely, parading, public symbolism and the legacies of the past.[41] Although many commentators believed that the latter would prove to be the most contentious,[42] in fact, the section on dealing with the past was the only part to receive substantive support among the parties of government. The notion of resilience marks the foundation of Haass/O'Sullivan's set of policy proposals for dealing with the past. 'Northern Ireland is blessed with many advantages and virtues', they write (strangely, for a policy paper, the document's paragraphs are unnumbered and the style, written presumably for a collective Executive voice, anticipates agreement. The 'final' document is actually the seventh draft, which negotiators took back to their parties). 'We have a hard working, resilient population', they go on to explain. Despite this, however, the persistence of historic divisions creates an imperative: 'we must find our own way and our own means to [a] higher ground. A civic vision is needed'.[43] The object that that vision is focused on is 'reconciliation', which, for Haass/O'Sullivan, is concerned with

> . . . the transition from a divided society to one that is whole, from a wounded society to one that is healed . . . a harmonious society, one that does not forget the past but is not held back by it as we are today.

Haass/O'Sullivan proceed to set out a complex institutional framework to achieve that vision. It consists of a number of key features. First, Haass/O'Sullivan prioritize the principle of individual choice in psychiatric and trauma care, but avoid defining who is eligible for that care ('[o]ur understandings of the word "victim" . . . [are] closely tied to our different narratives of the conflict, which are not presently reconcilable'). Second, they explain that '[s]incere acknowledgements are a foundational step in the effort to contend with Northern Ireland's past'. Haass/O'Sullivan state that interpretation should not predetermine or prejudge any such acts: 'Our disagreements about the meanings of past events', they write, should not stand in the way of individuals and groups acknowledging those events, their role in them, and the fact that they had a profound impact on society'.[44] Although what exactly an act of 'sincere' acknowledgement may look like is not specified, Haass/O'Sullivan give a detailed outline of what they understand it to consist. It should, they argue, 'be more than saying sorry: 'Saying sorry is necessary but not sufficient'; instead, a full acknowledgment would entail admission of responsibility, an expression of 'understanding of the human consequences for individuals and society, and include a sincere expression of remorse for pain and injury caused'. They also argue that '[s]tatements of regret and reconsideration' ought also to be 'welcome'.[45] It is uncertain as to how this understanding of remorse differs from regret – after all a perpetrator of violence may express sorrow at the hurt their actions caused without disavowing the putative rationale that inspired them to inflict that hurt in the first place; with the implicit threat being that unless circumstances continue to change to their liking, occasions for carrying out terror may recur. This seemingly self-evident situation is not alluded to by Haass/O'Sullivan in either their treatment of acknowledgement or of storytelling, which they claim has, in Northern Ireland, begun to 'develop a methodology . . . and to establish good practice'.[46] In calling for the establishment of an oral history archive, Haass/O'Sullivan reveal a similar political naiveté to that which informs their treatment of acts of acknowledgement. Such an archive, they state,

> . . . will be free from political interference. It will not seek to interpret people's narratives or attempt to create any single narrative of the past. It will, rather, be a collection of individual narratives – a vital primary resource for future historians, genealogists, and writers who will interpret the myriad histories of Northern Ireland.[47]

Aleida Assmann outlines several dangers associated with such a lack of political nous. For example, she argues memory often acts like a club: 'The only memory that is important is the guilt of the other, and establishing that guilt is seen as wiping out one's own guilt'. Although she speaks explicitly to the idea of a club as something to hit one's opponents, of course, as alluded to earlier, national identity is itself a kind of selective memory club, defining what narratives and beliefs about the past are acceptable and which are taboo. Again, she argues that such a decontextualized approach leads to competition between claims of victimhood. 'Placing one trauma in a privileged position' she argues, 'can serve to eclipse another trauma'. This should not be understood that there is no hierarchy of victimhood, but rather, that the very idea of victim status can be easily mobilized to cover up a multitude of sins. As Assmann goes on to explain, the appropriation of claims of suffering on the part of perpetrators work to 'cover up' what is worse with what is bad. Importantly, Assmann does not negate the individuality of the experience of historical violence, but she warns against what might be called a reifying of memory and narrative through the impulse to conform to broader ideologies, whether they are based on nationality, community or reconciliation: 'Everyone has a human right to his or her memories. That, however, does not exclude the necessity to place such memories that have been articulated and recognized on a wider horizon'. It is only through 'retrospectively placing them in a larger context', she argues, that they can 'be made compatible with other memories.[48] The lessons seem relatively clear: oral history archives provide a repository for information, but, as Jerome deGroot points out, the 'consuming' of history is not simply a passive process[49]; rather, we participate in learning about the kind of history that validates and valorizes our own identity and in so doing reproduce favoured myths and stories. The Dúchas oral history archive on the republican/ Catholic-dominated Falls Road in west Belfast, for example, contains virtually no references to the IRA's policing of 'its' ethnic strongholds[50] – including its practices of suppressing claims of sexual abuse perpetrated by its members, or Sinn Féin's preferred option of bringing rape victims and their perpetrators together in a restorative justice conference to adjudicate who was telling the truth. Instead, the archive is replete with stories concerning British army injustices.[51] This is not to deny the truth of the latter, but rather to highlight the naïveté inherent in the notion that storytelling archives are somehow separated from ethnic politics or that they provide a means to facilitating reconciliation.[52]

The potential ethnicization of the past that is contained in Haass/O'Sullivan's valorization of experience and storytelling is, arguably, offset by their commitment to empirical research and forensic investigation in other areas. They propose, for example, to set up a 'Historical Investigations Unit' (HIU) to amalgamate and 'streamline' police investigations into unsolved murders and which will refer cases to the Public Prosecutions Service that will decide if there is enough evidence to pursue prosecutions. Although they argue that an amnesty process must be avoided, they acknowledge that, on the basis of precedents (such as the cases of the 'disappeared' or the Bloody Sunday Inquiry), information in relation to such cases may only be forthcoming if it is not admissible in subsequent court proceedings.[53] The proposal is that the HIU will operate alongside, but completely separate, from what would presumably be a larger umbrella institution – the Independent Commission for Information Retrieval (ICIR). This latter body consists of several interlocking strands and is geared towards 'increasing the availability of information'. Thus, Haass/O'Sullivan explain that 'creating opportunities to retrieve as much information as possible is essential to helping victims and their families, and to contending with the past. Only through gaining the fullest picture of what happened during the conflict and why can Northern Ireland begin to constructively confront its past'.[54] In essence, the ICIR would act as an institutional repository for collating and reporting information outwith the judicial system:

> Given the importance of their [perpetrators'] information to the future of Northern Ireland, the [ICIR] will therefore be empowered by law to offer 'inadmissibility' or 'limited immunity' in both civil and criminal courts to those providing information in connection with the incidents described.

The proposals go on to state that such a policy 'renders statements given under such conditions inadmissible in court and protects an individual from self-incrimination.' Despite that inadmissibility, they claim that the idea is 'not . . .

an amnesty in any form. Statements given under these conditions simply cannot be admitted as evidence against the person giving them or anyone named in those statements'. A (narrow) definition of amnesty does not apply because those statements will not 'provide protection against prosecution or the pursuit of civil damages through evidence derived from other sources, or against prosecution for other acts'.[55] The fundamental idea, therefore, seems to provide a balance between information recovery through confidentiality and victims' rights to pursue prosecution. The ICIR falls short of the South African model by not including the principle of full disclosure, which, negotiators felt, would not be realistically possible.[56] Instead, the ICIR would be empowered to offer any individuals named the opportunity to participate in its case inquiries, 'to deny, clarify, or confirm their involvement and secure the limited protections offered by ICIR where possible. If they choose not to participate, they will suffer no penalty'.[57]

The ICIR will also provide broader reports on what Haass/O'Sullivan term 'themes' or 'patterns' by convening a specialist unit that would include 'lawyers, historians, and other academics'[58]. These themes would be suggested by the empirical evidence or by another specialist body, the Implementation and Reconciliation Group (IRG) (comprising politicians, civic society organizations, lobby groups and victims' representatives). Haass/O'Sullivan suggest that themes should '[o]ffer meaningful insight into the political and strategic context of events during the conflict; involve serious human rights violations; or [that have] left a legacy that is particularly important for the work of reconciliation'.[59] This, like the IRG, may essentially become a toothless tiger. Thus, the idea is that the thematic unit can operate for three years, after which time it should produce either a report or an update of its work. The Haass/O'Sullivan document contains the critical proviso to this workload that a final report may be mothballed:

> In an extreme condition, [the unit] could decide to issue a report only stating that the level of participation [among key protagonist groupings] was not sufficient to allow for a meaningful assessment, clearly identifying those organisations whose failure to cooperate frustrated its task.

In other words, the thematic unit may become a tick-box exercise involving academics and transitional justice practitioners with no outcome and minimal political effect – this scenario, of course, would depend on non-cooperation on critical issues alluded to by Haass/O'Sullivan, such as 'disappearances' and 'ethnic cleansing' on the part of republicans, and the collusion of state forces on each side of the border by the British and Irish governments. It would also depend on the group's constitution and its ability to not leak sensitive and embargoed material.

Conclusion

An indication of the limitations of dealing with the past in Northern Ireland can be located in Gerry Adams' long statement in response to allegations that Sinn Féin, the IRA and members of the organization Community Restorative Justice Ireland were complicit in holding investigations into claims against a republican that he raped a young woman, the grand-daughter of one of the founding members of the IRA, Mairia Cahill. In his response to a BBC Northern Ireland documentary exposing the investigation and attempted cover-up (the IRA concluded its interest in the case by placing Cahill and her alleged rapist in a room together, before placing him under house arrest and threatening to shoot him; allegedly, if the decision had gone against Cahill, the verdict would have been the same), Adams explained that the IRA 'on occasion shot alleged sex offenders or expelled them' during the Troubles.[60] But he went on to state that the 'recent publicity surrounding the case of Maíria Cahill has brought this particular issue to the fore in public consciousness'. The IRA, he claimed, conducted an investigation into the rape allegations at the time of their surfacing, but the 'IRA has long since left the scene so there is no corporate way of verifying this'. As one journalist pointed out, the statement raised more questions than it served to answer: '[any] process on the past is pointless if there is "no corporate way of verifying"'.[61]

Ideas about answerability, verification and clarification can give way, once again, to questions about the meaning given to perspective. For the implications of Adams' assertion – namely, that responsibility for the past can be sidestepped – is, as Martha Nussbaum points out a curiously restrictive, and, in this case, self-serving, conceptualization of the term. Ultimately, it gives way to an undercutting of relations between past, present and future, for, as Nussbaum points out, if we can just 'shirk' our responsibilities for past actions, then any kind of teaching or lesson learning becomes meaningless. She uses the example of a parent saying to a selfish child, 'From now on, treat others fairly' and not 'From now on, do things *differently*'. Although the former may incentivize a child to act differently, it creates confusion because the child 'really doesn't learn about fairness since she doesn't learn what she did unfairly just now'.[62] Thus, leaving experience of the past in a de-politicized realm, as Adams' implies is where it is, gives a particular meaning to the very notion of 'dealing with the past' – one that is based on narrowly defined presentist and instrumentalist considerations; in other words, the idea that 'From now on, we'll do better'. This logic speaks to the almost imperializing, all-subsuming force of Rancière's police order in that the 'counting' or ordering of political reality is accomplished according to established objectives, and unwelcome histories, experiences and points of view are deemed inadmissible. The point is, however, each time that that logic reproduces itself – in this case, through the repeated assertions that the plaintiff never carried her complaints into court – it draws ever more attention to itself and that very act of drawing works to make clear the injustice of delimiting justice in this way. The Rancièrean response, this chapter has argued, is to return to responsibility as a reversal of self-serving, narrow, confusing and presentist interests and, instead, to place its meaning on those who have been rendered most vulnerable and marginalized by political violence.

Notes

1 Young, *Responsibility*, p. 78.
2 Ibid, p. 88.

3 Martha Nussbaum, 'Foreword', in Ibid., p. xxi.
4 Ibid., pp. xxii–xxiii.
5 Ibid., p. xxiv.
6 Duncan Ivision. 'Historical injustice', in *The Oxford Handbook of Political Theory*, edited by John S. Druze, Bonnie Honig and Anne Phillips (Oxford: Oxford University Press, 2006), p. 511.
7 Bernhard Schlink, *Guilt about the Past* (London: Beautiful Books, 2009).
8 Dominick LaCapra, 'Fascism and the sacred: Sites of inquiry after (or along with) trauma', in *The Future of Trauma Theory: Contemporary Literary and Cultural Criticism*, edited by Geert Baleens, Samuel Durant, and Robert Eagleton (Abingdon: Rutledge, 2014), p. 34.
9 Bernhard Schlink, *The Reader*, translated by Carol Brown Janeway (London: Weidenfeld & Nicolson, 1997), pp. 132–133.
10 Ranciere, *Names*, p. 3.
11 Ibid., p. 8.
12 Ibid., p. 2.
13 White, 'Foreword', pp. vii–viii.
14 Chambers, *The Lessons of Rancière*, p. 113.
15 Rancière, cited in Chambers, Lessons, p. 114; original emphasis.
16 Chambers, ibid.
17 Rancière, *Names*, pp. 25–26.
18 Ibid., p. 26.
19 Ibid., p. 29.
20 Ibid., pp. 29–30.
21 Ibid.
22 Chambers. *Lessons.*
23 Omar G. Encarnación, *Democracy without Justice in Spain: The Politics of Forgetting* (Philadelphia, PA: University of Pennsylvania Press, 2014).
24 Christine Bell (2003) 'Dealing with the Past in Northern Ireland', *Fordham International Law Journal,* 26: 1095–1147.
25 See, for example, the opening pages of Bell's *On the Law of Peace: Peace Agreements and the Lex Pacificatoria* (Oxford: Oxford University Press, 2008).
26 Diarmaid Ferriter, 'Pouring water on the flames of what-if-history', *Irish Times*, 27 September 2014. Available at www.irishtimes.com/culture/heritage/pouring-water-on-the-flames-of-what-if-history-1.1943189?page=2; accessed on 6 October 2014.
27 Richard J. Evans, *Altered Pasts: Counterfactuals in History* (London: Little, Brown, 2014), p. 58.
28 http://sluggerotoole.com/2014/09/29/the-what-ifs-of-our-past-play-a-part-in-dealing-with-it-today/; accessed on 10 August 2015.
29 Judith Butler, *Precarious Life: The Powers of Mourning and Violence* (London: Verso, 2004), p. 33.
30 See Roinn an Taoisigh/Department of the Taoiseach 'National Commemorations Programme: Decade of Centenaries, 2012–2022: Appointment of Advisory Group on Centenary Commemorations' [2012]. Available at www.taoiseach.gov.ie/eng/News/Archives/2012/Government_Press_Releases_2012/National_Commemorations_Programme_Decade_of_Centenaries,_2012–2022.html; accessed on 14 April 2014.
31 See Decade of Centenaries 'Initial Statement by Advisory Group on Centenary Commemorations' [n.d.]. Available at www.decadeofcentenaries.com/initial-statement-by-advisory-group-on-centenary-commemorations/; accessed on 14 April 2014.
32 Mary E. Daly and Margaret O'Callaghan (eds.) *1916 in 1966: Commemorating the Easter Rising* (Dublin: Royal Irish Academy, 2007).
33 Ronan McGreevy, 'Historian queries decision to invite royals to 1916 commemorations', *Irish Times*, 14 April 2014. Available at www.irishtimes.com/life-and-style/health-family/historian-queries-decision-to-invite-royals-to-1916-commemorations-1.1760992; accessed on 6 October 2014.

34 Edwards and McGrattan, *The Northern Ireland Conflict*, p. 57.
35 Alvin Jackson, *Home Rule: An Irish History, 1800–2000* (London: Weidenfeld and Nicolson, 2003), p. 268.
36 McGrattan, *Northern Ireland*, pp. 77–88.
37 David McKittrick, Seamus Kelters, Brian Feeney, and Chris Thornton, *Lost Lives: The Stories of the Men, Women and Children Who Died as a Result of the Northern Ireland Troubles* (Edinburgh: Mainstream, 1999), p. 1473.
38 Gordon Gillespie (2004) 'The Origins of the Ulster Workers' Council Strike: Structure and Tactics', *Études Irlandaises*, 29(1): 129–144.
39 Bonnie Honig, *Antigone, Interrupted* (Cambridge: Cambridge University Press, 2013), p. 3.
40 Ibid., p. 119.
41 The document is available at www.northernireland.gov.uk/haass.pdf (hereafter cited as Haass/O'Sullivan); accessed 11 October 2014.
42 See, for example, Alex Kane, 'Northern Ireland is in big trouble and Haass can't fix it', *Newsletter*, 19 August 2013. Available at www.newsletter.co.uk/news/northern-ireland-is-in-big-trouble-and-haass-can-t-fix-it-1–5402351; accessed on 11 October 2014.
43 Haass/O'Sullivan, p. 19.
44 Ibid, p. 22.
45 Ibid. p. 23.
46 Haass/O'Sullivan, p. 35.
47 Ibid., p.36.
48 Aleida Assmann, 'Europe: A Community of Memory?' *Twentieth Annual Lecture of the GHI*, 2006. Available at www.memories.uni-bremen.de/files/2011/03/Assmann_Europe-A-Community-of-Memory-2007.pdf; accessed on 13 October 2014.
49 Jerome De Groot, *Consuming History: Historians and Heritage in Contemporary Popular Culture* (Abingdon: Routledge, 2009).
50 See, for example, the investigative reporting of Eilis O'Hanlon for the *Sunday Independent*: www.independent.ie/irish-news/alleged-rape-victim-to-tell-bbc-show-of-ira-attacker-30656910.html?utm_source=indoshare&utm_medium=socialoremail&utm_campaign=indoshare.
51 McGrattan, *Politics, Memory, Identity*.
52 See Cahal McLaughlin, 'Where politicians fail, storytellers address the Troubles in Northern Ireland, *The Conversation*, 28 October 2014. Available at http://theconversation.com/where-politicians-fail-storytellers-address-the-troubles-in-northern-ireland-33335; accessed on 30 March 2015.
53 Haass/O'Sullivan, p. 29.
54 Ibid, p. 30.
55 Ibid, p. 34.
56 Private correspondence.
57 Haass/O'Sullivan, p. 31.
58 Ibid, p. 35.
59 Ibid, p. 33.
60 Gerry Adams, 'How republicans dealt with allegations of child abuse', *Léargas*, 19 October 2014. Available at http://leargas.blogspot.co.uk/; accessed on 24 October 2014.
61 Brian Rowan, 'Is the IRA really beyond answering?', *EamonnMallie.com*, 21 October 2014. Available at http://eamonnmallie.com/2014/10/can-hiding-behind-ira-now-gone-away-brian-rowan-cahill-case-adams-blog/; accessed on 24 October 2014.
62 Nussbaum, 'Foreword', pp. xxii–xxiii.

7 Conclusion: lessons from Northern Ireland

If, following Nussbaum (as outlined in the previous chapter), we take lessons to be a meaning-giving practice, which links the past to the present and the future, then what lessons can we draw from Northern Ireland to the politics of trauma and the ethics of responsibility? I wish to sketch an answer to this and draw together the themes of this book in two sections. First, what can Northern Ireland illustrate by way of examples to be avoided? And, second, what positive steps can be taken forward to avoid some of the pitfalls in understanding and re/presenting trauma, responsibility and community that have been covered in this book?

Revising the Troubles

The term revisionism has a problematic history in Ireland.[1] Divorced from the international resonances of Holocaust denial, the Irish revisionist debate concerned arguments between historians and literary critics during the 1980s and early 1990s, and, at times, among historians themselves. With hindsight, the division might be seen as to do with the 'proper' representation of the Irish past. For example, with little time for nationalist grandstanding over traumatic narratives and catastrophic tropes, historians established themselves on an empirical footing. The political effect was seen, however, to be 'revisionist' of Irish mythology and gave rise, on the other hand, to the dialectic of literary critics and practitioners, particularly those associated with the Derry-based Field Day project, arguing that the Irish historical experience ought to be viewed through a post-colonial lens of alienation, disempowerment and subjection. (The division was not, of course, so neat in practice –historian Brendan Bradshaw and political scientist Brendan O'Leary launched critiques of 'revisionist' historians, whereas literary critic Edna Longley published a robust attack on nationalizing tendencies within cultural studies.)[2]

Without wishing to add what would be perhaps a third reading of the term, I suggest that dealing with the past in Northern Ireland has given rise to new forms of revisionism. Read through the Irish lens, it may be more accurate to describe these forms as anti-revisionist; read through the international context, however, they are closer to the repainting and relativizing of the Nazi experience that characterizes what might be seen as more commonplace understandings of the notion of historical revisionism – see, for instance, those deployed in the *Historikerstreit* in 1980s Germany. This anti/revisionist approach is at its core characterized by the sidestepping of the Deleuzian injunction against speaking for others. Because of this, its political and societal effect is to push to the margins of public debate and policy the historical experience of those affected by political violence. The process arises through the narration of the conflict. Narratives give meaning to experience, but the fact that that meaning, as Rancière points out, is saturated with political import does not necessarily condemn narration, I would argue, to an eternal recycling of police orders. In Rancierean terms, narratives can give voice to the part-without-part and can restore a positive political character to lives that have been damaged by violence and betrayal or that remain outside of the political mainstream. They can also be resistant to the subsuming tendencies of that mainstream, described by Rancière as the paradox of nothing existing outside of the count.

The historical narrative accomplishes this, Rancière explains, by bringing together two truths: the truth of events (facts arranged in a chronological order), and the truth of explanation (argument or discourse). What he terms the 'new narrative', the 'narrative that is not one',[3] brings to the fore those who have been rendered voiceless by the tides of politics, violence and history. In Rancière's description, the historian brings 'the poor' into visibility by speaking for them; taking Michelet as emblematic of this unveiling, he argues that the historian 'invents the art of making the poor speak by keeping them silent, of making them speak as silent people'. But the continuing paradox of historiography is that 'the historian keeps them [the poor] silent by making them *visible*'.[4] Arguably, the paradox is circular and self-referential: 'the poor' can be made visible by whomever decides who 'they' are. In his foreword to Rancière's text on historiography, Hayden White seemingly supports this reading, but misses its political implications – namely, that favouring any 'poor' works to place means in support of ends (any individual or group can, presumably, be 'rescued' from oblivion or condemnation). Thus, for White, Rancière's text places Michelet on the same modernist ground as Joyce, Woolf and Proust in 'auguring' an elision of science and literature. Rancière's text, then, should, he argues 'be taken neither literally nor figuratively; his own mode of address is to be taken as neither active nor passive; and his assertions are to be taken as neither denotative nor connative'.[5] This seems, to me, to miss the importance that Rancière affords to paralepsis in the construction of historiography. As he explains, '[p]aralepsis fraudulently represents what is not admissible to represent'. It is here, precisely, that historiography meets the politics of trauma in that it brings into focus that which is left outside mainstream concerns (the count).The kernel that is paralepsis, in other words, works to give voice to that which is rendered silent; it speaks through but not for the part-without-part or those who have been marginalized by history, politics and terror. Rancière describes this speaking-through-but-not-for as an impossibility of re/presentation:

> The impossibility of imitation produces the silent witness who holds the truth of science, who holds this truth without herself having the power to deliver

> it. The figure of the one who would speak – the legitimating agency of the narration – becomes that of the silent witness – the legitimating agency of knowledge.[6]

History, then, for Rancière is the opposite of relativism; rather it is grounded in the (dual) acknowledgement of event and interpretation. What he calls the 'theory of the silent witness' depends on the disjuncture created by paralepsis, but it remains a partial event. This is because history making also incorporates what might be called, in Rancièrean terms, the 'theory of heresy', namely, the 'catastrophic vision, in which history comes to the point of refusing to accept its object'.[7] The 'heresy' of revisionism, Rancière argues, lies in the confusion of event and interpretation – of empiricism and ideology. The confusion arises, in part, from the ambiguous nature of narrative as something with or without a beginning, middle and end, as something in which what is left out is sometimes more important than what is included.

The first form of confusion that anti/revisionist narration of the conflict takes may be termed the myth of ambiguous culpability. The focus of the narrative in this case is on claims of collusion between the British state and loyalist and republican terrorists (groups and individuals). One example can be found in the angry response of the victims group Relatives for Justice (RFJ) to a keynote speech by the Secretary of State for Northern Ireland, Theresa Villiers, MP, in May 2014. RFJ denounced Villiers' speech as 'disgraceful' because it 'sought to distract from the state's duty to account for their actions by saying that the focus on any future truth process should be on those who were most responsible for the violence'. RFJ's complaint with this was that Villiers

> . . . also referred to the state "only" being responsible for 10 percent of deaths during the conflict . . . This 10 percent figure does not take into consideration collusion . . . when that is calculated at a conservative figure it would take that 10 percent to around 30 percent.[8]

In fact, the secretary of state actually called for a new process that would provide the scope

> . . . to write in from the start the need for an objective balance and with proper weight and a proportionate focus on the wrongdoing of paramilitaries. Rather than the almost exclusive concentration on the activities of the state which characterises so many of the processes currently underway.[9]

The myth of culpability centres on numbers and how they are being used to set agendas. It is the meaning behind these numbers that is fundamental to this framing battle. But the politicization of the issue is, arguably, only exacerbated by inaccurate attribution. The origins of the 'only' claim, for instance, seem to stem from an interview that the director of RFJ did shortly after the Villiers speech where he stated that the

> . . . propaganda myth that the state is only responsible for 10 percent of all killings throws up two key points: it ignore[s] the reality of collusion that when factored into the equation accounts for the state being culpable for approximately a third of all killings. And that is only what we know at this point without a truth process.[10]

The political effect is to manufacture a version of reality and to throw the onus of responsibility on to particular actors. In the process, a certain confusion enters into the debate due to the shift in focus from motivations to numbers. There seems to be little doubt that individuals and groups of soldiers and policemen were involved in 'running' suspected terrorists and either through act or omission were guilty of directing murders; however, the shift to a numbers debate, although critical for the purposes of transparency and accountability, ignores the radically different strategic visions and policy directions of the state forces and terrorist organizations.

The second form of anti/revisionist confusion can be called the myth of heavy lifting. This follows the same logic of valorizing 'community' over society that was mentioned in an earlier chapter. It can be seen in restorative justice advocates' affirmation of community policing, but it can also be seen in explanations of the ending of the conflict where paramilitaries are portrayed as having made personal sacrifices. One example of this is the assertion that in 'working-class republican and loyalist communities . . . ex-combatants are largely regarded as having "done their bit" on behalf of their communities'.[11] The uncertainty regarding what 'done their bit' refers to ultimately works to confuse society with community. The narrative suggests that the peace process was brokered by paramilitaries who carried 'their communities' and the hawks in their movements forward away from violence. The notion of peace as privilege is thus invoked implicitly by the threat that the paramilitaries could return to killing if democracy does not work out as they hope. A double substitution occurs within the confusion created by the myth of heavy lifting. First, communal is substituted by community, and the notion that the conflict was driven by ideas that were communally or ethnically inspired is deferred in favour of a focus on self-defence and a lack of political alternatives. Second, society is substituted by community. Here, the focus is on peace as capacity building at a local level to the deferral of the societal implications that such policies may have. In other words, the confusion between society and community works to hollow out any notion of a civic or a public sphere in favour of communal visions.

A third form of an anti/revisionist approach to the past might be termed the myth of crisis. In this case, the past is something to be dealt with as a policy priority and an interpersonal imperative. Putative 'crises' concerning revelations about events or the actions of politicians during the Troubles are seen as 'clear' evidence of how 'fundamental addressing the legacy of the past is for the legitimacy and stability of Northern Ireland's political institutions'.[12] The framing issue at stake in this instance is the deferral of the links between the call for 'addressing' and the ideas of 'legitimacy and stability'. This is because, arguably, the very notion of dealing with the past within a large-scale policy framework is one of the most destabilizing issues within Northern Irish politics. As alluded to earlier, the Belfast/Good Friday Agreement consociational institutions were designed explicitly to ensure elite stability and carefully avoided any divisive commitments on the part of the Northern Irish political parties to tackling legacy issues. It is no surprise, then, that division and contention occur between those parties when they are called on to legislate in the area of dealing with the past. The patina of legalistic respectability that ostensibly underpins the calls from transitional justice advocates to provide an answer to the 'recent crises' masks a discourse that is structurally biased towards moving away from that status quo. The myth of crisis, therefore, sits on top of a transitional discourse, which itself is in constant movement, part of which is a reinvention of the territory upon which political debate takes place. One recent example is the (re)definition of the basic terms of debate that are used in talking about the past. Brewer et al, for example, defend their use of the term 'ex-combatant' by referring directly to how former paramilitaries understand themselves:

> The term 'ex-combatant' is contested by former combatants themselves, in part because it suggests their times of active engagement are past . . . they very much like to think of themselves as remaining involved in their community's broader struggle for justice. But others believe it is a victors' term (worse still, a favoured term of the British), used judgmentally to condemn.[13]

Others could, alternatively, argue that taking former paramilitaries' favoured terms at face value is similar to recognizing Mafioso as 'soldiers'. Further, one could argue that such terminological interventions serve, in part, to confer (retrospective and contemporary) legitimacy and, again, respectability, to those whose ideas and actions were rejected by the vast majority of the population of Northern Ireland throughout the conflict.

Silent witnessing

In taking forward lessons from the Northern Irish case, I wish to suggest that the 2013 Special Advisors (SpAd) legislation represents one outworking of the types of ideas about responsibility and moving beyond the past. That legislation is, in effect, a very limited act of lustration that bars individuals who have served over five years in gaol (termed 'serious offences') from holding publicly funded offices of political patronage – namely, being special ministerial advisors in the Northern Ireland Assembly. Yet, as a piece of positive discrimination, it calls into being that which would otherwise be all but ignored, not acknowledged or spoken of. As such, the SpAd legislation works at a symbolic and political level by way of *paralepsis* – it creates a legal and political category that exists by way of reference:

the reference being the violent actions that were committed by individuals during the Troubles and the deaths and bloodshed that followed from those actions. The import of the legislation, then, is to speak through those references and bear witness to the absences from the conflict.

The legislation was precipitated by the appointment of the former Irish Republican Army-woman, Mary McArdle, as Special Advisor to the Minister for Culture, Arts and Leisure in 2010. McArdle had served 18 years of a life sentence for her role in the murder of a 22-year-old teacher and attempted murder of her father, a judge. The appointment was controversial, especially given that McArdle's accomplice had never been convicted; McArdle's explanation that the murder was a 'tragic mistake' was seen as further evidence of an ambivalence towards the justification of the killing.[14] The appointment was seen as a way of rewarding McArdle for her silence – see, for example, the evidence given to the Northern Ireland Assembly by Ann Travers (the victim's sister).[15] The bill seeks to address issues such as this by prohibiting persons with serious criminal convictions (defined in law as five-plus years) from holding unelected public office. Fundamentally about political patronage, the bill represents a form of lustration and draws a line to say that certain events in the past were and remain outside the bounds of societal acceptability. It also redraws the relationship between legislators and the people they represent, and acts, arguably, as a mechanism of positive discrimination, favouring the rights and needs of victims of violence over and above those of perpetrators. Opponents of the bill claim that it is anti-peace. In his evidence to the assembly, for example, Professor Peter Shirlow argued that 'as somebody who believes in conflict transformation', he opposed the legislation. 'If a constituency is prepared to engage, move forward and challenge itself', he argued, 'it should be included in society'.[16] The underlying political effect of the framing is to equate peace with progress: sacrifices must be made for the sake of good governance. The relationship of governing to governed is, thus, again rendered distinct and questions of accountability from the latter to the former do not feature.

As pointed out earlier, the Northern Irish consociational system veers towards crisis politics when confronted with symbolic issues that it was not designed to deal with. 'Legacy' issues seemingly require a certain flexibility that seems not to be a part of that system. This is because consociational systems fasten together otherwise polarized and segmented blocs and their elites within a single policy-making framework. Consensus on decision making and implementation becomes, paradoxically, the only option as agreement is created through a system of checks and balances (veto powers in particular) and a subsequent tampering of ethnic sentiments. Within this system politics becomes effectively de-politicized: the culture of openness, transparency and debate that is commonly understood to be the hallmark of politics becomes deferred through the procedural requirement to reach consensus – an inversion of Heaney's 'Whatever you say, say nothing'. The element of crisis contained within this arrangement is that it is impossible to suppress issues such as victimhood, truth recovery or the search for justice forever and that cases such as that of McArdle will inevitably appear and recur.

The question of how to deal with such appearances and recurrences goes therefore to the heart of any democracy. They constitute a fundamental dilemma over what the roles of politicians should be and how ordinary citizens are represented and re-presented by political elites. In his contribution to the *Federalist Papers*, James Madison drew explicit links between political representation and popular participation. For Madison, the paradox of democratic government resides in the fact that it has to be simultaneously *for* the people and *of* the people. It must necessarily involve ordinary citizens and communities in the processes of governance, while also observing a system of checks and balances to ensure that one group does not exercise unfair, unjust or unethical sway over another:

> To secure the public good and private rights against the danger of such a faction, and at the same time to preserve the spirit and the form of popular government, is then the great object to which our inquiries are directed.[17]

Madison's point echoes in the oral evidence of Professor Brice Dickson to the committee. Human rights law, in his opinion 'would allow states a certain margin of appreciation' in deciding on employability protocols for special advisors or ex-paramilitary prisoners. Professor Dickson and his colleagues argued for an 'individualised approach' – a point that was reflected in the Human Rights Commission's interpretation of the treatment by the European Court of Human Rights on lustration and domestic restriction of employment rights. The Madisonian corollary to that proposition is the question of how to balance those individual rights with societal ones. Mr Mitchel McLaughlin, Member of the Legislative Assembly (MLA), alluded to this in his response to Professor Dickson's arguments:

> We have great sympathy with and sensitivity for the individuals who have been hurt as a result of the actions of others, but we also have an absolute duty to try to move beyond post-conflict into reconciliation processes such as truth recovery to deal with the fact that there are many victims in our community who have never had redress.[18]

The issue of how to move forward as a society, building a sound infrastructure for future generations while acknowledging the divisions, hurts, grievances and injustices of the past, lies at the heart of the legislation. Although this involves issues of rights and issues of ethics, it is fundamentally a political question: it creates polarization and debate and is, perhaps, ultimately unsolvable. This is not to say the issue should be ignored, nor is it to indulge in sentimentalizing of the notion that we should agree to disagree. The point deserves consideration, for arguably the legislation works as a check of its own against a slide towards equivalency; particularly, the suggestion that there is no distinction between state killings and those of extra- or anti-state forces. Three points follow from this. First, there is the issue of accountability: despite the failings of the British state to persecute those culpable for heinous acts of murder and terror against individuals and whole sections of society, it is subject to the law. Mr McLaughlin and Sinn Féin implicitly recognize this in their calls for the state to admit to its actions. There results an immediate moral confusion. For, just as the state is accountable before the law (that is, before the legal process), the idea that loyalist and republican volunteers should also give evidence before an independent or international tribunal becomes mere rhetoric: those groups are unaccountable to anyone but their own codes of ethics; apart from outside coercion, they are not under any compulsion to partake in a truth and reconciliation process. Second, the consequence is not just moral confusion between the distinction between accountability (the law) and murder – there is also a political effect to equivalency: namely, that the state is accountable, paramilitaries are not. The effect is to weight the political process in favour of paramilitaries. This is not to say that the British and Irish states were not culpable of atrocious actions (and omissions). It is rather only to point out that the playing field becomes uneven through the application of an implicit system of double standards. Third, not all voices are equal. Contrary to Mr McLaughlin's otherwise laudable promotion of acknowledgement, 'understanding' is not synonymous with justice. In other words, some stories are more easily told than others and victims – namely, those marginalized and muted (if not silenced) through political violence – start from a point of disadvantage vis-à-vis their perpetrators. Equalizing that disparity remains radically different from fostering an equivalence of experience. Within this understanding, acknowledgement and (uneasy) understanding fall short of redress or justice and may, through repeated reference, create a discursive framework that militates against actually achieving justice or uncovering the truth about what happened to victims.

Madison's response to the question of balancing individual rights against the need to create a coherent, cohesive polity was straightforward: either the elite (what he referred to as the majority faction) contains itself or it is made 'unable to concert and carry into effect schemes of oppression'. In a way, Madison's point brings the book full circle: *The Politics of Trauma and Peace-Building* has attempted to unpick some of the assumptions surrounding the (undoubted) need to build robust, stable and transparent institutions in societies transitioning from violence to peace. I have argued that consideration of the politics of trauma sheds light on some of the limitations of a narrow proceduralist or institutionalist approach to peace-building, however, and, instead suggested that a more substantive vision of democratization ought to incorporate questions of societal responsibility. The key dilemma within that vision, however, remains the possibility of remarginalizing or re-silencing those who have suffered from political violence and terror.

The paradox that I wish to finish with is that legislation may provide one response to that dilemma. The SpAd legislation does this by evoking the ethics of societal responsibility in a Rancièrean sense of speaking through but not for those who have suffered. In this light, the SpAd legislation, I argue, speaks to a form of silent witnessing: a witnessing to the silent rejection of violence that characterized the majority of responses to the Troubles, but also a reminder of the silences involved in fellow travelling, turning a blind eye or 'sneaking regard' that enabled terrorists to persist in their campaigns for so long. It is also a witnessing to the silences that ensued from those campaigns: the intimidations, exiles and deaths that marred Northern Irish society for three and a half decades. The legislation witnesses to the special privilege that elected politicians bear as being responsible to their voters but also society at large. The legislation, in short, acts as an embodiment of the themes of responsibility and ethics in post-conflict societies that run throughout this book. Certainly, the SpAd legislation is not without its problems – one of which being the fact that it was deemed necessary in the first place – but, I suggest it provides a minimalist and more realistic approach to dealing with the past than much of what is contained in the politically limited and ethically problematic reconciliation and transitional justice literatures.

Notes

1 Gkotzaridis, *Trials*.
2 McGrattan, *Memory*.
3 Rancière, *Names*, p.43.
4 Ibid, pp. 45 and 46 (original italics).
5 Ibid, p. xix.
6 Ibid, p. 55.
7 Ibid, p. 91.
8 Relatives for Justice, 'Adams arrest is positioning on truth end game', 2 May 2014. Available at http://relativesforjustice.com/adams-arrest-is-positioning-on-truth-end-game/; accessed on 27 October 2014.
9 The Northern Ireland Office, 'Theresa Villiers addresses church leaders on moving Northern Ireland away from the politics of identity to focus on the politics of delivery', 16 April 2014. Available at www.gov.uk/government/speeches/moving-politics-forward; accessed on 9 March 2015.
10 Francesca Ryan, 'Victims confront Villiers over past', Belfast Media Group, 22 April 2014. Available at http://belfastmediagroup.com/victims-confront-villiers-over-past/; accessed on 27 October 2014.
11 McEvoy and Shirlow, 'Re-imagining DDR', p. 41.
12 Louise Malinder, 'Dealing with Northern Ireland's past: A guide to the Haass-O'Sullivan talks', Open Democracy, 8 May, 2014. Available at www.opendemocracy.net/5050/louise-mallinder/dealing-with-northern-ireland%E2%80%99s-past-guide-to-haas so%E2%80%99sullivan-talks; accessed on 9 March 2015.
13 John Brewer, David Mitchell and Gerard Leavey, Ex-Combatants, Religion and Peace in Northern Ireland (Basingstoke: Palgrave Macmillan, 2013), p. x.
14 BBC News Online 'Mary McArdle – Mary Travers murder a "tragic mistake"', 2 June 2011. Available at www.bbc.co.uk/news/uk-northern-ireland-13625007; accessed on 9 May 2014.
15 Northern Ireland Assembly Official Report: Hansard. 'Civil Service (Special Advisors) Bill: Ann Travers/Catherine McCartney Briefing, Committee for Finance and Personnel', 21 November, 2012. Available at www.niassembly.gov.uk/Assembly-Business/Official-Report/Committee-Minutes-of-Evidence/Session-2012–2013/November-20121/Civil-Service-Special-Advisers-Bill-Ann-TraversCatherine-McCartney-Briefing/; accessed on 9 May 9, 2014
16 Northern Ireland Assembly Official Report: Hansard, 'Civil Service (Special Advisors) Bill: Ann Travers/Catherine McCartney Briefing, Committee for Finance and Personnel', 21 November. Available at www.niassembly.gov.uk/Assembly-Business/Official-Report/Committee-Minutes-of-Evidence/Session-2012–2013/January-2013/Civil-Service-Special-Advisers-Bill-Briefing-from-Professor-Peter-Shirlow/; accessed on 9 May 2014.
17 James Madison, Alexander Hamilton and John Jay, *The Federalist Papers* (London: Penguin, 1987), p. 124.

18 See Máire Braniff and Cillian McGrattan, 'The Civil Service (Special Advisors) Bill: Democratic Implications and Considerations', written evidence to the Northern Ireland Assembly, 2013. Available at www.niassembly.gov.uk/globalassets/documents/finance/special-advisers-bill-submissions/other-papers/10.democratic_implications_consideratin_dr_braniff_and_dr_mcgrattan.pdf; accessed on 9 March 2015.

Index